THE MIND OF A SPIDER

Trisha St. Andrews

This is a work of fiction. Names, characters, places, and incidents either are the product of the author's imagination or are used fictitiously. Any resemblance to actual persons, living or dead, events, or locales is entirely coincidental.

629Publications.com
www.TrishaStAndrews.com

Copyright © 2015 Trisha St. Andrews
All rights reserved.

Dedicated to the memory of my beloved father, Donald Stuart Phillip Weatherhead, 1924-1997, who continues to be an inspiration and guiding star in my life.

Also dedicated to the memory of my dear friend Michael Goodrich, 1947-2015, who cared so much about my characters' fortunes and misfortunes in *The Heart of a Lynx* that he spoke of them as if they were real.

CHAPTER ONE

Fairy tales do not tell children that dragons exist.
Children already know that dragons exist.
Fairy tales tell children that dragons can be killed.
—G.K. Chesterton

"She's alive. I know it," she cried as she slammed her hand on the granite countertop.

Trina Shanihan McClaren stood in her country kitchen in Lincoln, Nebraska. Her bare feet clawed the cold, ceramic-tiled floor as the heater hissed through the ventilator, unnerving her with an associative vision of an escaped snake residing in her kitchen wall. She stared out the window, focusing only on the daunting task before her.

She needed help—from all of them. She needed the strength of passionate, injured women with a common mission. Strength in numbers, strength in purpose. But without Tess's support, engaging Tess's two sisters in this quest for justice was next to impossible. Tess was the key, the trigger point, the catalyst to set justice in motion. Justice. That straight-forward, honorable word that implies moral rightness. That respectable, civilized concept that at times is fringed with revenge. Trina's instinct for reprisal would be masked in conversation as justice, simply justice.

In an hour the sun would shine its solar spotlight and set ablaze the red sugar maple outside her kitchen window. Soon the children would be up. It was time to reign in her fury and compartmentalize it in a box marked OPEN LATER. Upstairs in a *Town and Country* bedroom, surrounded by stuffed animals and storybooks, her children, Cristin and

Elizabeth, slept beneath a fairy-tale mobile and a ceiling covered with glow-in-the-dark stars that glimmered like luminaries softening the darkness, and lighting the way to a faraway land. They were untroubled and unmarked by life's brutal twists from which Trina had protected them ... so far. When Trina and her little sister Cristin were their ages, they'd lived a carefree life at a time when no one locked the doors to their homes or cars, and yards weren't enclosed with block walls to keep strangers out; a time when security systems were only installed in businesses in edgy neighborhoods; and a time when everyone knew their neighbors. But try as she had, she couldn't replicate her early childhood for her daughters. The world was more sophisticated, complicated ... scarier.

She was relieved that her husband Bryan was gone for a few days because she needed time to think. Bryan, a freelance nature writer, was fly-fishing in Montana, experiencing the Gallatin River that he had so loved as a kid. His favorite book, Norman Maclean's *A River Runs Through It*, had been a constant source of reference throughout their nine-year marriage. At her prompting, he'd left for a week to visit Montana, to recapture his childhood memories and witness its supernal beauty as an adult with a keen eye, keen ear, and keen pen. He was "haunted by waters." How many times had she heard that phrase? Every time he said it, she'd think, *I'm haunted by fire.*

She tacitly vowed that when Bryan returned, she would tell him that she'd contacted Tess. He wouldn't be pleased.

Her focus broke when she heard the girls' footsteps above her, scampering in their room. As if by rote, with one hand she opened the refrigerator to survey the sandwich choices for their lunches, and with the other, she turned on the television to Fox News where the female broadcasters all seemed to be attorneys who stepped out of a *Victoria's Secret* catalog. The latter observation was not her own, but Bryan's, who commonly remarked, "Where do they find these women?"

"Mommy, can I wear my green dress to school today?" Cristin, with her golden ringlets unbridled by hairclips, stood in the doorway.

Trina walked to her daughter and nuzzled her face in Cristin's hair to smell the residual scent of strawberry shampoo used at bath time the night before; in Trina's mind, the smell of a clean child ranked right up there with hearing a baby giggle.

"No, honey. Uniforms every day, remember?"

"Ohhhhh," she groaned.

"Cristin, please help your sister get dressed. Breakfast is ready and we have to leave in twenty minutes. We have blueberries this morning," she said with an intentionally tempting voice.

She and Bryan had switched the girls out of a public school to a private religious school over the summer. Not that they were particularly religious but the violence in the public schools across the country was so frightening, they decided a private school was safer. Actually, she decided and Bryan acquiesced. He lived by the axiom "you can either be right or you can be happy," which when shared with other couples in a social situation, guaranteed raucous laughter from the men, and smiling approval from the women. In this instance, Trina was unyielding about the private versus public school dilemma. So he'd let it be. Amen.

After breakfast, Trina supervised the gathering of backpacks and distributing of lunchboxes, then ushered the girls into the family SUV and secured their seatbelts. It was then that she noticed the morning. Sunny, with autumn pollen sprinkling the air like pixie dust, minus the magic. Elizabeth sneezed, a reminder to Trina to talk to their pediatrician about her daughter's allergies which always worsened in the spring and fall. *Add it to the list.* The newly-lacquered asphalt on the street in front of their home would soon lose its odor and luster with time and wear, and be saturated with the moisture of snow, creating new potholes, just in time for more maintenance the following summer. Some things were predictable. Some things were not.

The girls' chattering in the back seat reminded her of how she and her sister had shared everything ... before her sister Cristin's death ten years ago. Trina and Bryan had agreed to name their first-born daughter in memory of her sister, so they spoke Cristin's name every day, a constant reminder of the cherished life that had been cut short.

"Mommy, we're here. Cristin, will you take off my seatbelt?" Elizabeth asked in her tiny, little-girl voice.

Trina parked the car, opened the door closest to the curb, helped the girls exit onto the sidewalk, and kissed each of them on the tops of their heads, sneaking sniffs of their shampoo one more time. She watched Cristin hold her younger sister's hand, reminding her of how close she and her own sister had been. The playground monitor acknowledged the changing of the guard by waving to Trina who alertly stood at the curb. *One can't be too vigilant.*

When she arrived home, she poured herself a cup of coffee, sniffing its fresh-roasted aroma. She sat down in her winterized porch with the screened windows open so she could feel the breeze while she reflected on the facts that compelled her to make the call to Tess. She stared into space, focusing on nothing except her usual suspects of thoughts as if they were in a police lineup. She needed to identify her next move, and be one moment closer to a restful night's sleep, and be one moment farther from the racing heartbeat that recently dominated her days.

Let's go through this again like I'm telling my story to a detective, she thought to herself as she ceremoniously placed her coffee cup on the glass-top table.

Three years ago, I read a book called Gone, written by a woman named Tess Monson Parker, Monson being the last name of my biological mother whom I'd never identified or contacted. I am adopted. You can imagine my surprise when I recognized a character named Cristin Shanihan, which could not have been coincidental, as it was my sister's name. I flew to Minneapolis to meet the author. After sharing the coincidences between her story and my life, she confirmed what I suspected, that her character was someone I had known who had used information from my past to connect with Tess, and more invasively, had used my sister Cristin's past to start a new life.

Cristin died in a fire at the home of Hunter Cross, a girl from our high school. Hunter's parents also died in the fire. It had bothered me for years that after the accident, Hunter had abruptly left town. No one else had given it a second thought but an inexplicable intuition nagged at me for years that Hunter knew how that fire had started. I just couldn't figure out how she had been involved ... or why ... until that day in Minnesota. It became insidiously evident. Hunter Cross killed my sister, and her parents, stole my sister's identity and began a new life. On top of this shocking discovery, I learned that Tess was my biological aunt ... which until that time, neither of us knew. Her sister Katie was my birth mother who had put me up for adoption as an infant. My having read Tess's book only because her maiden name was Monson led me to my biological family.

Tess appeared shocked to meet me, her niece, for the first time, and then learn that the woman Tess knew as Cristin Shanihan who had lived in her home, was not only a fraud, but may have been a murderer. The only saving grace that day was learning that Hunter Cross was dead, killed in a plane crash. So the case was closed and for the first time in years, I slept through the night, no longer stalked by nightmares.

Trina stopped to take a sip of coffee and chewed the taste until it only lingered on her breath; then continued her telling of the facts as she knew them.

Before I met Tess, I believed that the only possibility of finding Hunter was to recognize her artwork, published in an art magazine or hanging in a gallery. Hunter used to talk about how she wanted to be a famous artist, and during high school art classes, I'd witnessed her Munchian "Scream" style of painting which was disturbing. Disturbing because it was grotesque and dark, but uniquely recognizable. For years, I subscribed to art publications, in search of her demonic style as a lead to tracking her down to prove or disprove my theory, but when I heard she was dead, I quit looking for her paintings.

But over time I'd developed a penchant for art and hadn't unsubscribed from my magazines. Then one day, unsuspecting and off-

guard, I noticed a published painting that indicated she might not have died after all. I felt a sharp quickening of panic slice my gut. I slid off the edge of my chair onto the hard floor, boneless, mindless.

Trina shivered and breathed rapidly, as she did every time she thought of that moment. And as usual, she momentarily couldn't connect the dots to her next thought.

But then it became clear what to do ... tell Tess. Yes, that was the right thing to do, the first step. I sent Tess the publication and have now given her enough time to digest its implications. If Hunter Cross is alive, we need to hunt her down.

It was now time to make the call.

Trina summoned her courage, her heart pounding. The subject was too sensitive to leave as a message. She held her breath as she dialed, hoping that Tess would answer the call. The phone rang three times before Tess picked up her receiver.

"Hello. This is Tess."

"Yes, Tess? This is Trina, Trina McClaren. Did you receive the package I sent to you?"

"Yes."

"Can you talk right now?"

"No."

"I'm going to give you my cell phone number and need you to call me when it's convenient. Soon. Do you have a pen?"

"Yes." With the cell number received, Tess hung up the phone.

Trina quickly inhaled and exhaled a number of times, as if finishing a Pilates workout. She refilled her coffee mug and sat back down in her porch to revisit related conversations that she'd collected in her mental vault.

Having replayed it so many times in her mind, she recalled an interchange with her high school counselor like it had taken place yesterday. He'd responded like a typical school counselor not wanting to get involved ... certainly not taking her seriously.

He'd said, "Trina, when people suffer a loss of this magnitude, it's natural to look for someone to blame. Lashing out to find an explanation, a scapegoat, a tangible reason for a tragedy so sudden is normal. But what you're telling me doesn't make any sense. Hunter has been an excellent student, well-liked, with no indication of aberrant or violent behavior. I think you need to let go of this hysterical notion you've conjured. And I suggest you don't talk to the students about this. It would only be unsettling, and colossally unfair to Hunter's reputation, were she to return."

Blah, blah, blah. He wouldn't even consider that Hunter might have been guilty of a crime. Trina had wanted to scream, but composed herself to maintain the illusion of stability. But at that point, her internal grief and frustration had metastasized to anger. That's when she'd gone to her parents. Unwilling to even consider that there had been foul play, they'd asked that she not mention her "insane suspicions" again. So she kept her theories to herself and buried them in the basement of her subconscious, somewhere deep and inaccessible … or so she thought. From time to time, they'd creep up the stairs and knock on the door of her mind, forcing her to open it just a crack to hear them present their doubts. *Where had Hunter gone without a trace? Why hadn't Hunter ever contacted the family of the girl who had died in the fire with her parents? Why would Hunter Cross murder her sister? What had she to gain?* Those were the haunting questions. Despite the fact that there was no evidence, the tormenting uncertainties corroded Trina's spirit like salt water on iron.

But now there was an explanation. Cristin's identity was the prize, the motivation for a murder that had been adeptly masked as an accident. Trina was certain of it.

When she'd shared her thoughts with Bryan, he'd asked her to "let sleeping dogs lie," his exact words.

"Maybe Hunter's painting was discovered and published by someone who passed it off as her own for financial gain," he'd suggested.

"Maybe," she'd said, "but how will I know if I don't try to find her? I hope it is a crook or a plagiarist on the other end. I truly do. That would put my mind to rest, knowing that she did die in that plane crash."

Trina precisely recalled his response as if it had been directly recorded on her brain's hard drive. "And if you don't find a plagiarist and do find Hunter, what then?" he'd continued. "Didn't you tell me that this woman from your past almost single-handedly destroyed the family in Minnesota? I don't like seeing you consumed by conjecture, Trina. Even if you're right, the potential consequences could irreparably damage someone. Call me paranoid, but I think it's a bad idea."

He may be right, she acquiesced. Paranoid or prophetic, Bryan had spoken his peace, and she had taken note.

She walked to the porch window, absorbing the smell of a wood-burning fireplace that traveled on the breeze from a neighbor's home. The familiar scent uprooted a memory.

One summer years ago, her parents had rented a lake cabin for a week, a log cabin surrounded by Norway and white pines, birch, spruce, and butternut trees, as high as one could see. She and her sister listened to the sounds of boats and loons and voices talking on the other side of the lake, words traveling across the water like skipping stones. The sisters quietly swung in the hammock, not talking, but listening, trying to decipher the faraway conversations as if they were spies, decoding an important secret. When the voices faded, they giggled and swung higher, trying to turn each other out of the hammock. In the morning, they ran down to the dock and watched the minnows, wishing they had a fishing pole to catch a sunfish and surprise their parents. In the evenings, they slipped off to the pond behind the cabin where lily pads served as jumping stations for the frogs that lived among the reeds and cattails. At night, when they sat around the campfire, they sang songs learned at church camp and took turns telling scary stories. Cristin always told stories about monsters as she'd been an imaginative child, and more fearful than Trina, but that's what made her stories so thrilling. The scent of burning pine and eucalyptus logs teased their senses, saturated their clothes and hair, and embedded Trina's senses with a love for her sister. Anytime she smelled a fire burning, she could almost feel her sister's leg pressing against her own as they sat on the campsite log together.

Returning to the present, Trina breathed a whiff of burning wood through the sieve of her porch screen and whispered, "Don't worry, sweet sister. The time has come to find the monster. There will be justice."

CHAPTER TWO

Life shrinks or expands in proportion to one's courage.
—Anais Nin

Tessa Monson Parker needed to fortify her spirit before making the imminent call. She walked into The Healing Life Center, an eastern medical office in Minnetonka, Minnesota. The air was still and steeped with the scent of jasmine. The meditative music combined sounds of birdsong and lightly falling rain. The wood floors were clean and shiny. To the left was a parquet chest with twenty square drawers, probably containing Asian teas, essential oils, candles, and herbs. To the right stood a large vase embossed with periwinkle prints of bridges, flowing water, and a charming Chinese village. However, the crowning centerpiece of the room was a large wooden dragon which spewed a mist of incense, humidifying the air like a rainforest at dawn. On the countertop, a tall, simple arrangement of purple orchids greedily absorbed the moisture provided by the mythical, snorting sculpture.

She was early for her acupuncture appointment so she took a seat in front of a floor-to-ceiling window that overlooked a koi pond in an amply-birched forest. White-crowned sparrows flitted and flirted with the water and freshened their feathers. The fish in tones of gold, orange, and spotted white, looked bored but unafraid, two emotions Tess would settle for that morning. She loved Minnesota, its native beauty and at times, its imported beauty.

Voices of quiet Chinese dialects spoken behind bamboo sliding doors added to a feeling of mystical authenticity that forty-nine-year-old

Tess had entered another world, an ageless world of knowledge and potent powers of the ages … possibly, a panacea, bestowing clarity and answers. She knew better than to think there was a quick fix for her anxiety, but hoped to dissipate her level of apprehension. She felt fortunate to live in an era and a country where so many options were available for mental and physical health. This morning East would meet West.

An hour later, although more relaxed, Tess walked out of the office, realizing that the pressures she felt could not be relieved by needles, or any other magic or mystic power. She needed to call the person who had visited her three years ago, and who had requested not to have any further contact for everyone's sake. But now this person had sent her a package that could turn Tess's life upside-down … again. She needed to call Trina, her niece, her sister Katie's long-lost daughter, and the sisterless victim of the woman Tess had known as Cristin Shanihan.

That afternoon while her husband Ren was at work, Tess placed the call. Every number was like a step toward an unknown but treacherous fate, and yet she continued to press each button. No one was forcing her to dial. It was a strange human phenomenon, to witness oneself, moving forward through an uncomfortable act, but moving forward nonetheless … like driving to a root canal appointment.

When the phone rang, she almost hung up but braced herself to listen to the voice on the other end.

"Hello?"

"It's Tess, Trina."

"Tess. I saw the Minnetonka area code and figured it was you. Thank you for calling me back."

The pause was excruciating but Tess outwaited her niece who finally cut to the chase.

"Tess, I think Hunter Cross is alive. I need your help finding her. We need to tell your sisters."

Tess watched her right hand start to tremble. "Why would you want to do that? You told me that you would not cause trouble for my family, that your visit to see me ended with us. We agreed that no one else would be privy to our meeting because it would be too unsettling for both of our families. I honored that arrangement, Trina. I didn't tell anyone, not even my husband. And if my sister Katie knew that I'd met you and hadn't shared this fact, my relationship with her would be dead."

"I'm sorry, Tess, but circumstances have changed. We now think that this person is alive. It changes everything."

"I don't know. This whole theory is so upsetting and I wouldn't give it any credence except …" Tess paused, gulped air so hard that it stuck in her throat.

"Except what?" Trina asked.

"Except for the name on the painting … Yvette."

"Why is that disturbing? She could have chosen any name."

"But she didn't. She chose Yvette."

"What are you saying?" asked Trina.

"When she was living in France, my sister Tia's friend dropped dead on her kitchen floor. She was only twenty-two."

"And?"

"Her friend's name was Yvette. She was a Swiss girl studying in Grenoble."

Tess withstood the attentive silence on the other end of the phone. Trina had now heard the incriminating link which pointed closer to the fact that her theory was valid.

"Did they know each other, Yvette and your *Cristin*?"

"Yes. They were introduced by my sister Tia."

"So this monster has moved on and assumed the identity of Tia's friend? Am I hearing you correctly?"

"It appears that way, doesn't it?"

"Yes it does, compounded by the fact that this magazine print was published in Switzerland. That's where she is, Tess. She's in Switzerland."

Tess felt like she was moving through a car wash, slowly clicking forward with no vantage point and a sloshing sound in her ears. She could barely hear Trina's voice in the background.

"But what about the plane crash? She died in a plane crash," Tess said.

"That brings us to another issue," Trina continued.

"What's that?" inquired Tess, hoping beyond hope that it was something more uplifting or positive, but not holding her breath.

"If she is alive, how did she survive a place crash in a remote section of the Pyrenees? And if she did, who rescued her and why didn't she contact Katie's family? After all, she was married to Katie's son Shep, right? I've thought about this a lot. She was never on that plane, Tess."

"But she was logged in on the manifest and her clothes were found scattered on the mountain."

"But they didn't find her body," Trina stated.

"No, but the snow is deep and doesn't melt at that altitude. They often don't recover all the bodies in a plane crash. That's what they told us." Tess could hear the desperation in her own voice.

"That's probably true. But how do you explain her painting being published, years later, by an artist named Yvette?"

"Oh, Trina. You're implying that she planned the plane crash that killed Shep."

"That's right. I am. It makes sense. And that's why both Tia and Katie should know that this beast may be alive. I know she stole my sister's life. I know she killed her, and if I can't prove that, maybe we can prove that she killed others."

"We're not private investigators, Trina. I wouldn't know where to start."

13

"Tess, help me find this murderer. Hunter Cross deserves to be punished."

"I don't know, Trina ... and please, we know her as Cristin ..."

"You're right. If we're going to find her, we'll need to stop calling her either name. From now on, she's Yvette, okay? To use the other names will be too confusing, especially because my seven-year-old daughter's name is Cristin. Are you willing to help me find Yvette? I must tell you that I'm going to search for her with or without your help, but it will be easier with combined forces; and in the event I was to find her on my own, the rest of your family would hear about it on the news anyway."

"This is so unnerving," said Tess, who paced around her kitchen island, wearing an invisible energy path into the hardwood floor.

Trina remained silent.

"All right, but if I'm going to help you, we need to agree on something. I must reiterate; when you contacted me a few years ago, you asked that I not tell my sister that I'd met you because you didn't want to complicate her life or your own parents' lives, for that matter. I honored your request and never told a soul we had met, Trina. But now, you're putting me in a precarious position because you want me to tell my family that you have contacted me. I don't want this to backfire. You must agree that as far as anyone else is concerned, this is the first time we've spoken. This must be our story: you found my contact information on my website because you read my book. You emailed me with your suspicions and your discovery of the painting in the art periodical, and I called you. It's the only way I can face my husband and my sisters. It's very important to me, Trina. Do you agree to this?"

"Of course, Tess. Of course I do."

"Okay, with that said, I'll speak to my husband. That's as much as I can promise right now. Send me your picture, a picture of *her* as the girl you knew and introduce yourself, as if we've never spoken. Include your telephone number and ask for me to call you. Communicate clearly

14

what you believe to be true and include a picture of the painting you found in the magazine. I'll call you tomorrow."

"You're doing the right thing," Trina said in an affirming voice.

"Let's both hope so," Tess replied. She hung up and reflected on the web she was weaving. She hoped that she wouldn't become entangled as a victim, unable to extricate herself from her own creation.

That evening, Ren walked in the door at 6:30. By 8, Tess had spilled the details of her story. Any loopholes that Ren may have found in her relaying of the story were unspoken, probably eclipsed by the shock that the woman, who had lived under their roof and shared their lives, was not only alleged to be a murderer, but was most likely alive. Ren, being the skeptic he was, asked a barrage of questions which Tess was able to answer. When he saw the photo of Trina with *Cristin*, he admitted that Trina had to be Katie's daughter and Trina had indeed known *Cristin*. Tess shared the emailed magazine photo of the painting, signed "Yvette," which Trina had scanned to Tess's computer that afternoon, and the pieces of a gruesome puzzle fit together.

"So what are you going to do with this information, Tess?" Ren inquired.

"Trina wants me to talk to Katie and Tia, because she thinks they should know that Shep and Yvette's alleged murderer may still be out there. My sisters thought she was a liar, not a killer."

"So what do you want to do?" he asked, emphasizing *you*.

"Rennie, I don't know ... that's why I'm talking to you about this nightmare."

She wrung her hands, clasping them together until she could feel her nails bite her palms. "She's going to pursue this hunt whether I agree to join her or not," she said, shaking her head. "If Trina finds her, it will all come out, and I will be guilty of withholding this critical information from my sisters. I don't think I could survive it."

"So that's probably your answer, Tess."

"To tell Katie and Tia?"

"I know it's painful but you need to weigh how much more painful it would be if they find that you had knowledge of this theory and chose not to share it, to say nothing of not telling Katie that her birth daughter has contacted you. Your sisters are grownups, Tess. You don't need to keep secrets, especially of this magnitude, to protect them ... from what? The truth? Would you want them to protect you from the truth?"

"But that's just it. What if none of this is true? ... What if she didn't kill Shep or Yvette? ... What if she died in the plane crash?"

"She did steal Cristin Shanihan's identity. She's not exactly lily white," replied Ren.

"But it doesn't make her a murderer."

"No, it doesn't. Tess, you need to decide which risk you're willing to take. To tell your sisters of your suspicions and find out she is dead, or withhold your suspicions and find out she's alive, possibly still a threat, and you knew about it all along. The third option is not to tell them and Trina might discover that she's dead, no harm done. But are you willing to chance it?"

"All right, all right. You're right. When you put it that way ..." Tess paced the room as she spoke. "So I'll call Trina in the morning. I told her that I needed to talk with you first, Rennie. Do you think I should call my sisters or should I see them in person? Alone or with Trina?" Her speech was peppered with short anxious breaths. She knew she was capable of making these decisions on her own, but felt more secure deferring to her husband's guidance and blessing.

"Which way would you prefer to be told if the shoe was on the other foot?" he asked.

Tess's eyes closed then opened wide, focusing on the ceiling.

"In person ... alone. Asking Trina to join me may be too much of a shock. But definitely in person ... at least with Katie. After I tell her, I'd probably call Tia ... but seriously, now that Tia's living in D.C., I might as well take the quick trip down from Boston. What do you think?"

"I think you're on track. And remember, all you're signing up for is disclosing the possibility that Cristin, now possibly Yvette, is alive.

That's step one. After the theory is disclosed, they may not want to pursue it. If so, Trina may be on her own. But if your sisters are going to join forces, be thinking of what your plan will be, Tess. Whom will you employ to find this phantom artist and what proof do you really have? Enough to involve the police? If you become involved past this disclosure phase, you should speak to legal counsel before you take the next step. Agreed?"

"You're right. But one step at a time. Tomorrow I'll call Katie and book my trip to Boston." Despite her deep yogic breathing, her nerves felt serrated as her tension escalated. "I have to stop thinking about this, Rennie. Can we talk about something else?"

"Fine by me. How about our tickets to *La Traviata* tomorrow night? Anna Netrebko is singing the role of Violetta."

"Grazie, mio marito."

"Prego, mia amante."

It was the perfect distraction. Italian opera sung by a Russian diva, and particularly, this Russian diva. Netrebko was strikingly gorgeous with an angelic voice and a talent for acting to boot. Tess loved the flourish of the bel canto style. She loved nothing more than this graceful, charming opera, with its sweeping orchestral style and embroidered characters that loved, hated, and betrayed one another with intense emotion. Much like real life.

That night as she lay in bed, she remorsefully reflected on the fact that she'd not told Ren that she'd met Trina in their home three years ago. With the heart of a lynx described in her Native American medicine cards as the keeper of secrets, she'd protected her niece's identity merely because Trina had asked her to do so. She thought to herself, *Why was it that my need to be polite to a stranger could trump my instinct to be forthcoming with my husband and my sister? Why did I feel obligated to keep Trina's identity secret? because she asked me? because I didn't want to upset my family? because I didn't think they could handle it? because I didn't think I'd get caught? because I felt in control?*

Each layered question peeled away until she felt uncomfortably transparent, vulnerable. Each question felt more damning. So she wrapped herself in her writer's cape and impersonalized her responses. *Human nature is fascinating. I'll have to write about it someday.*

CHAPTER THREE

Our doubts are traitors, and make us lose the good we oft might win,
by fearing to attempt.
—William Shakespeare

Bryan arrived home the following afternoon, with stories of his Montana travels and his delight with the photographs of flora and fauna, people he'd met, and history he'd uncovered. His expertise was interviewing inhabitants of the areas he visited, and writing captivating stories with the bounty of nature as his backdrop.

After he'd settled in, they sat on their bedroom balcony which overlooked a timbered area, the most private lot they could find on the outskirts of their Lincoln, Nebraska, suburb.

"I want to hear about your trip, honey. Although you do know you'll have to repeat everything for my mom. She loves your Montana stories," Trina said, urging her husband to open the conversation.

"Well, it had a precarious beginning like I told you on the phone … with what I now call airport insecurity. But once I started driving, it felt like home. So you know me. I like to go off the beaten path. First, I went to Deep Creek Canyon off Highway 5. Those lodgepole pines and Douglas firs. I took my best photo of a peregrine falcon there. Took a beauty of an elk munching willow and a couple of bucks with full racks lying in a meadow near the Gibbon. I even captured stellar shots of a northern harrier, let's see, a Clark's nutcracker, and a western tanager. Mmm. Mmm. Those were satisfying."

Trina smiled, unable to envision the foreign-sounding birds with the strange-sounding names.

"Then I visited the Madison River Canyon Earthquake area. That was sobering. The site of a natural disaster where there's staggering geological evidence of an earthquake's destruction. Trina, I don't know if I ever told you this, but that earthquake rocked that valley, causing a massive landslide to block the Madison River, and creating Quake Lake, where a forest of trees is still submerged in water with tree tops breaking the surface. It is a sight to behold."

Trina sipped her lemon-drop martini, didn't say a word, but nodded her head.

"I stayed in some campsites along the Gallatin and talked to rich fly fishermen as we stood side by side in our hip boots. Bought a new pair of hip boots. The fishing was awesome. The Gallatin River, winding through those meadows, and carving valleys through those mountains! Well, it takes your breath away, honey. I set out looking for indigenous characters, visited a couple of hole-in-the-wall saloons and only found rich cowboys … actually Californians dressed like cowboys. That was disappointing."

Trina interjected with a mischievous smile. "It sounds like a target-rich environment for a single gal wanting to land a rich fisherman or rich cowboy, doesn't it?"

"I guess." He dismissed the comment, failing to see the humor. "On the last night I slipped over the border into Idaho to Henry Forks Lodge for a great meal. I may have been a tad underdressed."

"Didn't you go to Yellowstone, baby?"

"Yes, if the truth be known. I tried to stay away for as long as I could because I like the roads less traveled, but I love Yellowstone. Despite the commercialization and crowds, it is still one beautiful patch in God's quilt. We have to take the girls there soon."

"Don't you think Elizabeth is too young to remember a trip like that? She's only five. Cristin would remember, I think."

"I vividly remember a trip to Toadstool Park when I was six. Well, maybe not vividly, but if I take pictures, it will help their recall, don't you think? Besides, we'd probably have to wait for summer anyway and they'd be six and eight by then."

"Sounds like a plan." Trina realized she was agreeing more enthusiastically than she might have, had she not needed to tell him about her contact with Tess Monson Parker that morning. *Oh the machinations of a determined mind.* She wasn't actually conniving. As her father had taught her, manipulation had a bad rap. Its definition was to manage shrewdly, which she had every intention of doing. She was merely setting a stage, lining up agreeable muses in the wings.

"Bryan, I need to tell you something, something you're probably not going to like."

"That doesn't sound good," he said, as he settled back in his chair, stretched out his legs and placed his feet on the wicker ottoman.

"I contacted Tess Parker, my aunt in Minnesota. I sent her *The New and The Obscure* issue, that magazine with Hunter's painting in it? I thought she had the right to know that her Cristin was probably still alive."

"Possibly, Trina, not probably."

"Well, how else am I going to know if I don't follow the one lead I have? In ten years, I hadn't a single clue as to how to find her. In ten years, Bryan. That's a long time. I've asked for Tess's help."

"What did she say?"

"She called this morning and said she told her husband last night. She agreed to tell her sisters and is flying to the East Coast at the end of the week to talk to them."

"And then what?"

"I guess we all meet to assemble as many facts as we can and hire a private investigator. We can't very well go to the police until we have something concrete."

There, it was said and a *fait accompl*i. It was akin to the feeling that it was easier to ask forgiveness than permission, although she wasn't asking for either.

Bryan was silent.

"Say something," Trina prodded.

"What do you want me to say? You can't undo what you've done but you could leave it alone. However, I can tell you're not going to. In my mind, you're ankle deep in Mississippi mud. You've decided to follow up on this wild goose chase so I'll stay out of your way. I'm not going to quarterback you on this one."

Bryan paused, then continued, "Trina, I'm only going to say this once. Sometimes your suspicious nature is your undoing. Be careful."

Trina nodded deliberately.

"How much is this investigation going to cost? Who's going to pay for it?"

"I don't know. I was hoping my aunts or my mother know someone. I'll ask them."

"Your mother, Trina? You have a mother. Dori Shanihan is your mother."

"You know what I mean, Bryan. I love my mother. I mean my birth mother, Katie."

"Are you going to tell Dori what you're doing?"

"Of course. I've already thought it through. She knows I met Tess, but at that time, we thought there wouldn't be any more contact. Hunter was dead and there was no reason to meet the rest of the family, including Katie. Now I think Hunter is alive. I have no idea how Mom and Dad will react, but I can't worry about that. I'm doing this for my sister."

"Your sister died ten years ago, Trina."

"Okay. I'm doing it because she was wronged ... her identity stolen, and she was possibly murdered ... and there should be justice in her memory. Bryan, if you'd been murdered, would you want me to drop it if I had a clue as to where your murderer was?"

"No. But you wouldn't be pursuing the murderer for me. So be honest about your motive." He paused. "I just hope you're not disappointed, honey. I hope you either find nothing or proof that this person really is dead, so you can get on with your life. Remember, you have a husband and two children who love you. I hate to see you concentrating on the condiment when the main course is right here. Don't miss what's important, Trina."

"I won't. I promise. I just know she's out there, Bryan. I just know it. It makes sense to me. Doesn't it make sense?" she asked.

"Anything makes sense if you believe it."

CHAPTER FOUR

No one can say of this house, there is no trouble here.
—Asian proverb

Before Tess arrived at Katie's doorstep, she faced the fact that she was, once again, a deliverer of shocking news. This time the news was not an omission of truth, the discovery of which had left Katie emotionally numb and bereft for years; but rather, a message of possible hope and redemption … although still shocking. Katie was fragile and had recently shared with Tess that through what she termed "the Cristin ordeal," she'd lost a quarter of her body weight, a third of her ability to sleep, and half of her faith in humankind. But the two sisters had incrementally, gently, found their way back to each other after their estrangement seven years ago.

Tess traveled under the auspices of having found a great deal on a Delta fare. There had been no benefit in planting seeds ahead of time as to the purpose of her trip because the truth would sprout to the surface soon enough and this way, Katie couldn't agonize in advance. Tess clothed her own timidity in a cloak of strength and goodwill.

Katie lived an hour from the airport so Tess hailed a taxi. The autumn day smelled of woodlands, and the cognac-tinted, slanted sunlight fluted through the flitting oak and maple leaves like a spinning kaleidoscope. Tess hadn't visited Boston since Shep's funeral and although she'd seen Katie's new home at the reception, it wouldn't feel like home. The former abode in Wellesley was home, but ah, that clock had struck its time. New chapter. As the cab approached the townhome, her heart thumped, her temples pounded, and the pulse in her wrists metronomically joined the body's rhythm section. The finale was nearing and it was time to excel. She'd learned from experience, that no matter how many times she'd simulate a strenuous conversation, it always took on a life of its own, sometimes surprising her with its grace, but more often rearing an ugly head that couldn't be contained or decapitated.

The taxi stopped. The female taxi driver to whom she hadn't said a word since she'd given the address, announced, "Ma'am, we're here."

"Do I have to get out?" Tess asked rhetorically.

"Unless you want me to take you back to Logan." She paused. "Tough trip, huh?"

"Yep ... tough trip ... sorry." Tess looked at the fare and paid the driver.

"Good luck."

"Thanks. I'm going to need it."

Tess climbed out of the car, grabbed her purse and carryon, and closed the car door. She felt as if she were having an out-of-body experience, as she waved goodbye to a nameless taxi driver, delaying her about-face which would lead her to Katie's front door.

About face. Forward, march. Left, right, left, right, left, right. Halt. She heard the doorbell ring as she pressed it.

Katie opened the door and stood with open arms, welcoming an embrace. And there before Tess stood an adult Trina, with the same green eyes with flecks of gold, and auburn hair to her shoulders. She shook off the image and hugged her sister.

"Come in. Come in," beckoned Katie. "The tea is on, Irish blend of course. Ingrid is on her way ... she doesn't live far from here and runs every morning ... training for the marathon, you know. Heidi's in Dubai on business but Ingrid is so excited to see her Aunt Tess."

"Wonderful," Tess heard herself say as she computed whether she would share her news with Ingrid as well. In an instant, she deciphered that Katie's decision to meet Trina and/or find Yvette should be Katie's decision. Whether she shared it with her daughter was her business, not

Tess's. Making that decision, Tess somewhat relaxed, as if having been given a reprieve from imminent sentencing.

The morning passed quickly. Tess heard about Katie's new job as a travel agent which provided a backdrop for some hilarious stories about working with the public. She then heard about Heidi's job finding exotic cars for wealthy car enthusiasts, and Ingrid's position as a stage manager for a repertory theater in the city, something she should have been doing for years. Heidi had a steady boyfriend and Ingrid was engaged to a man from Connecticut; so Katie appeared ebulliently happy for her daughters.

Ingrid arrived, sweaty and fit, took a few minutes to clean up, and joined the sisterly coven for a delicious, healthy lunch of salad, salmon, and sesame seed pull bread, followed by a catch-up session, cataloging the events in Minnetonka and Boston in the past year.

It was evident that Ingrid and Katie had grown closer. Katie beamed as Ingrid talked about her fiancé Adam because he was all that was on her mind.

That evening, when the sisters were finally alone, Katie lit a fire in the fireplace.

"Remember what Dad used to say, little sister? *One log won't burn, two logs might burn, three logs will burn, and four logs make a good fire.*"

"Like it was yesterday."

They wrapped themselves in shawls that their mother had knit, and Katie brought out photo albums of their childhood.

When she could no longer put off the inevitable, Tess found the right moment to change the subject.

"Kate, I have a picture I need to share with you." She reached into her purse, took out the photograph that she and Ren had found in Cristin's drawer seven years ago, and handed it to her sister.

Katie instantly recognized Cristin and raised her voice. "Why are you showing this to me? Why are you bringing her up?"

"Please, Katie, look at the other people in the photo."

She studied the photo with the date of May 7, 1994, printed on the perimeter.

"This girl looks like me ... but that's impossible ... as a young girl, I never knew Cristin and these girls are in their mid-teens. I was in my early thirties in 1994, married with three children ..."

"Four children."

"Why are you bringing *that* up? What is this?"

"Look at the photograph ... closely ... please."

Katie stared at the photo, boring her eyes into the face of the girl who strikingly resembled her. "But all of my children look like their father," she whispered in disbelief.

"Not this one, Kate."

After an interminable pause, she asked, "What is her name?"

"Trina, as in Katrina."

"The name I gave her," Katie whispered.

"Yes, her adoptive parents honored your name."

"Oh my." She hesitated. "Oh my." She paused again. "Where is she?"

"She lives in Lincoln, Nebraska, married with two daughters."

"She knew Cristin? How do you know all of this?" Katie suddenly stammered accusingly.

"She read my book, Katie. She recognized the story about Mum's stolen locket, and tracked me down, wanting to know if the story was true. I hesitated to tell her anything but she insisted that she had information that we'd want to hear, so I listened."

"What are you talking about?"

"It all makes sense. The picture you're holding? Ren and I found it years ago. We recognized Cristin but didn't know the other two girls. I remember thinking that this one," pointing to Trina, "looked familiar, but we weren't looking for your daughter, so I blew it off. I scanned this photo to Trina and she identified the third girl as her sister. But the point is ... Trina knew Cristin and she's looking for her."

"Cristin's dead. Did you tell her that Cristin is dead?"

"Yes, I did but … okay … let me back up." Tess breathed deeply, folded her hands and clasped them as if to brace herself. "Trina believes that the person we knew as Cristin killed her sister and assumed her identity."

"She was a murderer? What was her sister's name?"

"Cristin Shanihan."

"What was her real name?"

"Hunter Cross."

"Oh. This is too much. What does it matter anyway? Cristin … Hunter … whatever the hell her name was … she's dead," Katie screamed.

"That's why I'm here, Katie. Trina doesn't think so … and neither do I."

Tess watched the blood drain from Katie's face like a mask changing colors before her eyes. Katie's confusion had turned to terror.

With the sound of panic in her voice, Katie said, "Well then…I'm missing something. Why in the world would you think *she's* alive?"

Tess took the evidence that she'd tucked into the crease of the sofa and slapped the folded magazine on the coffee table.

"This is why! Trina found this painting reproduction in a recent art magazine," emphasizing the word *recent*. "This painting is hers."

"So maybe someone stole it. This doesn't mean she's alive. She died with my son in the accident!"

"Katie, that crossed my mind too but there's one other piece of incriminating evidence. The painting … it's signed 'Yvette.' "

"So? What does that mean?"

"Remember hearing about Tia's friend Yvette in Grenoble? Cristin also knew her. Yvette was found dead on her kitchen floor prior to the plane crash."

"So? What are you saying?"

"I think, we think, that she's living as an artist named Yvette in Switzerland."

"And you're saying she killed two people."

"Yes. But Katie, think about it ... who else ...?"

The pause seemed unending as the single question telescoped into its painful but obvious answer. Suddenly Katie panicked like a person locked in a lion's cage. She jumped up from the sofa, vigorously exhaling with a battery of huffing outbursts. She began to shake her hands like she was playing invisible castanets. "Oh my God, oh my God, she's responsible for my son's death? And she's alive?"

"If she'd wanted to be found, she would have contacted us. She wanted to lose herself which begs the question *why*. I'm sorry, Katie. I couldn't keep this from you and maybe we're wrong. I hope we're wrong. But we don't think so."

"Who else have you told? Have you told Tia?"

"No. I've told Rennie, and Trina has shared this with her husband. I'm going to fly to D.C. on Thursday to talk to Tia. It will be up to you and her whether or not you want to become involved in finding this Yvette. But I should warn you that Trina will pursue this, whether you want to be party to it or not. And Katie, Trina is a beautiful young woman. She's so much like you."

"You've met her?"

Tess caught herself. "On the phone ... but I can tell." She tacitly begged God's forgiveness and continued. "She's determined like you would be, and her voice ... well, she sounds just like you."

Katie shook her head, then buried her face in her hands as if she wanted to hide her potential involvement and make it disappear. "I don't know what to say. I need to think about this. I'm not prepared to make a decision. It all needs to sink in." She took a string of deep breaths, like a speaker preparing to go on stage. "When are you seeing Tia?"

"The day after tomorrow."

Katie dropped to the sofa. "I thought this God-awful ordeal had come to an end. I can't imagine opening it up! But Shep's death? I want her to pay."

"Then we'll need to find her, Kate. If we're all in agreement, our combined forces will be stronger than just one person searching for this monster who seems to slip away like a stealth vulture as soon as she's taken what she wants."

"What does she want?" Katie screamed. "What DOES she want?"

Katie put her hands on her knees to brace herself and pushed down to stand as she audibly exhaled. Hunched over with her head hanging, she leaned into Tess's chest and hugged her. Then she whispered, "I don't want to talk about it anymore. I want to go to sleep ... if I can. But I want to be with you when you tell Tia on Thursday. Maybe by then I'll see things more clearly. Good night."

"Goodnight" was all Tess could muster as well. She followed her sister down the hallway. They turned into their rooms precisely at the same time, like prisoners entering their cells for the night. Tess closed her guest room door and noticed that on her blue pillowcase was a white rose with a lacey white ribbon and a note. She opened the envelope and read.

Dearest sister,

I'm so happy that you're here. I have looked forward to us being together again more than you can imagine. We've been through so much but now we can put everything behind us and just be sisters. Nothing but special memories from now on, Katessa. I love you so much.

Always and forever,
Katrina

Tess read the words three times, undressed, and climbed into the huge oak-framed bed that had been Ingrid's childhood bed and in the family for years. Knowing she would not easily fall asleep, she started cataloging the events that had led to this dramatic turning point. *If I hadn't invited "Cristin Shanihan" into our home, Shep and Yvette might still be alive. If I hadn't written the book about* her *entry into our lives,*

30

Trina never would have made the connection and contacted me. If Trina hadn't seen the painting in the art publication, we would not know that Cristin may be alive. Woulda, shoulda, coulda. Under the floorboards of her intuition was the tell-tale heart of the matter which beat so percussively, it was impossible to ignore ... the signature "Yvette."

But herein lies the rub, she thought. Maybe their relentless pursuit of Yvette would be the bitch's undoing. Granted, nothing could ever undo her vicious deeds but perhaps, just perhaps, she would pay. *Enough. Enough*, Tess thought, as she slipped into sleep like a seal from an ice floe into the sea.

CHAPTER FIVE

One equal temper of heroic heart,
Made weak by time and fate,
But strong in will,
To strive, to seek, to find, and not to yield.
—Alfred Tennyson

Two days later, Tess and Katie arrived at a seventh floor townhome, off DuPont Circle, which Tia had recently rented. The building "had history," which sounded like a euphemism for old, but according to their sister, her interior had been modernized with Brazilian hardwood floors and stainless steel appliances. Besides which, as she had communicated with Tess, its location was a fabulous metropolitan area with great Metro access, and she'd grown accustomed to walking everywhere in France, so why not? Walking was better for her general health, great for her butt and legs, and not purchasing a car was better for her bank account. Win, win, win. She had texted Tess the night before that she'd be home late but that the key would be under the mat. It was.

Tess and Katie nested in the two extra bedrooms, and as directed through the copious notes in the kitchen, reminiscent of a scavenger hunt, they helped themselves to the deli meats and salads while admiring Tia's European art, music, and book acquisitions, definitively French. An entire bookshelf was devoted to books written in French. But then again, Tia was a translator in the nation's capital, so speaking, reading, and thinking in French was, by necessity, second nature to her.

"Our little sister has grown up, *n'est-ce pas?*" Katie remarked.

"*Mais oui.*"

"She's even displayed copies of your books, Tess." There on the coffee table were Tess's compilation of short stories and the book that was about to change their lives, ironically entitled, *Gone*.

Just as Katie had lit the sandalwood-scented candles and turned on the electric fireplace, Tia burst into her living room like a surprise guest at a birthday party. "What are you doing here?" She ran to hug Katie. "I thought only Tess was coming."

Just then, Tess materialized from the hallway. "We thought we'd surprise you!"

"You have!" Tia squealed. "This will be the perfect night! I'm so happy you're both here."

The guests exchanged furtive glances that were not translated by the translator, and pinot noir was opened in celebration of their reunion. In quick-witted conversation that is spawned by excitement, the women bounced from Ingrid's engagement to Tia's job to Tess's current writing project. But it wasn't long before Tia broached the operative question to Katie.

"When did you decide to come?"

Katie glanced at Tess, took a deep breath, and paused before answering. "The night before last. I hadn't realized that Tess was flying here after her visit to Boston and I wanted to see you too. Actually, I wanted to be here when she told you something that she's discovered."

"Oh, that sounds intriguing. Do tell." Tia's wide, smiling eyes urged her sister to continue.

Tess relayed the story in efficient detail without giving Tia a moment to respond. It was easier that way, having replayed the scenario dozens of times the night before, and feeling more confident with Katie next to her.

"I'm in shock. You are certain this is true?" Tia asked as she stood up and started pacing the living room floor

"No. But we believe it may be … the painting is the clue. Tia, you said you saw her art in that studio in Grenoble. Does this look like her painting?"

Tess pulled out the magazine.

"Yes. But Shep, my darling sweet nephew. Oh, Katie, this has to be horrible for you. I'm so sorry."

Sitting on the sofa, Katie didn't reply, but with eyes downcast, was obviously overcome with emotion.

"Oh, Katie. I don't expect you to say anything. I'm sorry. I won't talk about that right now. And Cristin killed Yvette? That never occurred to me either. If I hadn't invited Cristin to France, and she'd never met Yvette, my friend, my beautiful friend Yvette would be alive? *Mon Dieu.*" Her eyes welled with tears.

"Tia, you can't blame yourself. You can imagine how I feel, having invited her into my life, and subsequently our lives. It is what it is but the question remains—-do you want to open up this ugly drama? Or should we leave it alone? What's your gut instinct?"

"My instinct tells me we need to find her, bring her to justice. We're talking about three people that we know of … how many others have there been? Yvette was right about her. I wish I had listened. She's a monster. If what we think is true, she will kill again. We can't stand idly by. We have to do something."

"Then we're in agreement?" Tess's eyes darted between her sisters.

"What does Ren think?" Tia inquired.

"He felt that it was up to the two of you … and Trina, because you three were the people whose lives were most heinously violated."

"That's right. Trina." Tia looked at Katie with wondering eyes. "How do you feel about meeting your daughter? Our niece."

"At this point, I think it's a foregone conclusion. We should meet her ... together. I know my girls will be thrilled. I'll be nervous. But we all knew she was out there. We just haven't put a face or personality to her."

"Here's her picture, Tia," Tess offered, taking the old photo out of her purse, feeling its serrated edges.

"Oh my. Katie. She looks like you. Exactly like you."

"I know. I know," said Katie who then gnawed her lower lip." I think I need to rest," she continued, then walked to her room, leaving her sisters to quietly commune.

The following day, Tess called Trina to inform her that the three sisters were aligned and would meet her as soon as the cosmic dust had settled. At Tia's prompting that evening, it had been arranged that the trio would visit a wine-tasting art studio called Arte e Vino on Pennsylvania Avenue. Tia had taken art lessons for months and wanted to share the experience. A novel concept, a marriage of two delights, art and wine ... why not? However, the underlying motive for the visit that night was to speak to her teacher whose husband was a private investigator. They had to start somewhere.

"Arte e Vino is within walking distance from here," Tia explained. "It's a good thing because since the presidential election is only six weeks away, the traffic in D.C. is intense. No one's predicting the outcome, except for the occasional far left or right-wing zealots."

Tess picked up the gauntlet and remarked, "Remember after 9/11, how popular George W was? Those days are gone. With the war in Iraq, healthcare, gas prices...."

Katie chimed in. "Don't forget the national debt."

Tess continued, "Of course. I mean, really... what else can we pile on this plate of national crises? Whether it's for the better or not, the country wants a change."

"Maybe it's my age or maybe it's living in D.C.," continued Tia, "but I've certainly become more politically conscious, and frankly, the country appears to be decomposing into a divisive, unforgiving populace. But enough politics." She clapped her together and said, "Let's go!"

Arm in arm, the sisters left the building and headed toward their destination. It had been a rainy day so leaves clogged the gutters and squished under their feet like mushy compost. Rain puddles reflected amber street lights and twilight humidity compressed the air, reminding Tess of Minneapolis. She wondered what Ren was doing.

Arte e Vino's Italian ceramic-tile flooring was draped with pods of canvas, mottled with and smelling of paint drippings and turpentine. The walls were plastered with art, painted by young wannabes, professional artists, and everything in between. Sarah, Trina's art teacher, met them at their station with a smile that could melt cold butter. After introductions were made, the wine was ordered. Cheese and crackers were delivered to their table, around which stood three easels with canvases set up for the sisters. When everyone was settled, the art lesson began.

"Tonight is Improv Night," the raven-haired Sarah began. "What is your experience level, ladies?"

"Well. You know how amateurish I am," Tia said teasingly. "I've discussed this adventure with my sisters but their experience is even less than mine ... so you have a group of beginners, Sarah. Sorry."

"No problem." She twinkled. "Let's start with something simple like a basic landscape. Or would you prefer something more modern, like an expression of feelings through color and line?"

Tia said, "That sounds more doable to me. Maybe less embarrassing. But a sip of my wine would be the best start."

"It's going to take more than a sip for me," stated Katie, laughing out loud for the first time in a couple of days.

"Help yourself. I want you to have a good time tonight," said Sarah.

"Sarah, I think you'll need to start at the beginning ... like in Genesis," said Tess, throwing her head back and laughing heartily.

"I think you'll surprise yourselves, ladies," Sarah said like an encouraging teacher. "I have an idea. Is there something that you share in common? After all, you are sisters. There must be some common theme you'd like to express. If you have any ideas, shout them out."

The women looked at each other for tacit permission. In a round robin free-for-all, they took turns, venting their emotions like a barrage of enemy fire. "Rage! Disbelief! Anger! Fear! Confusion! Helplessness! Vengeance!"

"Whoa, whoa, whoa! What's going on, ladies?" Sarah's stunning smile faded.

"Sorry about that, Sarah," Tia said, with a gritty face and firmness in tone that defended the validity of their exclamations. "We have discovered that someone who has wronged our family, whom we presumed was dead, may still be alive. As a matter of fact, Sarah, maybe you could help us. Didn't you tell me that your husband is a private investigator?"

"Well yes, he is …"

"Would it be possible to speak with him? We're in the dark. We think she's in Switzerland but it's complicated. She's had a string of aliases. We don't know where to start. We've never done this before."

"Of course," Sarah replied. "I'll talk to him this evening. Do you even want to continue with the painting?"

The Monson girls chimed in a dissonant but resolute shout. "YES!"

They had possibly located a private investigator, which had been their mission. Now they could lose themselves in painting what they felt, and drinking their wine. *In vino veritas.*

That night, before Tess and Katie's departure the following morning, they surveyed and studied their paintings. Tia suggested that she store them in D.C., and when the object of their rage, their fear, their vengeance, was behind bars, they would convene at *Arte e Vino* once again to release more uplifting feelings of relief, justice, and peace of mind onto new canvases. They all agreed.

Close to midnight, after intoxicating and intoxicated conversation, they burned down. Their combined memories, hurt, and anger, lay on the table like bags of evidence, ready to convict their target. They had no idea how they would do it, but they were committed to doing whatever it took to find her. No turning back.

Just before retiring, Tess spoke. "Isn't it ironic that the pent-up feelings we unleashed tonight on canvas might be similar to the feelings she experiences all the time when she paints?"

They nodded their heads in inferred consideration. Had they found a common denominator with the person they were about to hunt? The mere thought made their communal skin crawl and the room shiver.

CHAPTER SIX

The pedigree of honey
Does not conquer the bee;
A clover any time to her
Is aristocracy.
—Emily Dickinson

By mid-October, the rendezvous was set. Trina, Tess, and Katie would fly to Washington D.C. to stay at Tia's. That time of year, the nation's capital had the most temperate climate of their four cities, which wasn't saying much, but it was latitudinally the farthest south. Katie and Tess agreed that this should be a private time among the women, so intermittent pop-ins from Ingrid or even Ren could be disruptive. Tia's place was large enough, quiet enough, private enough.

D.C. was chilly and windy that week. Tess rented a car basically for the long weekend's airport shuttles. After all, there was a possibility they wouldn't even leave Tia's townhome, except to eat or go for a walk, and if they did, the Metro was convenient. Katie and Tess arrived a day before Trina to prepare for the meeting. Katie seemed particularly nervous to meet her daughter; Tia, excited to meet her niece; and Tess prayed she could disguise the fact that Trina and she had already met.

The three sisters used the time to prepare food with Tia directing her two sous-chefs in the kitchen. The Eagles reunion DVD blared while the girls intermittently sang, danced, à la *The Big Chill*, and sipped Virginia's famed cabernet franc.

Tess sampled the goat cheese and plum chutney on a cracker, "Whew…spicy," she remarked Then she picked up her wine glass and said, "I feel so cosmopolitan, so D.C."

Rolling her eyes, and lifting her chin with feigned old guard arrogance, Tia remarked, "Well, you know, they say Virginia may be the Napa of the East."

"Who's 'they'?" asked Tess.

"You know, they ... those in the know," Tia responded, striking a pose as if she were model in an advertisement in *Vogue*.

Katie laughed. "I believe you. This is delicious. I wonder if Trina drinks wine, or maybe she's a bratwurst and beer girl."

"I bet she's a chameleon like I am," said Tess. "I'm a brat and beer girl in the right setting. Put me in a football stadium at a Gopher/Badger game, and there's nothing in the world better than a steaming brat rolled in sauerkraut and smothered with mustard ... and a cold beer."

"Who is this person masquerading as my sister?" Katie laughed.

Tess defended her position. "I'm serious. And any self-respecting Nebraskan loves brats and beer, I guarantee it."

"Why do you say that?" Katie persisted.

"You're not serious. Did you know that when the Nebraska Cornhusker stadium holds a capacity crowd on game day, which is every game day by the way, it becomes the third largest city in the state? They're not sitting in the stands and sipping viognier. They're a football lovin', brat and beer nation."

Katie cleared her throat as she tapped the rim of her glass. "Which brings me back to my question, or at least what I implied ... do you think Trina will feel comfortable with us?"

"Only as comfortable as we make it for her, girls," said Tia, as she suddenly swept through the room, removing a few books written in French from the coffee table.

"I agree," said Tess. "Besides which, she's as refined as any of us."

As soon as the words left her lips, she heard her slip of the tongue.

"How do you know? You haven't met her," Katie commented in a voice that dared a response.

In Tess's mind, the statement hung above them like a sinister thundercloud, but only for the seconds it took for her to blow it out of the room.

"I've talked to her. I can hear it in her voice. She's one of us. And by the way, I should clarify. She was born in Nebraska, raised in Iowa, and then she married a Nebraska boy so they settled in Lincoln. That's all I know. You can ask all the questions you want tomorrow."

Tia broke the ensuing silence. "Well, I for one, am very excited to meet her. And sisters of mine, we do have a possible contact in Switzerland which we can talk about tomorrow when Trina is with us. But past that, I'm just glad we have a chance to meet her. I'm hungry. The smell of the soup is driving me crazy."

"Wait, wait, hold your horses," Katie interjected. "We have a contact in Switzerland? Tell us now."

"It came in an email yesterday from the PI, the husband of my art teacher? It's just a name of someone who might be a lead, that's all. I'll print it out in the morning so we can wrap our minds around it."

"Okay, sounds good," Katie responded. "I'm tired and I'm hungry. Let's eat."

After dinner, the weary sisters hugged each other and called it a night.

Tess didn't fall asleep for what seemed like an hour. She was nervous on many levels. The perils of a conscience. She hoped that her prior meeting with Trina wouldn't surface, like an affair not being discovered. *Sometimes people did get away with an indiscretion. Let this be one of those times*, she prayed, asking God to give her a spiritual mulligan.

The last thought of the night that she would recall when she awoke in the morning was something an old, beloved friend had once suggested. Tess would have to string her own pearls of experience, one pearl at a time. In the recesses of her mind, she felt dread that the string could break, scatter, and shatter on the floor of her life.

The following day, Tess offered to retrieve Trina from Dulles, considering she had rented the car, was the initial contact, and the only one who had spoken to the girl. Not being intimately familiar with the city, Tess gave herself ample time to drive to the airport. As she left Tia's building, she saw a young black girl jumping on a pogo stick on top of a manhole. She hadn't seen or thought of a pogo stick since she was a child. It was a snapshot from her past, like tying newspapers in bundles with twine for school paper drives (*where did those papers go? who bought them? and for what reason?)* Her mind wandered as she admired the elegance of D.C. architecture, so different in style from Minnetonka, Minnesota. She then revisited the image of the girl on the pogo stick and the manhole. Hadn't she read about exploding manholes in Washington D.C., something to do with methane gas? She'd have to ask Tia about that one.

By the time she arrived at Dulles and parked her car, she was reasonably certain that Trina's plane had landed. It was three years past 9/11; she couldn't meet the plane. Terrorists 1, Homeland 0.

Next to the baggage claim, she saw Trina, dressed in a camel winter coat, trimmed in faux fur, camel leather gloves, high brown boots, and a camel skull cap crowning her long auburn hair. Tess was once again struck by Trina's resemblance to Katie, the mother she was about to meet for the first time. The women hugged, and she instantly realized that anyone having seen them at the baggage claim area would suspect they had met before.

They had a little over a half hour together in the car to speak privately.

"How are you feeling about this meeting?" Tess asked

"I'm a bit nervous to meet my mother and my aunt, I must admit. But it's hard to separate my apprehension from my excitement. Don't ask me to name just one emotion right now."

"Well, on this end, Katie is very nervous but Tia and I are excited to welcome you into the family. Whoever would have guessed that we'd be meeting under such a bizarre set of circumstances?"

"Tell me about it," Trina wryly remarked, smiling her mother's smile.

"And Trina, remember this is the first time we've met in person, all right?" She cleared her throat. "By honoring your request not to share your visit to my home three years ago, I withheld from them. It's complicated sometimes. You try to do the right thing, and no matter what you do, you're letting someone down. Do you know what I mean?"

"Completely. Don't worry, Tess. I've got it. My husband and my parents are the only people in the world who know that I visited you but if they ever meet you or any of my bio family, I'll make sure they know not to mention it."

"That's critical, Trina."

"I understand," said Trina as she smoothed her coat over her knees.

Shortly after their intense recitative, they parked the car in Tia's parking garage and ascended to what would be the boardroom for the next couple of days. Tia opened the door and with her standard enthusiasm, hugged Trina, and introduced her to her birth mother. Tess muscled the luggage.

After they agreed that they not go out for dinner, they took off their shoes, changed into casual clothes, and settled into the plush sofas in the living room.

Tia served hors d'oeuvres and drinks, and the sharing fest began. The sisters started tentatively by sharing their family backgrounds which Trina seemingly not only enjoyed but was hungry to hear.

Out of the blue, Trina said, "I've been thinking about what to call you. Aunt Tess comes pretty naturally. Is that okay?"

Tess smiled and nodded.

"Tia," Trina continued, "we're practically the same age, so is it all right that I just call you Tia?"

"Sure, that's cool," Tia responded with a subtle giggle, glancing at her sister with an I'm-younger-than-you look.

"And Katie, I'd like to call you by your first name because I have a mom, the woman who raised me. Is that okay with you?"

"Yes, of course. Trina, may I ask you … have you had a good life?" Katie asked.

Trina smiled. "No one could have been luckier than I am. My mom and dad are wonderful people."

Katie beamed. "You have no idea how good that is to hear. You can't imagine how often I have thought of you during these years, hoping and praying that your family was loving and you were safe. What are your parents' names?"

"Sean Daniel and Kathryn Doris Shanihan. But they go by their middle names, Daniel and Doris, actually Danny and Dori. I hope you meet them someday. They're such good people and I know you would like them."

"Do they know you're here? With us?" asked Katie in a timorous voice.

"Yes. I told them that I talked to Aunt Tess but hadn't met any of you and that was the purpose of this weekend." Trina smiled as she nodded her head gently at Tess.

"Do they know why you're here?" Tess asked, trying not to sound too pushy but knowing the question needed to be asked.

Trina spoke to all of them but addressed Tess.

"Yes, after I read your book, and then found the painting, I realized she might be alive. There were just too many coincidences to ignore, so I called you. Then when you identified the photo I had of Hunter as the person you knew as Cristin Shanihan and you saw the print signed 'Yvette', I realized that the situation was more monstrous than I had suspected. So I had to tell my folks. They were devastated to hear my theory. Mind you, I had mentioned it years ago, but they must have been in hysterical denial, as they had only a vague recollection that I'd ever inferred that she might have been responsible for my sister's death. I had no proof so I just dropped it … until now."

"Did they know Hunter?" Tia asked.

"They knew who she was but they didn't remember having met her. She was our school friend but never came to the house," Trina replied.

"How did you leave it with them?" asked Katie.

"They're apprehensive about my pursuing the matter but they've accepted that I need to do this to honor the memory of my sister. She was a beautiful person. I miss her so much. The death of our Cristin left huge holes in our lives. No one ever expects that their children, or sister, will die so young ... especially under such tragic circumstances. My parents are not strong enough physically or emotionally to do what I feel must be done, although my father in his younger years would have pursued this, I know it. But that's why I'm so grateful to meet you and work together to bring this evil thing to justice."

"What can you tell us about her? We just knew an imposter. What was she like growing up?" asked Katie.

"Well, she was beautiful, physically, that is, but you know that. She loved to draw and she liked gardening. Sounds pretty innocuous, doesn't it? Did you ever see that movie *All About Eve*? She was Anne Baxter, seemingly pure and trustworthy, and beneath a scrupulous façade seethed an unrelenting, heartless bitch. If only I had suspected how devious she was. But I didn't. I'm so sorry."

Tess spoke first.

"There's no way you could have known, Trina, just like I didn't suspect, nor did my husband, Tia, or Shep. No one knew. As naturally trusting people, we aren't suspicious of seemingly good people ... trust can be an asset or a detriment."

"I know that one from experience," Trina agreed.

Tess continued. "It's one of life's inequities. To see the best in people sometimes comes back to bite us. But sometimes when we do see the best in people, it's the break they need and they rise to the occasion. Go figure. What's a girl to do?"

From the corner of the sofa Tia quietly said, "Yvette knew. Yvette warned me that she was no good but I didn't believe her."

"But Tia," Katie responded, "she had everyone fooled. Even if you'd told Shep, he wouldn't have believed you."

"Katie's right," said Trina. "She was a pro. She is a pro. I'm sure we all beat ourselves up for not putting it together. No matter how many times I replay it in my mind, why didn't it occur to me that the necklace and letter that you'd left for me, Katie, were missing around the same time my sister died and Hunter left town? And then the story of the necklace and letter showed up in Aunt Tess's book, and I knew I'd found her. She used that letter to embed herself into Aunt Tess's life. Thank goodness I read your book. But why didn't I see it earlier? I was so naïve."

"And grieving, Trina. You were unsuspicious and grieving. Don't forget that," said Katie, in an attempt to comfort her daughter.

Trina faintly nodded.

After all the helpings of guilt had been self-served, Tia changed the course of the conversation.

"So everyone, let's get to the central nerve of the matter. We're in agreement that we must give it our best shot to find if this person who is the cause of so much tragedy in our lives, is alive … I don't even like to say her name…it sets me off … so what shall we call *her*?"

"How about *it*?" Katie offered

"How about *monster*?" Tess responded.

"How about *bitch*?" Trina chimed in with authority.

"Well, I see we don't need a thesaurus." Tia snickered and regrouped. "How about *Yvette*?"

Everyone nodded in agreement.

"Let me tell you what my PI has suggested." With her hands punctuating every word, Tia addressed her sisters. "Remember the art teacher Sarah at Arte e Vino? We spoke about her husband Charley helping us?"

She then clenched her fists and dropped them into her lap, and turned to Trina. "Sorry, Trina, my sisters and I have talked about this but …"

"Aunt Tess filled me in," said Trina as she tucked her feet under a sofa pillow.

"Okay. Good. First of all, he only has a license registered in Virginia so he can't practice as a private investigator with the resources we'll probably need in Europe. Besides, the job would not only be geographically undesirable because he's married with a family here, but it would be prohibitively expensive for us. However, the good news is that he has a banker friend, a Herr Hiller, who owes him a favor. Apparently a couple of years ago, Hiller's girlfriend absconded with a sizable chunk of Hiller's euros, and he suspected that she may have flown to D.C. where her sister lives. This gal was a few peas short of a casserole and within a few weeks, she was located by our very own PI, Charley Backstrom, who turned her over to the police. So my point is … Charley has asked Hiller to check bank records for an Yvette Vandal, hoping to glean an address or some semblance of contact information. Let's hope that privacy laws in Europe aren't buttoned up. Meanwhile, Hiller also knows someone in the Swiss Customs and Immigration office, so he's checking for passport usage in the past three to four years under that name."

Tess cleared her throat. "This is good news, very good news."

"Yes, it's a start but I have a feeling there may be numerous trails of bread crumbs that could disappear before we get there," Trina said, with mouth pursed and brows furrowed.

Katie's voice resounded. "This is like scratching a lottery card with hope of winning." She stood up and began pacing.

"Do you have a better approach?" questioned Tia, sounding a bit annoyed.

"No. I don't. I'm sorry. I just wish we knew how this was going to end before we begin. I want it to be over. I really don't have the stomach for it."

"No such luck, big sister," Tia remarked.

"So, is there anything else we can do now?" asked Trina.

"No, I think we need to hear what Herr Hiller comes up with. After we do, anticipating that he will uncover some clue as to her whereabouts, one of us should go to Europe. There's nothing like boots on the ground, so think about that. But in the meantime, let's enjoy our time together. My name is Tia and I'll be your tour guide in beautiful downtown Washington, D.C. Are you ready?"

The communal "yes" resounded.

"Tomorrow I thought we could visit the new World War II Memorial that was opened to the public last April. And then we could do some sightseeing, you know, walk down the mall and hit some of the museums? How does that sound?"

"Wonderful," said Trina. "Let's have a toast to the success of Herr Hiller, and then I need to clear the cobwebs and hit the hay. Oops, I just heard that ... it's a Midwestern expression. What can I say?"

They laughed and after their collective toast to their success, Trina dismissed herself and disappeared into her room.

When out of hearing range, Tess whispered, "Katie, what do you think of her?"

"I can't lie. Right up to the moment I met her, I questioned the wisdom of this rendezvous. But the instant I laid eyes on her, I knew it was right. It's like the first time you look at your baby and instantly love her. I love her. Already. There's so much catching up to do. But tomorrow is another day."

Tess smiled.

"All right, Scarlett, it's definitely time for bed."

CHAPTER SEVEN

False face must hide what the false heart doth know.
—William Shakespeare

Sofia awakened to the sound of water spilling through flumes into her enormous Olympic-sized pool, with designs of golden Vestal Virgins inlaid on an aqua-stoned pool floor. She loved her pool with statues of Roman emperors on each corner and a fountain in the middle with her virile champion, Neptune, standing guard with his trident. Morning was her favorite time, especially when the weather was glorious. As her head pressed against a cool Egyptian cotton pillowcase, she gazed through the tall, paned windows to see Italian cypress trees, swaying together in the celestial breeze that had inspired poets for millennia. She'd paint the scene one day, she thought, but then again, landscapes weren't her style.

From time to time, she allowed herself the luxury of reconstructing her complex fabrication of a life. This was one of those times. Her collage of disparate lives was truly her masterpiece, the living, breathing art of random identities, adeptly woven, with the cunning skill of a spider.

She was born Hunter Cross of Muscatine, Iowa, a nobody from nowhere.

She became Cristin Shanihan of Minnetonka, Minnesota.

She married and assumed the role of Cristin Shepherd for a few but lucrative months.

She then transmuted into Yvette Vandal, a wealthy, mysterious, young woman living in Switzerland.

She now existed in the persona of Sofia Gherardini, the wife of a wealthy, powerful Italian from Castiglione, Italy, who lavished his wealth on his young, insatiably lusty wife. Far across the sea, she had successfully transmigrated from a world where her identity could be traced to a new world where no one would ever find her.

One January evening in 2001, at the home of a Swiss attorney Clement Germond, Rudolpho Gherardini, twenty-five years her senior, was introduced to Yvette Vandal, a beautiful, young artist, recently relocated from France. The introduction was not by chance, but by her personal manipulation. He was the man who could change her life once again, not once and for all, but again. He was the perfect mark in that he had the legal savvy to expunge her history, rename her, and protect her. She knew the precise moment he saw her that her life would be transposed.

During the six years before she met Rudolpho, she had lived lives about which he would never hear. But on the morning she agreed to be his wife, her intricate plan blossomed like a lotus.

Lying in bed, with her slender, warm back pressed against his cool chest as he spooned her, she stole the opportunity to be mystifyingly silent.

"What's the matter, *mia colomba*?" he asked in his beguiling Italian accent.

"Nothing," she responded.

"I don't believe you. Talk to me," he insisted.

"I'm frightened," she replied, tasting the bitter excitement of deception.

"Frightened? Of what?"

"I can't tell you, Rudolpho. I can't tell anyone. Please don't ask me again."

"But you are safe with me, *colomba*."

She rolled over on the white satin sheets to face her rescuer. She covered her mouth with her right hand, and stared at him, begging with her eyes for him to persist.

"Talk to me, Yvette. I want to help you."

"Rudolpho, I need to disappear. Someone is looking for me and I'm afraid."

"That can be arranged. We've talked about this before, my darling. Marry me. You will leave Switzerland and reside in Italy as my wife. You will have a new name, and no one will find you unless you wish to be found. No questions asked."

"It's more complex than that, Rudolpho."

"What do you mean? It appears simple to me.'

"If there was any chance of Yvette Vandal being traceable ... well ... I couldn't bear my past tarnishing your reputation."

She wrapped her long, slender legs around his hips and sat up on him, her wide eyes begging for his benediction. Then she lowered her full bare breasts to press against him and placed the side of her face next to his left cheek.

"You cannot harm me, I assure you, *mia colomba*. So it's settled? You will be my wife?"

"Yes, Rudolpho, yes," she whispered.

Within the week she'd closed her Swiss post office box, packed her personal items, walked away from her lease and furnishings, and emptied her bank account. Once she chose her new name, Rudolpho exploited his connections to provide her with a new passport which she used crossing the border from Switzerland into Italy through Locarno. On that day, at his insistence, Rudolpho drove because he wanted her to see the famous Italian countryside and practice her Italian before meeting the household staff. Fortunately for Sofia, she spoke the language with *panache*, and if frustrated, her patient, Umbrian husband-to-be spoke brilliant English with a disarming Italian accent.

"Tell me about your estate, my darling," she said to Rudolpho after taking in the shifting vistas of rolling olive groves, and braids of cypress-lined vineyards twining the landscape. "Surely, it could not look like this," she teased.

"No, give it another four months and it will look quite different." He proceeded to describe golden hills appliquéd with circular bales of hay, acres and acres of sunflowers, and fields of red and yellow poppies. "I can't wait for you to see your new home. We have a view of the lake; a woodland grove with mushrooms, nuts, and wild boar; a vineyard for our wine; and a ranch to supply us with fresh beef, pork, lamb, chicken, and eggs."

"Really? And a garden? I'd love to tend a garden."

"But of course."

"How many people do you have on your payroll?"

"On my estate staff? Dozens."

"And otherwise?"

"You needn't be bothered with the family business," he said.

Sofia bristled at his tone of voice but tabled her objection and opened her Italian dictionary to look up *colomba*. It meant dove.

"By the way, *mia colomba*, I like your new name … Sofia." He smiled.

She smiled. Sofia Cassandra Maria Gherardini. She chose it most deliberately. Sofia meant wisdom. Maria meant beloved, but Cassandra translated as "one who entangles men." Her nature was sandwiched between perfect disguises, even in name. But no one would ever know that her name choice was so contrived.

"Tell me about your childhood. What were you like as a child?" Rudolpho had asked.

"There isn't much to tell. I didn't have any brothers or sisters. I left home as soon as I could because I knew there was a better life waiting for me." She didn't mention that she lived on a farm, isolated, with few friends.

"I loved art. I drew and painted in my discretionary hours." She didn't mention that at twelve, she picked up her pencil and began sketching grotesque faces and physiques of her molesting teacher and disbelieving parents.

"We must hang your art in our home, Sofia. We could have a salon to introduce your art to our world."

"That's so kind. But that was a chapter of my life I've finished. I'd much rather garden, Rudolpho. It's a tremendous creative outlet for me." She didn't mention that her need to be lost in the world prohibited her from flaunting her art. After all, she didn't need the money, and any notoriety could conceivably compromise her anonymity.

"We'll make sure you have the most beautiful garden in Umbria. Cyrano, our groundskeeper, will be at your constant disposal. When you were a little girl, did you have any pets?" he persisted.

"Yes, I had a kitten named Sugar." She didn't mention that animals were her only companions until she became angry at the world.

"What happened to Sugar?" he asked

"She died." She didn't mention that Sugar was her first victim, drowned in a potato sack in a stream near the farm. Nor did she mention the three-legged dog named Tripod that she tied to a stake in a neighbor's fallow field and left to die.

"Well, animals die young but they can be wonderful companions. I'm quite fond of animals. You can tell a lot about the character of a person by how they treat animals," Rudolpho continued.

"I suppose so," she replied. She didn't mention that her schemes to injure or kill animals gave her a sense of superiority, a feeling of control. *After all, they were only animals.*

"At what age did you leave home?" he asked.

"About seventeen," she responded. She didn't mention that she'd killed three people and stolen an identity before she left town.

"How did you come to be so accomplished, *mia colomba*?" he asked.

"I'm a natural," she stated with a coquettish smile while she squeezed his arm. She didn't mention that she suffered through awkward years and practiced composure, cunning, and charisma by imitating movie stars and powerful celebrities.

"You are so beautiful, Sofia. My world will adore you," he said.

Why was it that people responded so positively to beautiful women? she thought. "I don't want to talk about myself, Rudolpho. Tell me about your family ... your son."

"Nicolai. We call him Nico. You'll meet him soon enough. He's a few years older than you. He lives on a lake at the opposite end of the estate and keeps a penthouse apartment in Firenze. He races his speedboat, skydives, and spends far too much time in Monaco, gambling, wining and dining with the beautiful people, if you ask me."

"I'm so happy you are a more private person, Rudolpho. I don't want to be in the public eye."

Within hours they entered the Gherardini property, Bellaterra, which was more in every way than she had imagined. "Do you see these olive fields, Sofia?" He paused to bask in her nod. "They are mine. Do you see those grapevines on the hills to your right? They are mine also."

Sofia took note that he had not said ours and immediately asked, "Where is our house?"

"The next turnoff leads to our home. You're charming when you act like a little girl. Be patient."

She nervously twisted her ring, feeling like a little girl, anticipating a visit to Cinderella's Castle. After what seemed like an interminable amount of time, she saw the gates, the bronze-filigreed gates, proclaiming the entrance to a walled mansion which was about to be hers. These would be the walls that would insulate her from the rest of the world, and this was the gate that would be guarded night and day. She felt her heart relax, and she embraced the reality of this fairy-tale chapter of her now perfect life.

As they approached the structure, Sofia exclaimed, "Rudolpho, this isn't a home, it's a castle."

"Indeed it is, *mia colomba*."

In front of the castle entrance was a line of uniformed people, assembled to greet them. Sofia was about to meet the household staff.

The door of the car was opened by a strikingly tall young man, and she heard him say, "How did you enjoy your drive, Signor Gherardini?"

"Very much, thank you, Lazio. Sofia, this is our footman, Lazio."

"*Buon pomeriggio*, Fabio," she replied in her finest Italian accent.

"Lazio, Signorina Sofia."

"My apologies, Lazio then."

Sofia was pleased that her translation of his words was so simple, as she would probably always think in English. She extended her long, lean leg out the car door, planting her heel into the gravel drive, and offered her hand to Lazio.

As she stood, Lazio relinquished her hand to Rudolpho who proceeded to the receiving line to introduce her to Mateo the butler, Flaviano the driver, Cyrano the groundskeeper, Lucia the head housekeeper, and Chinzia the head cook. "Be especially good to Chinzia if you want eat well," he whispered. "You'll meet the rest later. Thank you, ladies and gentlemen. You can go about your duties. Mateo, please ask Gianni to unpack the car and bring the luggage to our bedroom."

Upon entering the foyer of the manor, a servant who looked to be Sofia's age, twenty-five or so, offered them cool limóncellos in slender fragile-looking glasses. "And your name is …?"

Lucia interceded. "This is Pia, Signorina. I have taken it upon myself to prepare a list of the servants' names. I have taken the liberty of leaving it in your room."

"Thank you, Lucia."

Walking through a labyrinth of rooms, she mirthfully asked her betrothed if he had a map of the castle.

"Oh, I suppose there is one somewhere but you'll catch on in time. I'll be leaving for Rome in the morning so you can spend a couple days exploring the halls and acquainting yourself with the staff and our routine. I'm sure you can use a few days to decompress."

"You're leaving me, Rudolpho?" she asked coyly, thinking what a gift it would be to be alone.

They adjourned to their master suite, to rest after their long drive.

The following morning she woke to an empty bed. Rudolpho had "evaporated" into another region of Italy, and she was on her own. The sound of the fountain in the pool outside her window percolated like music, and she half expected a water show to begin when she appeared at the window.

On the escritoire, she noticed a book of French Impressionist paintings. She picked it up and remembered her mother's art books which she had loved during her childhood. She'd spent hours combing through them, entering the world of Monet, his mist-veiled haystacks and sun-drenched water lilies, or was it sun-drenched haystacks and mist-veiled water lilies? She'd dreamed of sailing boats on the Seine, the cloud-saturated cathedral at Rouen, the hills of Normandy, and lilies of Giverny. She'd stared at the farms, flowers, rivers, and churches in the paintings, all of which were generically in her town in Iowa. But they weren't the same. She'd wanted the real thing. She'd longed to travel to the places that inspired these artists and see the exotic landscapes of Europe. And now she was there.

She dressed, then found her way to the copper kitchen as she quickly named it. Copper pots and pans hung from the ceiling, and copper designs were etched into the Italian-tiled walls. Chinzia offered her breakfast but Sofia declined the cook's efforts and said she'd wait until lunch to eat. The cook appeared not to be amused, as she demonstratively dumped her culinary masterpiece into the trash.

Surveying the castle was Sofia's top priority. She found the reception halls, adorned by gorgeous, canopied ceilings, many of them hand-painted. She waltzed through two dining rooms, one apparently for small gatherings, and the other she surmised, could hold up to 200 people. A gold-gilded corridor led to a richly decorated eighteenth-century-style salon that perhaps Rossini or Verdi had visited. She'd have to ask. One of the most surprising finds of the day was the armory in the cellar, furnished with armor and metal antiques, and walls accented with Gherardini family crests. There she also found an amply-stocked wine cellar. The pavers and walls were cool, dark, and delightfully dungeonish.

Upstairs, the guest rooms were lavishly furnished and frescoed, each with their own marble bath and hand-painted ceiling; some with a wrought-iron spiral staircase to the bed; and each with a balcony overlooking the surrounding hills, displaying the Gherardini acreage like a banquet table.

The exterior was Italian limestone, and the crowning glory was a fifth-story rooftop that stretched the length of the castle. There she discovered the bell in the bell tower that had rung every hour the night before. The grounds were glorious: a tennis court; two swimming pools; lime, olive, and cypress trees; sculpted shrub gardens with life-sized topiaries; an eighteenth-century stone fountain; an arboretum; a Roman cistern, and an Italian-style hedge that reminded her of a terrifying scene in the movie, *The Shining*.

When she found the garden, she planned her strategy within minutes. A garden AND a greenhouse. How could she be so lucky? She'd always had a garden: in Iowa, at Tess's house in Minnetonka, in France, and in Switzerland. Sometimes it was as small as a patch of earth or a window box. But under the radar, she always had a garden.

By the time she found her way back to the kitchen, Chinzia, having so ceremoniously tossed the breakfast, was tossing an antipasto salad and simmering a tortellini soup. Life was good.

The only time Sofia left the grounds during Rudolpho's business trip was to have Flaviano drive her to the bank in Perugia to wire funds to a Cayman Island account and reserve some working funds in the account set up by Rudolpho under the name of Sofia Gherardini. And poof! Yvette Vandal was gone.

CHAPTER EIGHT

Man is not what he thinks he is, he is what he hides.
—André Malraux

By Sofia's request, Rudolpho and she were quietly married with Nico standing up for his father, and Mariana Scardina, a long-time family friend and wife of Rudolpho's attorney Santino, standing in as the witness for Sofia. It was legal and it was over in a matter of a quarter of an hour.

Then there was the matter of Nico. Nico, Nico, Nico. A delicious temptation from the moment she'd laid eyes on him. Despite his immediate attentions, she didn't encourage him. He was far too visible for Sofia to claim, even behind the scenes. As smart and manipulative as she was, she'd boxed herself into a life of relative anonymity, at least on the world scene. Her *modus operandi* was to shy away from photographers and refuse interviews. Nico was in the public eye. She would lead a lavish, grandiose life within her self-prescribed limitations. That was the rub. She dared not be famous.

It wasn't long after she arrived at the estate in the spring of 2001 that it appeared that Nico's lifestyle had changed dramatically. He seemed to find reasons not to leave the area and spent more time with his father and his father's intoxicatingly beautiful new wife. Within weeks, he let his impassioned desire for Sofia be known to her, and she decided to use it to her advantage.

Sofia confided in Nico, without particulars, that her past life had complications which she preferred not to revisit; that whatever steps they took to be together in the future, she was to remain out of the limelight. She wanted no notoriety. He complied and they became discreet lovers. By year's end, they had landscaped their relationship with grand designs, discovering that they had much in common, including a tacit disloyalty to Rudolpho and a vision of their mutual dominion over the Gherardini estate.

By June of 2001, Sofia had gained weight, which she attributed to Chinzia's pasta, homemade bread, and a personal penchant for limóncello. It wasn't until Rudolpho teased her about her tummy that it occurred to her that she might be pregnant. She was horrified at the possibility. She'd gone to great lengths to ensure she would not conceive a child … except once.

She initially believed that if she was pregnant, she would terminate the pregnancy without Rudolpho knowing. But that might prove difficult, considering that she was a stranger in a strange land, and Rudolpho was a prominent name in the area. Her solitary hours before meeting with the doctor had afforded her time to reconsider the long-term benefits of having a child. She was, after all, a woman with vision, never having been discouraged by events, but rather, driven by potential benefits of circumstance.

By the time she returned from her medical appointment, she wore her pregnancy as a merit badge. Rudolpho was thrilled at the prospect of being a father again, and she was no longer a trophy wife, but a soon-to-be adoring mother. No one would know that it was not her nature to nurture. Delightful concepts like nanny and boarding school were in place, so other than the actual birthing, Sofia's duties would be over. Motherhood could be a form of cover. The child would be a decoration, as well as a marital security, nothing more.

If the truth was known, she despised being pregnant. The thought of something growing inside her and being pulled out was repulsive, to say nothing of the fact that her body would be grossly distended for months. Not anticipated on the radar was the morning sickness, an unforeseen and most unpleasant inconvenience, the particulars of which she fortunately wouldn't vividly recall after the baby was born. She never remembered what the flu felt like either, until it struck again, but a pregnancy would never reoccur. A quick trip to a doctor in another city when Rudolpho was out of town would guarantee that.

One benefit was the frequent visits from Nico who, under the auspices of a caring stepson, visited his fragile stepmother/lover almost every day. It was obvious that he not only didn't recognize her pregnancy as an impediment but didn't have a clue as to how devious she could be. He brought her bouquets of hortensia, what Americans called hydrangeas, because they were full and beautiful, and their fragrance didn't aggravate her nausea.

In February of 2002, Sofia gave birth to a baby boy, and named him Luca Franco Gherardini. His middle name, an Italianization of Franz, appealed to her sense of irony to pay homage to her late husband whose fortune had paved her way to a life of untraceable identity and extreme wealth. With the birth of Luca, Rudolpho had another son, the child had a nanny, and Sofia had leverage.

During Luca's first year, Sofia nurtured, not her son, but the plants in her garden. She designed the large garden with apparent but feigned enthusiasm. There were no financial constraints, and her artistic eye created fragrant, floral abundance. She worked with Cyrano the groundskeeper to whom she gave directives to tend and supervise her design. But the second garden was, in fact, a greenhouse which was explicitly her domain, which housed plants in elevated, rectangular containers. The greenhouse was a restricted area, *verboten*. No one else was allowed to enter and she alone had a key to its locked door. Within its opaque glass walls, she grew castor bean, rosary pea, and two plants from South Africa, wintersweet and blood flower. Outside the greenhouse, she lined the perimeter with familiar fuchsia oleander, and spurge laurel, a common ornamental shrub with attractive waxy leaves and gloriously scented flowers. What these plants had in common was not only their beauty, but their toxicity to humans when ingested.

From the beginning, her cunning with the plants had served her well. In Iowa, she'd drugged the people at the farmhouse before setting fire to it; in France, she'd disposed of the menace Yvette; and in Spain, she'd drugged the pilot and her late husband prior to their takeoff. Their death circumstances had never been questioned.

By the time Luca was a year old, Rudolpho was not well. Month by month, he became increasingly infirmed, less able to manage business or attend social engagements. Nico became more involved in the Gherardini business; Rudolpho, more doting on Sofia and Luca; and Sofia, more doting on her ailing husband. By the following year, Rudolpho seemed to be an invalid. And all the while, Sofia tended her gardens, trimming and cutting plants from the greenhouse which dissolved in hot tea and soup without a trace.

As Rudolpho's life gradually faded, Sofia made plans. She and Rudolpho met with his financial advisor, Santino Scardina, and made sure that his affairs were in order. Sofia was to be the beneficiary of half the estate, with Luca as secondary beneficiary if anything were to happen to her. Nico was invested with the other half, also naming his only brother Luca as his secondary beneficiary, if Nico were to suddenly die, in which case Sofia would act as the executrix until Luca came of age. Rudolpho's wife and children were well cared for, and in return, they were deferentially attentive.

In the winter of 2004, Luca was to be three years old in a matter of months, an adorable child with her dark hair and his father's Mediterranean skin and fiery brown eyes. The nanny, an unattractive girl of nineteen named Auriane, cared for Luca day and night, and dutifully brought the child to see his mother daily for an hour, no more, sometimes less. Some days, the visit was too much trouble, but she kept her appointment most of the time. Sofia appeared to be a good mother which pleased her husband and reinforced her maternal job description.

One evening, while they were all together in the dining room, Rudolpho asked his son if he was planning to sell his penthouse in Firenze.

"Why do you ask?" Nico replied, leaning into the question.

"You're never there anymore. I'd like to see you get out more. There was a time when you were never here. Now I see you every day. I hope it's not because of me, Son."

Nico glanced at Sofia, and addressed his father. "Of course it is, Father. You aren't well and of course, I'm concerned. It angers me that the doctors can't determine what's wrong with you. You're too young to be this frail."

"Never mind, Nico. I plan on sticking around for years but I want you to live! Don't you agree, Sofia?" he asked emphatically, obviously expecting an affirmative response.

Sofia stood. "Of course, darling. Would you like another cup of tea?"

"Yes, please. It is soothing," he replied.

That night, after Rudolpho had retired, Sofia went for a ride in her red convertible Ferrari to get some air. She arrived at Nico's lake house to undress, decompress, and redress before her absence became suspicious to any of the help. No one ever saw her leave, except for Jonas, the gatekeeper, and he appeared to like his job.

Returning to the estate, she stopped before making the turn into the gate, she refreshed with coral lip gloss, and wrapped a coral/green chiffon scarf around her head, to obscure the just-got-out-of-someone's-bed appearance.

As she rounded the corner to Bellaterra's gate, she remarked, "Jonas, it's a beautiful night, isn't it? I love to take a drive after Signor Gherardini goes to bed. The fresh air clears my head. I must ask … why do you stay so late every night?"

"I want to make sure you safely return, Signora," he replied.

"Oh, no need, Jonas. You should be home with your family. How is your family, by the way?"

"Very well, *grazie*."

"Good. Good night, Jonas."

"Good night, Signora Gherardini."

Sofia left the car outside for Flaviano to put in the garage in the morning. It was a clear, mistless night. The car would be safe. She hoped her repartee with Jonas served its purpose. She didn't like someone monitoring her moves.

****

At the gate, Jonas reflected on where one would go for a two-hour drive night after night, but it was none of his business. He had been under the Gherardinis' employment for fifteen years, and he needed his job.

CHAPTER NINE

There is no remedy for love but to love more.
—Henry David Thoreau

Christmas passed before the women had word from Herr Hiller. On the evening Trina heard the news, she was helping her daughter put the finishing touches on a poster board timeline of Nebraska explorers. Suddenly a FOX news station was interrupted with shocking videos of an Indian Ocean tsunami hitting Indonesia, Thailand, Sri Lanka, India, etc.

"Oh my God, Bryan!" she screamed. "Turn on the television upstairs. A tsunami … you won't believe the footage. Cristin, please go to your room, honey, and play with your sister for a few minutes."

The phone rang and she recognized Tess's number on the caller ID.

"Aunt Tess? Are you watching the news?"

"No. I hope I'm not calling too late. I just heard from Tia and offered to call you."

"Okay, well, you're going to want to turn on the news. From what I can gather, an earthquake of sizeable magnitude created a tsunami which has bludgeoned Southeast Asia. They're talking about a couple of hundred thousand people possibly dead."

"Oh, no. Okay. I'll call you back."

"No, please. I want to hear what Tia said. I'm just reeling in shock and need to compartmentalize my feelings for a second. Please, please, tell me what you know," Trina said as she looked away from the television screen to focus on her aunt's call.

"It's not great news, Trina. But it's news. An Yvette Vandal opened an account at Swiss National Bank in a village outside Lucerne in late 2000 and withdrew her funds in April of 2001. She didn't transfer them; she withdrew an undisclosed but 'enormous' sum of money in the form of a cashier's check to herself. Then she disappeared. The bank had a record of a post office box that was closed in April of '01 as well, but no forwarding address."

"What about the customs office connection Hiller had?" Trina asked.

"There is no record of an Yvette Vandal using a passport since 2000. It's as if she has disappeared, or has gone into hiding. There is one other thing I need to tell you, Trina."

"What? What?"

"Sit down for this one, if you're not sitting already. The passport photo of Yvette Vandal is the face of our killer."

Trina felt her knees buckle.

"She's alive! I knew she was alive! I knew it!" Trina felt her heart start to pound as she yelled the words, and dropped into her chair.

"You were right and it looks like she's disappeared again," said Tess.

"So what do we do?"

"I'm not sure but I think I'll take a trip to Switzerland to see what I can dig up. You can't very well leave your children, Tia can't leave her job right now, and Katie isn't a digger like I am ... my journalistic blood, I guess. I was thinking of asking my niece Lindsey to join me. She's studying pre-law and has a month off in January for winter break."

"That's a great idea! Isn't she your brother Troy's daughter? My cousin?"

"Yes, and she's very excited to meet you and your girls. Anyway, I was thinking that Lindsey and I could visit the village where Yvette kept the P.O. Box and probably lived. If she was conspicuously wealthy, maybe she attracted attention and someone might remember her. And perhaps we could visit that publishing house that published the painting. I just think someone needs to be there ... onsite, you know."

"I agree. When do you leave? How soon? It can't be soon enough from my vantage point."

Tess laughed. "As soon as I can. I'll keep you posted."

"Let me know if I can do anything from Nebraska. Aunt Tess, you have to find her." Trina glanced back at her TV and said, "And pray for those poor people on the other side of the world."

"I will, Trina. It feels so inequitable, so wrong that this woman is alive when so many innocents have died."

"Life isn't fair, is it? Thank you for the call, Aunt Tess. And Happy New Year."

"Let's hope it is," Tess responded.

The following morning, Trina looked out her window to see snow falling on Lincoln, a beautiful sight and welcomed visitor in the eyes of a photographer or artist, but a menace for anyone needing to drive a car. After the hour it took to plow the driveway and bundle the children in their snow gear, she delivered them safely, although slowly, to school. By the time she returned home, the promise of a hot cup of ginger tea beckoned to soothe her anxiety over the pressing discussion she needed to have with her mom. Now that there was definitive evidence that Hunter Cross was alive, it was time to make the call. After all, she couldn't very well be colluding with her birth mother and leaving her own mother, Dori Shanihan, out of the loop.

She dialed the phone and held her breath until she heard the phone pick up.

"Hi, Mom. I know this isn't our usual Sunday morning talk, but do you have a minute?" Trina nervously tapped the heel of her right foot against the kitchen floor, making a sound like a dog's tail banging.

"For you, dear, always. Let me turn off CNN. This tsunami footage is terrifying. Those poor people."

"I know, Mom, it's horrific." She paused and the structure of her planned finesse crumbled to dust. "There's something I need to tell you."

"Are Bryan and the girls all right?" Dori asked with an alarmed tone of voice.

"Yes, of course." Then Trina blurted, "Mom, she's alive. Hunter Cross is alive. We don't know where she is but we've identified her passport picture and presume she's taken off again, maybe under another name, and this time, hopefully, she hasn't killed someone for it."

"Oh, Trina." Dori gasped. "This is gruesome. Please leave it alone. I don't want you to get hurt."

"That's exactly what Bryan said."

"He's a smart man, Trina. Maybe you should listen."

Trina could hear the panic in her mother's voice. "Not this time, Mom. We're going to find this bitch and bring her to justice."

"You and Bryan?"

"No, and that's what I want to tell you. Remember a couple of months ago when I flew to Washington D.C. and met my birth mom Katie and my two aunts Tess and Tia?"

"Yes … you met your birth mother. I remember," Dori stoically stated.

The expected silence ensued.

"Mom, I can hear hurt in your voice. The only reason I met her—all of them—is that I needed their help. We had reason to believe Hunter was alive and now our suspicions have been confirmed. They have more recent information than I do, regarding her. They're good people, Mom. What I haven't told you is that we have reason to believe that Hunter Cross may have killed Katie's son Shep, along with some other people. I'll write this in a letter because it's very confusing."

"Aren't you jumping to conclusions, Trina? What makes you think she is responsible for someone else's death too?"

"It's a long story. They all thought she had died in a plane crash along with Katie's son whom she had married. But it turns out that she's not dead and didn't come forward to the family, but escaped to Switzerland with a new identity. I didn't want to upset you and Dad until we knew that for sure but I found out yesterday through a positive identification. She is alive."

"What's she like?" Dori asked.

"Who? Hunter?"

"Your birth mother."

"Oh. She's very nice. But Mom, you're my mother, not Katie."

Trina could practically hear Dori's throat closing from the lump probably lodging in her mother's airway. She knew Dori so well.

"Mom, we've talked about this before. It's only because of my sister's memory that I ever considered meeting my birth mother. I'm doing this for Cristin."

"You're doing this for yourself, Trina."

It was like hearing an echo. "That's what Bryan said ... but Mom, I'm doing it because it's the right thing to do. And I'm telling you because I don't want to keep secrets from you. How many times have you told me to give people the benefit of the doubt and have confidence in their ability to process difficult news? That's how you raised me, Mom. And that's what I'm doing."

There was a brief silence on the other end of the phone, then Dori spoke. "You're right, dear. You've done the right thing in telling me. So how do you propose to find this woman?"

"Well, Tess, Katie's sister ... and by the way, I'll add a miniature family tree in my letter so it's easier to understand, along with the details we've been able to piece together. Anyway, Tess and her niece Lindsey may be flying to Switzerland to investigate further. I'll just be waiting in Nebraska, so don't worry about me. I'll be here with Bryan and the kids the whole time, minding my own business, and not in harm's way, Mom."

68

"Well, thank God for small favors," Dori stated through an exaggerated exhale. "Dear, this has been a stunning phone call. I will explain it all to your father so you needn't run through the whole scenario again. Please send me that letter soon. I love you, Trina."

"I'll talk to you on Sunday, okay? I love you, Mom," Trina added, taking the opportunity to call Dori "Mom" every chance she could.

"Of course dear. Goodbye."

"Bye."

Trina hung up and surveyed the benefits of her call. It was interesting how her focus was on the delivering the news of Hunter Cross being alive. She surmised that Dori was only thinking of the increasing contact that Trina now had with her "other" family, particularly with Katie. Dori would always be her mother in every sense of the word. Katie might someday be an addition to the family, like a friendly neighbor, or a beloved cook, or an extra grandmother, but that's all. It sounded naïve but Trina hadn't the energy to think it through any deeper than that.

What she was actually thinking about was how much she wished she could be the one to accompany Tess to Europe.

CHAPTER TEN

It does not matter how slowly you go
as long as you do not stop.
—Confucius

The call Lindsey Monson received from her Aunt Tess to join her in Switzerland for three weeks could not have been timelier. January was her only respite from the year's classes and she'd hoped to take a month's sabbatical from studying anyway. Informed of the mission and being particularly interested in criminal law, Lindsey was a perfect fit.

Before she knew it, she was walking into an Irish pub in New York City called The Green Derby to connect with her Aunt Tess before their transatlantic flight and to sneak a visit with her Aunt Katie whom she hadn't seen in years. As she opened the door, a siren screamed by and the entire patronage turned their eyes to the door as if the appalling noise were announcing an important arrival. Her aunts waved to her from the rear of the pub.

After the greeting, hugs, and ordering had taken place, Lindsey blurted. "You know I've never been to Europe. I'm the only girl from my high school graduating class of ten who hasn't." Her expression appeared dramatically forlorn.

"Oh poor baby," Tess said with a commensurate theatrical flair. She and Katie laughed as if they'd been cued by a stage director.

"Okay, I guess I deserved that. Pretty pathetic, huh? I'm not exactly like … deprived." Lindsey continued. "But I did take a trip to Argentina with my family when I was nine. I wish I'd been older because I barely remember it. The photos help but honestly, like all I really recollect is a blur of humidity, strange language, and eating thick, juicy beef."

"I guess she was too young to remember the handsome Argentine men, right Tess?" Katie asked with a wickedly suggestive tone of voice.

"Are you referring to that delicious blend of German, Italian, and Latin? Yes, I guess she was too young. Such a waste," Tess added while picking up her drink and batting her eyes.

"You guys are so mean," Lindsey said as she giggled. "Maybe I'll have to make up for it and find like some rich, handsome European on this trip."

The aunts smiled at each other. Lindsey guessed that they were most likely recalling the sense of amorous adventure they'd both experienced as younger women. The thought made her smile.

"By the way, I booked a room for us tonight," said Tess. "Our *hotel du nuit* is a charming boutique establishment, The Inn at Irving Place. It's actually two townhomes joined together, furnished in the style reminiscent of bygone New York." She wrinkled her nose and whispered, "I stayed there once before and could feel the ghost of Edith Wharton in the parlor."

"Seriously?" said Lindsey with widened eyes.

"Lindsey, I should warn you. Whenever possible, your Aunt Tess will stay in hotels frequented by famous authors. It's one of her quirks," said Katie.

"I love ghosts," said Lindsey with a mischievous twinkle in her eyes.

Before she knew it, an evening of sharing ghost stories and eating the best corned beef and hash Lindsey had ever had vanished into a memory.

The flight to Zurich the following afternoon was long but well spent, devising their undertaking, their plan of attack. Their first four days would be pleasure driven and allow for adjusting to the change in time and altitude. On their fifth day, they would get to work. They had an appointment with Herr Hiller in the afternoon and on the following morning, they'd drive to Kussnacht, the village where they believed Yvette may have resided. Although they only had a post office box as a clue, they hoped to locate her residence and talk to neighbors. It was a town of only 8,000 people, so if Yvette had flaunted her money to any extent in a town that size, someone might know who she was and more importantly, where she went. Then again, maybe the trip to Kussnacht would be unnecessary, depending on what Herr Hiller had discovered.

At that point, the publishing house of *The New and The Obscure* in Lausanne would be their destination, about 150 kilometers from Lucerne and located on beautiful Lake Geneva. There would be some traveling. Lindsey hoped they'd make that trip because of the location. Fortunately, Switzerland was only 16,000 square miles, so it wasn't difficult to imagine getting from one city to the next quickly. However, when she looked at a topographical map, the southern half of the country was mountainous. Not foothills, but mountains … the Alps, the Swiss Alps, to be precise. Perilously rugged, precipitously steep, and imposingly beautiful. What an adventure it would be.

Somewhere over the Atlantic in the dark, Lindsey nudged Tess to see if she was awake. Tess responded with a questioning, "Hmm?"

"I know this is a discovery trip and we'll treat it very seriously, but Aunt Tess, do you think we'll have any time to sightsee while we're there? A little?"

"Of course, Linz. What do you have in mind?"

"Well, when we're en route to Lake Geneva, could we like visit one of the famous ski destinations? Like Gstaad? Or take the train to the Jungfraujock? or to Kandersteg?"

"Looks like someone has done her homework."

"Oh, Aunt Tess, these are some of like the most beautiful vistas in the world. I really am excited to see them … if we have time, that is."

"I agree. After all, we'll be there … the airfare has already been paid. Let's keep our eye on the ball until we make some headway, but I imagine we'll have time to play. Try to get some sleep, Linz."

Lindsey smiled and closed her eyes to visions of the Bernese Oberland, imagining all four seasons in the alpine valleys, the snow-covered monoliths and craggy massifs, the crunchy cold air and the dramatic contrast of white against blue, defying what any painter or photographer could capture as hard as they may try. Fighting to stay awake and daydream, somewhere between Greenland and Norway, Lindsey Monson succumbed to sleep.

Whatever regret she had felt about not remembering Buenos Aires, Lindsey forgot upon driving to the Dolder Grand. With turrets and spires in the tradition of German *Art Nouveau*, the hotel sat on 125 acres of gorgeous grounds, overlooking the city of Zurich, like God's celestial palace in the clouds ... and of course, once-upon-a-time, Thomas Mann and James Joyce had been regulars, according to Tess. Within minutes of arriving, Lindsey felt she could stay there forever and prematurely lamented the thought of their departure the following day. They made reservations for dinner at Kronenhalle where they were to experience consummate Swiss and French cuisine. In their hotel room, she paged through photos of Kronenhalle, walls dripping with paintings of Chagall, Matisse, Picasso, and Kandinsky... an art appreciator's dream gallery. They cleaned up, changed clothes, and set out to explore the grounds before the sun set.

They took a cab to the town below and arrived early at Kronenhalle so they visited the adjoining bar.

"Let's have a drink, Linz," Tess suggested. "We're early, and in case you want to eat something other than sausage and potatoes, I suggest you order an appetizer here. We must celebrate our arrival to bring us luck in finding the person we've come to expose."

Lindsey picked up a menu as she elevated herself into a perilously high chair, her legs dangling, feeling almost weightless from the higher elevation; the air was infused with the smell of delicious French sauce, possibly *Béarnaise*?

"The drinking age is eighteen in Europe, isn't it?" Lindsey smiled.

"I don't even know if there is a drinking age in Europe. Don't worry about it, honey. Order whatever you like."

"And how are you ladies this afternoon?" said a tall, Swiss man with a cleft chin, blue eyes the shade of glacial ice, and a voice articulating impeccable English.

"How did you know we speak English?" asked Lindsey.

"You are American. You look American." He smiled.

"How do Americans look?"

"Different," he diplomatically replied. "Would you like something from the bar?"

Tess intervened, possibly sensing that Lindsey was insulted. "Do you serve a specialty drink?"

"Yes, madam, our signature drink is *The Ladykiller*."

The women interlocked glances with slight smiles, acknowledging the irony. "Perfect. Bring us two *Ladykillers* please."

Traveling in Europe by train may have been expedient and theoretically convenient, but being responsible for one's luggage was a drag. Leg bruises from the banging bags were par for the course, as there were times when the bags could not roll: entering and exiting the trains, lifting them over high curbs or onto dollies when unable to find porters. Lindsey remained cheerful and gave thanks to the man who had invented luggage with wheels. Nevertheless, after taking the train to Lucerne and having to make their way to Vitznau, the American women were exhausted. The dismay Lindsey tacitly experienced upon leaving the Dolder and the difficulties of the day's travel, were eclipsed by the stunning beauty of their next hotel, the Park Hotel Vitznau. The elegant *Belle Époque* hotel was located on the edge of Lake Lucerne, which the Germans called Veirwaldstättersee, the Lake of Four Forest Cantons. Lindsey recalled a line from the movie *Contact* when actress Jody Foster, upon seeing indescribable galactic colors, said to herself, *they should have sent a poet*. She knew that her memory could not capture the grandeur of being there but the feeling she experienced, she'd reclaim in a moment.

That evening and both days thereafter, Tess and Lindsey lived in the moment on the set of one of nature's most beautiful backdrops. It was winter, so they bundled up and took strolls around the grounds. They enjoyed cocktails while reflecting on Mount Rigi and its mirrored reflection in the still waters of placid Lake Lucerne. On the morning before they made their exodus to a more moderate Lucerne hotel, they took a tram to the peak of Mt. Rigi to witness the sunrise. The sun rose every morning of Lindsey's life but she hadn't always noticed it. In fact, she'd rarely noticed it, but from that moment on, she vowed that amends would be made and attention would be paid.

On the fifth day of their journey, rested and resolute to begin their unearthing of Yvette's whereabouts, they settled at the stark, clean, and adequate Hotel Reinholt, a financially necessary letdown. From there they took a taxi to Herr Hiller's office at the Swiss National Bank, and with a mixed bag of anticipation and apprehension, they entered a charming wrought iron elevator and headed to the third floor. The building was old. Original hardwood floors with a yellow-patterned runway led them to Room 315 as they passed a colonnade of gold-framed paintings of former bank presidents, who probably believed that they would be immortalized by the painter. In actuality, no one ever saw them unless they were sent to the "principal" or his assistants on the third floor.

"I feel like we're following the yellow brick road and about to meet the Wizard," Lindsey remarked.

"We should be so lucky," said Tess under her breath.

"Are you nervous, Aunt Tess?"

"So nervous, I feel I can hardly breathe," she responded.

The door was open and there sat a receptionist with long, pewter-gray hair pulled severely into a ponytail that arguably cut off circulation to her brain. She wore a gray blouse and an unmatched shade of gray cardigan. "*Guten Tag. Mein name ist Gunilla.* Oh, excuse me, you are the Americans, I believe, Herr Hiller's next appointment?"

"Yes, I'm Tess Parker and this is my niece Lindsey Monson." As they stepped closer, they could see Gunilla's gray glasses rimming her gray eyes. No makeup.

She spoke into her headset, "Herr Hiller, your appointment has arrived." She punched the button and asked them to be seated. Gunilla then stood from behind her desk, revealing a gray skirt, gray hose and tidy gray shoes; then like a gray ghost, she disappeared into his office.

They glanced at each other. Cracking the tension, Tess whispered, "I bet she only serves Earl Grey tea, what do you think?"

They both giggled. Suddenly a jovial, heavily-whiskered man with ruddy cheeks, thick yellow teeth and a cockaded hairstyle that reminded Tess of a stellar jay, blew into the room with open arms like Liberace in his prime.

"Ladies, ladies, I'm so pleased to make your acquaintances. Please, please, come into my office. This way, this way, please."

His office was painted hunter green with yellow accents. The walls were covered with American football memorabilia. "You must excuse my decorating," he began explaining. "I'm a Green Bay Packer fan. I love American football. Bret Favre is my hero. Silly me, but my dream is to visit Lambeau Field although I hear that a season ticketholder has to die before his seat becomes available, and even then, a family member will most likely inherit it. But nonetheless, do you know any hit men? Ha ha. Just kidding."

The women smiled but didn't say a word.

"Well ladies, on to more serious business, the reason you are here. I have some good news for you. But first may I say that my good friend Charley from your country's capital was very helpful to me a few years ago. It is a great honor to have the occasion to return the favor. As you know, this Yvette Vandal trusted our bank with her fortune, or I surmise, at least a part of a greater fortune. Usually when one deals with these sums of money, there are considerably more funds stockpiled in other accounts. But nevertheless, Ms. Vandal withdrew her funds in April of 2001. But of course, this much you know. It is now January

2005, almost four years later. Banks in Europe request post office addresses as contact information, and thus, that's all we had. That P.O. Box in Kussnacht has been closed, also in April of 2001."

"However," he continued, "my contact at the passport authority/immigration office has found no use of the passport issued to Ms. Vandal since she entered the country in late 2000. I am glad to hear that by securing the passport picture, you have verified that we're looking for the correct person. But the conclusion I draw is that either she is still here with no traceable bank account or she has left the country under a different name. Four years is a long time to have not used a passport in Europe, especially for a wealthy and educated artist, so my best guess is that she's no longer here."

"Why do you think she is an educated artist, Herr Hiller?" asked Tess.

"Please call me Felix. You're very astute, Ms. Parker. This brings me to the good news. I took it upon myself to hire a friend, a Camille Karson, whom I implicitly trust, to do some research in this area covering 2000-2002. And ladies, we may not have a former address for the person you are seeking, but we have the name of someone who knew her."

All the while he spoke, he rapidly tapped his pencil balanced between two fingers, on his desktop, making an annoying sound, and adding to the tension

Lindsey took Tess's perspiring hand and clutched it like someone who was waiting to hear whether she was the first runner-up or the winner of a beauty contest.

"It appears that in early 2001, Yvette Vandal held a private art showing at the home of Frau Klara Zutter, a well-known patroness of the arts in Lucerne. I have met her throughout the years on numerous occasions and she is, I'm happy to say, one of our prestigious bank clients. I have contacted her, and she will be pleased to meet you at her home tomorrow at 10 o'clock. May I confirm that appointment?"

"By all means, thank you," Tess responded eagerly as she moved forward in her chair and nodded.

He continued. "*Mit vergnugen ... avec plaisir*. She is not privy to the reason why you are searching for Ms. Vandal, as I am not, nor do I want to be. I am clearly just helping an old friend."

Standing erectly and with an informal bow, he handed Tess a paper with an address, presumably Klara Zutter's address.

"Herr Hiller ...," Tess started.

"Felix," he responded.

"Yes, my apologies. Felix, this is astonishing news. You have been an indispensible help and we hope we can help you in kind some day."

"You're most welcome, ladies. It is highly unlikely that I'll need your help, but the "pay it forward" principle works for me. It's not often that one has the chance to reciprocate directly. While you're staying in Lucerne, if you need me, please do not hesitate to call. This has been a pleasure." He nodded and clicked his heels. "Let me see you out."

"*Danke*, Felix. We are so grateful."

"Remember, if you ever get a line on Packers tickets, I will fly to Green Bay, Wisconsin. Although I surmise that our Swiss cheeses may be a bit finer than the famed Wisconsin cheeses so I may pack my own," he said with a twinkle in his eye. "*Viel Erfolg*, ladies."

That evening, the women tabled their trip to Kussnacht, subscribing to the "bird in the hand" theory as their most likely lead. They treated themselves to a fabulous dinner of Weiner Schnitzel and hot potato salad at the charming Hotel Schweizerhof, a nineteenth century structure, renovated in 1999, and renowned for being Richard Wagner's favorite hotel. Lindsey knew that Wagner was one of Tess's revered German operatic composers, and that Tess was most partial to the magnificence of his *Tristan and Isolde*. So Lindsey was not surprised by the hotel choice. She rather expected that there was the ghost of someone famous and dear to her aunt's heart, roaming the hotel's corridors. *Hopefully, not Wagner's.*

Before the serving of the tiramisu, Tess brought up her love affair with Wagner.

"You mean his music, Aunt Tess, right?"

"Of course. I know nothing about him as a man, except that he was brilliant."

"He was like a megalomaniacal anti-Semite, you know," Lindsey proffered.

"No, he wasn't … was he?"

"Yes, I'm afraid so. Do you know that only two men in history have had more written about them? Jesus and Napoleon Bonaparte. I learned that in my Humanities 407 course. Wagner was like, a hedonistic, ruthless, arrogant, overall repulsive human being."

"First of all, I must take issue with your professor's biography list … what about William Shakespeare or Adolph Hitler? Surely more has been written about them than Richard Wagner. And secondly, if what you say about him is true, then my Wagnerian bubble has just burst. I think some things are better left unsaid, my darling girl," said Tess as she pushed herself from the table.

"Apparently it's true but my professor offered us some solace in how we viewed his life overall. Do you want to hear it?"

"Bring it on … before I get indigestion," Tess added.

"If you were ill, and you had a choice between two surgeons: one who was an average surgeon and true to his wife, or one who was an incomparably fine surgeon and a married womanizer, whom would you choose?"

"The latter, of course. Because my successful surgery would be more critical to me than his personal morality."

"Precisely. Despite his controversial personal life, was he not like one of the most influential, inspiring composers to have ever lived? A rhetorical question."

"Thank you for that, Linz. Now perhaps I can enjoy my Italian dessert while I contemplate my unfailing love for Wagnerian music, sitting in this gorgeous Swiss hotel, being served by our delectably handsome French waiter."

"Aunt Tess!"

"One can look, can't one?" Tess smiled at her niece.

Within an hour they were back at their hotel, Tess readying herself for bed, and Lindsey, not.

"Linz, aren't you tired? We've got a big day tomorrow."

"I'm so wired. Would you mind terribly if I walked to that casino a couple blocks from the hotel? It's legal for me to enter a casino in Europe and I've never been inside one. I'm curious. I promise to be back in a couple of hours, and like, I have my cell phone with me. We have extended coverage so it won't cost much if you need to call me."

"A casino? What would your parents say?"

"I'm almost nineteen. They'd say yes. I'm cautious. I'll just want to walk around. I don't even know how to gamble; I'll just look, I promise." She made a mental note that it was January 21, and she would look and act like she was twenty-one, not almost nineteen.

"Well, I suppose it's all right. Make sure you're back by eleven, okay?"

"I promise. Thank you."

Lindsey ran into her room and reappeared fifteen minutes later in a short, red cocktail dress, chandelier earrings, and four inch high heels; hair piled on top of her head, secured with rhinestone combs; and makeup that accentuated her lips, her eyes, and her flawless complexion.

"Va va voom! Cinderella in fifteen minutes," said Tess.

"I was shooting for Keira Knightley."

"You look dynamite, little one. Promise me to use good judgment. You're there to look, nothing more, right?"

"Right!"

"See you in two hours. Have fun," said Tess, as she peered over her reading glasses at her grown-up niece.

Lindsey swiftly left the room as if she were afraid her aunt might change her mind. Within three minutes she'd exited the hotel, feeling independent and cosmopolitan. It was relative to the feeling she'd had when she'd driven her family car by herself to pick up a girlfriend for the first time. A rite of passage. She thought of her cavalier response to Tess's question concerning whether her parents would have sanctioned her being alone at night in a foreign city, walking to a casino. They would not have approved. But her aunt had taken off the leash and treated her like a grown woman. Finally.

Lindsey entered the casino with eyes wide and heart pounding. Her girlfriends in California had described the Las Vegas casinos they'd seen firsthand, with fake ID's of course. This one was more European than the pictures she'd seen. First of all, everyone was fashionably dressed. In Vegas, people wore jeans and t-shirts and generally looked like a seedy, needy lot. This casino placed her inside a *Casino Royale* movie set. From the high-vaulted ceilings dripped low-hanging chandeliers. People gathered in groups, watching the action as if in a red carpet gallery at the Academy Awards. Lindsey walked with her shoulders erect and a serene countenance, remembering what her volleyball coach told her team when they went to the state tournament: *Act like you've been there before.*

Past the whirring of the roulette wheel, the raking of the craps table, the cranking of the slot machines, she twisted her way through aisles of poker tables, suddenly aware of what she wanted to see that night. James Bond, a real, live James Bond.

She made her way to a bar and ordered her first martini, shaken not stirred. With her prop in hand, she found her way to the blackjack tables, where women in designer gowns with no backs and low-cut bodices quietly watched handsome, wealthy, tuxedoed men in intense concentration. Lindsey stealthily took her place behind a man old enough to be her father, and watched, waiting for something to happen. There were few words spoken but chips in piles were manipulated, stacked, and lost.

Suddenly from another table came cheers of congratulations as someone had obviously won a tremendous amount of money. She looked up and there he was. James Bond. A gorgeous, young, dark George Clooney-type with a beguiling smile. She moved closer to watch the casino Adonis, surrounded by beautiful women, while obviously commanding the attention of the men at the table as well. As he stood, he saw Lindsey across the table, nodded his head slightly, and said *"Buonosera, Signorina."*

She smiled and nodded in response, feeling faint as the blood drained from her head. He turned, and with his entourage of the rich and famous, evaporated into the crowd.

She addressed the man manning the poker table, and asked, "Who was that man?"

"We don't give out names of our clients, *mademoiselle,*" he responded without as much as a glance her way.

A tall Old Guard woman with a burgundy silk scarf wrapped around her neck like a noose, probably to hide folds of septuagenarian wrinkles, interrupted. "My dear, I don't work here and I share your admiration. That was Nicolai 'Nico' Gherardini, AKA, Italian playboy, race car driver, gambler. Too much man for you, my dear, but isn't he delicious?" she mused with her eyes sparkling and mouth pursed in a minxish smile.

Lindsey was back at the hotel a half hour before Tess expected her.

From her bedroom, she called out, "Linz, you're back early. Didn't you have a good time?"

"I loved it, Aunt Tess. I'm just tired and want to feel great tomorrow when we visit Klara. I'll see you in the morning."

"Okay, honey. God bless you."

Lindsey Monson lay in bed thinking about Nicolai "Nico" Gherardini, the man who would forever be her James Bond. He had smiled at her. He had addressed her. He had thought she was special. *Too much man for me? Ha!*

CHAPTER ELEVEN

Every solution to every problem is simple.
It's the distance between them where the mystery lies.
—Derek Landy

Klara Zutter's home was in an exclusive section of Lucerne. The area reminded Lindsey of the Rolling Hills division of Palos Verdes in California, but accented with European style homes. Old World homes had always appealed to her in photos, and now she and her aunt were experiencing the glory of Swiss architecture firsthand.

Of course, one couldn't see the home from the street. The taxi drove them up a hill for what seemed close to a quarter mile before they could see the main house. Lindsey imagined that the drive in any season but winter was probably bordered with flowerbeds of seasonal annuals. She wondered what kinds of flowers they planted in Europe. As it was, the driveway was icy and the grounds blanketed with an overnight snowfall, which contributed to the freshness of the vision and the air. They were in Switzerland! Hansen, their Danish taxi driver, helped them from the car even though the snow on the driveway in front of the house had been removed.

Rather than a door bell, there was a door knocker in the shape of a lion's head which Tess used to announce their arrival. Frau Zutter, a tall, imposing figure, personally met them at the door and invited them into her parlor.

After introductions were made, Tess began. "You are very kind to see us, Frau Zutter."

"Please call me Klara. I hope I can help you. Please sit. Would you care for some tea?"

"Yes, that would be lovely. Your home is beautiful," Tess remarked.

"After we talk, perhaps you would like to see more of it?"

"Wonderful," Tess replied, as she watched Lindsey smile and nod her head in tacit albeit enthusiastic agreement.

From a silver teapot, part of a family heirloom service set, no doubt, Klara poured a hot, what smelled like mint tea. She wore thin, dainty white gloves and held her chin erect, even when bending to serve the tea.

"Tell me, how you know Herr Hiller at the bank?" she asked.

"He is a good friend of a friend of ours in Washington, D.C., and he agreed to help us find someone. I believe he has told you that we are looking for Yvette Vandal?"

"Yes, he mentioned it. I didn't know her well. She was an artist in the area for a short time who contacted me to hostess an art showing for her which I was happy to do."

"That was kind of you, Klara. Do you know where she is now?"

Klara cleared her throat. "Why do you want to know?"

"She lived with me for a while. She married my nephew, Lindsey's cousin, and we've lost track of her."

"I didn't know that she was married when she lived here," said Klara whose aristocratic chin seemed to remain on the same plane whenever she stiffly turned her head.

"Her husband died … in a tragic plane crash."

"I'm sorry. God rest his soul."

"Thank you, Klara."

"Have you considered that she may not want to be found?" Klara suggested. "Perhaps a tragedy of that magnitude caused her to break with her past and begin anew."

An awkward silence resulted.

"Ahh, if that's so, we'll leave it alone. But in the event there has been a misunderstanding that could be resolved, we thought that while we're in Switzerland on holiday, we would try to contact her."

"Well, I'm afraid I can't be much help. All I know is that she married an Italian man a few years ago, and I presume, moved to Italy with him."

"Italy? Do you know his name or where in Italy he lives?" Lindsey interjected.

Klara's trained chin made its move toward Lindsey who up until then had not said a word other than hello.

"No, I don't. I didn't attend the function where they met, but my friend and her husband, who hosted the gathering, would know. I could see if she would share that information. I don't think she knew the gentleman well, but as I recall, her husband was a business associate, an attorney. It was a well-attended event, which frankly, I was sad to have missed."

"Klara, we would so appreciate your asking her. Our whole family would be indebted to you," said Tess, smiling in deference to her hostess.

"Well, then it's settled. I will call her as soon as they return. They're on holiday, skiing in Austria right now, but should be returning sometime this month. Is there anything else I might do for you?"

"You've already been so kind. I do have one more question," replied Tess, not appearing overly eager. "We are traveling to Lake Geneva before heading home and hoping to contact the publishing company in Lausanne that published one of Yvette's paintings in their magazine, *The New and The Obscure*. Would you happen to know any publishers who might accommodate us with a contact name?"

"Quite possibly," Klara responded. "Email me when you arrive in Lausanne. I don't give out my cell number. My apologies. In the meantime, I will put out my feelers in the hope that I can help you." Klara handed Tess a calling card with her name and email address.

"We so appreciate your assistance, Klara. Here is my card with my email address and cell phone number in case you have any information before we contact you," Tess replied.

"Excellent. Come, let's have a tour of at least our lower level, if you'd like. I have something that might interest you."

Lindsey looked at her aunt, sensing her excitement and disappointment. They had a lead but there would be no immediate gratification. Once again, they would have to wait.

The tour was magnificent, like exploring a mini-Hearst Castle. As they walked, they learned that Klara was a widow and a passionate art collector herself.

As they strode down the west wing bordered with art from all over the world, Klara suddenly blurted, "This one. Do you recognize the artist?" She pointed her long, gloved second finger with the elegance of a duchess.

There was no mistaking the style or the artist—Yvette Vandal. She had taken up permanent residence in Klara's corridor, camouflaged as an innocent French artist. The Americans assumed their best game faces and nodded with feigned approval, as if comforted to see their family member's talent recognized in such an exquisite venue.

"I knew you'd like this one," Klara declared with a seemingly satisfied resolve that she was helping to heal a family.

A half hour later, Klara asked, "If there is no further business, shall I call a taxi to retrieve you?" Apparently the morning had served its purpose.

Tess and Lindsey couldn't fathom waiting in Lucerne for the mystery friend to return from Austria so they decided to see the Swiss Alps, giving Klara enough time to make a contact for them at the publishing house.

Their first destination was Jungfraujoch. En route, they rode on the highest railroad in the world, stopping to see an ice palace carved into a glacier, with permanent monumental ice sculptures. They visited the town of Grindelwald, merely for the love of the charming name, and stayed at the Victoria-Jungfrau Grand Hotel in Interlaken to bask in sumptuous luxury for a night. The rooms even smelled rich. They traveled on to Kandersteg where they rented ski equipment and skied for two days straight, breathing the brittle alpine air and exercising their large leg muscles to the point of pain. The snow was icier than the snow in Vermont but the vistas were incomparable, just like the photos they'd seen, but better. Before leaving the ski resort circuit, they hit Gstaad, to cap off Lindsey's dream vacation. They were too sore to ski but experienced Switzerland's winter pageantry like children in a winter playground. They slept beneath eiderdown quilts and ate melt-in-your-mouth dark Swiss chocolate every chance they could.

"We could become very large women if we keep eating this way, Aunt Tess," said Lindsey.

"We're on vacation," Tess retorted with a delightful, carefree tossing of her head.

"No one back home will believe this. How can you possibly describe how beautiful this is! And I love the languages. French is so suave, and German, so much fun. That ice palace we visited is called Eispalast in German. It's like so easy."

"I agree. The translation isn't tough but the pronunciation is a killer."

Lindsey took out her German-English dictionary and immersed herself in amusement while Tess checked her computer for an email from Klara.

"Oh good," said Tess. "We can make an appointment with a Wilhelm Bridenstine at the publishing office any time this week. I'll call tomorrow."

"Any news from the friend in Austria?"

"Not yet."

The women put on their pajamas and nestled next to the fireplace to absorb the heat, drink from brandy snifters, and gaze at the mountains outside their hotel window. Lindsey watched Tess take out a photo of her Uncle Ren and trace his face with her index finger. They'd been gone for two weeks and would be home in a week. Without diminishing the trip in any respect, Lindsey surmised that her aunt wished she could have shared the experience with her husband.

"Aunt Tess? I don't know if I've ever told you, but you're like the only person who calls me Linz. And I like it." Lindsey gazed at Tess pensively, if not a bit hesitantly, then asked the question that had percolated in her mind for years. "Do you ever wish you'd had children?"

Tess smiled, then sighed. "Oh, yes. If I'd had a girl, I would have named her Julia. A boy, Tristan."

"You would have made a wonderful mother," Lindsey said ... and paused. "You are like a mother to me."

"Thank you, Linz. I love you very much, you know."

"I love you too, Aunt Tess. My mother has always been preoccupied with her own life so I don't feel close to her like I feel to you. Don't get me wrong. I love my mom. It's just that ... like ... she's never there."

"I understand your feelings, Linz. Suzanne's world does tend to revolve around herself. I'm sure she'd do better if she knew how."

"That's kind of you. Since the divorce, it's been even worse though. Maybe she thinks I'm like grown now so her job is over. I don't know. I think being Senator Northrup's wife just added fuel to the fire. And my dad? I don't know what he's thinking these days. Like he's like dating 'a Brigitte' and she's only ten years older than I am!" Lindsey paused to consider Tess's reaction but before her aunt spoke, Lindsey apologized. "That was awkward. I didn't mean to be insensitive. My dad's your little brother ... and like, he's wonderful. It's just that it feels so weird, my parents not being together anymore. I'll get over it."

Tess smiled. "We don't always get what we want in life, Linz. But I'll share with you a secret that helps. If you have a hole in your life, the best way to fill it is to become what you lost. If you feel slighted in the parenting department, someday become the best parent you can be, so that your child's joy in having you in her or his life will somewhat compensate for your loss."

"I can do that."

"How is your brother adjusting?" Tess asked.

"Max? He's a guy. He's fourteen now, and since he was named to the junior national rugby team, he's preoccupied. Someone told me that guys compartmentalize their lives better than we do. What do you think?"

"Without a doubt. We women are an ocean of connectedness. Every cup of our experience spills into the sea of our existence and affects us, sometimes to a fault."

"Are you suggesting we, like, take a page out of the male manual for survival?" Lindsey asked.

"There are times, yes. But all things considered, I love being a woman."

"Me too, Aunt Tess. I suppose it's a good thing, considering we are."

"You're a quick study, Linz. Now let's get some sleep. Big day tomorrow."

Upon retiring, Lindsey thought about Tess. Perhaps her aunt's wanting a child was the reason she had let Cristin Shanihan, AKA Yvette Vandal, into her life in the first place. If so, Tess's Achilles heel had led to heartache, and almost ten years later was the reason they were in Europe "on the hunt." If this mystery woman had not come into her aunt's life, Lindsey would not be in Europe ... the whole puzzle was like a game of dominoes, every day, every decision, affecting the slant, the power, and the direction of each falling square. Just before succumbing to sleep, Lindsey thought about Nico Gherardini, the gorgeous dark-haired man of her dreams. *Where was he tonight? Was he thinking of her?* The dominoes continued to fall.

The publishing house was not a publishing house as either of the women had envisioned. It didn't smell of ink and paper and old books. It had an impressive postal code and that's where the word "impressive" ended. It was a two-room office with three employees who apparently handled the mail, made the decisions, and ordered the printing which was done off-premises. Herr Bridenstine was much younger than they'd guessed. Broad shoulders, thick hair, horn–rimmed glasses, extremely good-looking, and no hint of a smile or a sense of humor. He greeted them with reserved cordiality and a thick German accent framing his English words.

"Yes, ladies. How can I help you this morning?"

Tess began. "We are on holiday from the United States and trying to find a family member, Yvette Vandal."

"That sounds like a French name, not an American name."

"That's true. Yvette Vandal is her artist name. We knew her as 'Cristin.' "

"So how can I help you?" he asked with the emphasis on *I*. He appeared to be taking notes as he spoke.

"Last year you published a photo of one of her paintings, and as fate would have it, our niece Trina in Nebraska recognized it. Imagine that. I'm impressed by your magazine's circulation. Anyway you made mention of her so we had hoped you might know where she is. We've unfortunately lost track of her."

"Well, it just so happens I do remember *Mademoiselle* Vandal. I will never forget her. She was an extremely attractive woman with an extremely unattractive personality."

"Why? What happened?" Tess inquired.

He slowly put down his pen, folded his hands, and leaned forward deliberately, squinting his eyes with intensity.

"I met her four years ago at an art gallery function here in Lausanne. She was a beautiful woman, adamant about my publishing one of her paintings in our magazine. Well, at that time, it wasn't my magazine. My superior did not like her work and refused to publish her. Last summer I was promoted and finally had the say as to what we would and would not publish. I thought Mlle. Vandal would be thrilled. I couldn't find her, but because she had been so adamant, I thought I was doing her a favor by publishing a photo of her painting. Shortly after the issue was released, I heard from her. She was no longer on our mailing list so she must have picked up a copy at a bookstore. She was ruthless, quite ugly, if the truth be known. She had the audacity to threaten us with a lawsuit for not having contacted her before releasing the photo she had left with me years before. It never amounted to anything but gave us a scare. We're a relatively small publishing house that might not survive an expensive, drawn-out litigation. Live and learn. How was I to know that she had moved out of country and that she no longer wanted her painting published? She did say that she wouldn't be painting anymore ... her career was over. As far as I'm concerned, that's good news. I'm sorry to say it, but good riddance to her."

"We're sorry, Herr Bridenstine. We don't blame you for being angry. Do you perhaps have a forwarding address for her?"

"No. All I remember is that her scathing phone call was placed from Italy ... minutes before I left the office for a soccer match for which I was late. We lost the match, and I was in a doubly foul mood for the remainder of the week. If you do find her, perhaps you can teach her some manners."

"Thank you for your time. If you think of anything else that might help us locate her, please use the email address on my card." Tess handed him her card and the women watched him drop it on his desk like a hot potato.

As they left the building, Lindsey commented, "I think it's highly unlikely we'll be hearing from Herr Bridenstine, don't you?"

"If you don't mind my saying so, Linz, what that man needs is a good woman ... for an hour."

"Aunt Tess!" Lindsey giggled.

"Well, it's true!"

91

CHAPTER TWELVE

Pull a thread here and you'll find
it's attached to the rest of the world.
—Vadeem Vaslam

Upon their return to the U.S., Lindsey returned to school and Tess to her husband.

The others were contacted with the news that Yvette had moved to Italy, and Tess was waiting for an email from Klara Zutter, their only lifeline and only lead, regarding Yvette's specific whereabouts.

February in Minnesota was harsh. The snow, with an inch of crunchy ice on the surface, was too deep to tread. The air was brittle and the temperatures, brutal. The nights were dark and sometimes seemed endless. There were mornings when the cloud ceiling was so thick and low, she couldn't decipher dawn from dusk but for the fact that she'd just awakened. But there wasn't a day that passed that Tess wasn't grateful that she lived in a beautiful, warm home with the man she loved. She had missed him more than she'd anticipated.

"Rennie, on nights like this, I can't help but think about the homeless," she remarked one evening while cuddled up next to the fire with a fleecy blanket, laptop, and warm brandy. "Why don't they leave this freezing climate and live where it's at least warmer at night?"

"Tess, I'm surprised at you. They don't have the money to leave, or the means," he replied, as he looked up from his scientific journal, his glasses perched on the bridge of his nose.

"I think I'd just start walking until I reached a city that was more forgiving in the winter. It must be so ...," reaching for the right word, "grim. I read an article in the paper last week about a man who threw a rock through a store window so he'd be arrested and be able to sleep in a warm jail. There shouldn't be such inequities in living conditions."

"No one has figured that one out, honey. Our welfare in Minnesota is one of the most compassionate and liberal in the country. There are mental health issues, people born into poverty, and those not getting any breaks or direction. It makes you sick to think about it, I know. And then there's the problem that the more people feel they're entitled to, the less they work. Human nature ... or habit. Then the taxpayers who have jobs have to work harder, to make enough to support themselves and the non-workers. It's not a matter of spreading the money evenly. Someone has to work. It's a conundrum. But believe me, baby, although it's cold out there, Minnesota is already a welfare state. Let's hope that her bleeding heart doesn't bleed her to death."

Tess nodded, then checked her email again. This time there was news.

"Rennie ... Klara, Klara Zutter, the woman from Switzerland, has sent me an email! Okay, okay. Just a minute." Tess opened the email with excitement and trepidation. *What if there wasn't any news they could use?*

"Here it is. Do you mind if I read it out loud? It feels more real that way."

Ren nodded.

Dear Tess,

I apologize for not getting back to you sooner, but my friends Clement and Fiona Germond just returned from Austria last week. I gave them a few days to relax, but on your behalf, I called Fiona this morning. I have good news for you. Your niece married Clement's good friend Rudolpho Gherardini from Castiglione, in the Umbrian area of Italy. He is apparently a wealthy businessman so we know she is well-off and secure.

93

I don't have a postal address but she shouldn't be difficult to locate if you still wish to contact her. I'm only sorry that I couldn't get this information to you prior to your departure from Switzerland.
My best wishes to you and your niece.
It was a pleasure meeting both of you. Good luck.

Sincerely,
Klara Zutter

"Ren! We've found her!"

"Good work, Sherlock. You'll have to ID her to be positive. What's your next move?"

"Call the girls. We didn't know we'd get this far. I'm calling Lindsey first because she was there with me and its only 8 p.m., her time."

Not wanting to disturb Ren's concentration, Tess went upstairs. With fingers shaking and heart pounding, she called her niece.

"Linz! Thank God you're home. I just heard from Klara Zutter. Cristin ... I mean Yvette ... is in Italy."

"Aunt Tess, we knew that much already."

"No, let me finish. She married a man by the name of Gherardini from Castiglioni ... in Umbria. We've found her!" Tess heard her own voice saying the words but felt as if they came from a faraway place inside her. She couldn't believe it herself.

"Oh my God, what do we do next?"

"I'll call the others in the morning and we'll figure it out. Linz, our trip to Europe paid off. We did good, girlfriend." Tess squealed.

"What was that last name, Aunt Tess?"

"Gherardini ... G-H-E-R-A-R-D-I-N-I. I know. It's a mouthful. I'll call you tomorrow."

"No, wait. What was Gherardini's first name?"

"I don't remember. I left my laptop downstairs. Why do you ask?"

"Just curious."

"Sorry. I'll forward the email to you tomorrow, Linz. Good night, sweetie."

"Good night."

Tess hung up with a ceremonial flair of the wrist, then headed downstairs to rejoin her husband.

"Do you want to talk about it?" Ren asked while balancing the astronomy periodical on his knees and adjusting his glasses.

"Actually, honey, I just want to be quiet for a while and think."

"By all means. I'll contemplate the universe and you contemplate the fugitive ... there's a connection there somewhere, Tessa."

"My husband, the philosopher," Tess replied, smiling her sweetest, dismissive smile.

Reviewing the facts: *We know she is alive but still need to confirm that she and the bride of Rudolpho Gherardini are one and the same. We can't very well make an arrest yet. We need proof of wrong-doing. Is there proof beyond suspicion? Yes, there's identity theft. Will we end up hiring a private investigator in Italy to arrest her on different charges like the IRS did in the case of Al Capone? This monster has stolen two identities and we suspect has killed four people, and has staged her own death. There is no way she is clean but we need to prove it. We will have to bring in professional help. One step at a time, a positive ID being the first.*

Tess sniffed a trip to Italy in the immediate future. Maybe Tia or Katie could go this time. Trina had two young children so she was not a likely candidate. She'd call the girls in the morning, and in the interim, attempt to manage her adrenalin surge so she didn't short-circuit.

****

Under the same moon, Lindsey Tyler Monson lay awake, stunned, and with only one question in mind—was her James Bond the man whom this person had married? She'd only met the woman they'd all known as Cristin once, at her Aunt Tess's home at Christmastime in

1995. Lindsey had only been nine years old and much more interested in counting her Christmas presents under the tree than paying attention to the houseguest. Lindsey barely remembered her but she'd undeniably become a phantom who had come back to haunt them. Surely the world was not so small that nine years later she would see a man in a Swiss casino who had married her Aunt Tess's houseguest. It was too convoluted, but still possible.

Gherardini. Nico Gherardini. The reason she'd remembered the last name so lucidly was that it was the last name of the subject of the famous DaVinci painting, the *Mona Lisa*. Maybe Gherardini was a common name in Italy. What if the sexy man of her dreams who had greeted her with *"Buonasera, Signorina"* was the Gherardini? No, he couldn't be.

She hadn't shared her fantasy with her aunt while in Europe and really had no intention of telling anyone, anytime soon … unless Nico Gherardini became the focus of their investigation, but that was absurdly doubtful.

****

Within an hour of her waking, Tess had informed her sisters and Trina of the news. Immediately Tia had a plan. She would talk to Charley Backstrom to see if he had any contacts in the Umbrian area. If not, she would go to Italy to personally ID their target. And when she did, she would hire a local Italian private investigator. She couldn't foresee the details but she was confident she could figure it out. She couldn't very well hire someone without meeting him or her, and she couldn't very well have Mrs. Gherardini arrested without positively ID'ing her, to say nothing about not having charges that could be proven … yet.

Katie was scheduled to visit her friend Sondra in Vancouver. Trina had to defer to the others and stay home with her girls. Tess had already taken a hit for the team. It was Tia's turn in the tub, as her father used to say. She immediately put in for an emergency time-off.

That afternoon she talked to Charley who didn't know anyone in the business in central Italy, but he gave her some sage advice. Once she identified "the target," as Charley called *her*, Tia needed to befriend someone in the house, preferably a disgruntled employee, who could provide inside information about the goings-on within the family. But the target should never lay eyes on Tia, so she mustn't make her presence known in the town. Otherwise their plan would be foiled because the target's guard would be up and perhaps would leave town, thinking she was being stalked, or worse, discovered. If that happened, they might never find her.

But more critically, Tia could be in danger as it had already been determined that the hunted one was indeed dangerous. This was a thought she would share on a need-to-know basis, and her sisters and nieces did not need to know. If they thought it through, they would most likely come to the same conclusion, but no one at this point, had verbalized it, so it wasn't real. It was strange how nothing lived until it was given form, a massive concept to ponder another day. Besides which, she was the only one of them who could pass herself off as a European, rather than an American, which would be a clumsy tip-off. Being that she made a living as a translator, her French was exquisite, and with a little study she could charmingly fumble through Italian conversation. Only certain words might give her away as a foreigner, but at all costs she wouldn't admit to being American. She decided to leave in a week's time and set out on an adventure as an undercover agent, a job description she'd never entertained.

****

Feeling a bit guilty about not offering to accompany Tia to Europe, Katie adhered to her plans and flew to Vancouver to visit her best friend Sondra. Two years earlier, Sondra had married a hockey sportscaster from Vancouver, the home of the Canucks, so they'd settled in the

Northland. As Sondra put it, Vancouver was a glorious city with the most moderate climate in Canada. Yes, it rained. Yes, it snowed. But when it cleared, it was God's country and Sondra was hooked. She and her husband had met on a television studio set where he was being interviewed and she was visiting her girlfriend Dani, a makeup artist. They were introduced before he "went on," after the show they "went out," and were married four months later. Sondra loved telling the story and Katie loved hearing it.

"At our age, you know when it's right," she said. "And Katie, you'll find Mr. Wonderful. I have no doubt."

"Not at fifty-one ... I don't have the energy." Katie sighed. "But I'm happy for you. Truly. Can't wait to meet him. It's so good to be here, Sondra. Dabbling in the travel agent business is fun but I was tired of booking everyone else's trips. It was time for me to travel and I can't think of anywhere I'd rather be."

Sondra smiled as she stared at the flickering candlelight from her vanilla-scented candles on the silver tray displayed on her coffee table. "We've been through a lot in our shared lifetimes, haven't we?"

"Actually I have something important to tell you. You don't know the half of it," Katie added. In the few minutes that followed, Sondra heard the extent of what her friend knew about the person they knew as Cristin Shanihan—her ultimate deception and probable existence.

Sondra stared straight ahead, with eyes moving from side to side like a Felix the Cat clock, as she digested the shock of the news.

"I don't believe this," she uttered, wide-eyed and open-mouthed.

"Believe it. Tia is flying to Italy this week to positively identify her."

"Why Tia?"

"Number one, she'll assimilate into the local scene better than the rest of us without calling attention to herself. Number two, she speaks French, so she won't stand out as an American and blow her cover. Number three, she was able to get the time off work; and number four, and arguably, the most important point, she's a bloodhound, always has been."

"Well, I think it's awfully brave of her."

"I agree. I wish I were more of the adventurous type. I'm just not cut out for traipsing around the globe, searching for a murderer. I'd hate to think I'm a coward though."

"Oh, don't be silly. This is hardcore. Why don't you just hire a PI?"

"We will, but Tia will do it over there after making the identification."

"Knock me over with a feather. The bitch is alive." Sondra paused, and looking at Katie's expectant face, she added, "And you've met your daughter. What is she like?"

"She's wonderful, Sondra." Katie smiled. "She even looks like me. And even if we don't find this monster, at least we've found Trina. I'm excited for you to meet her."

"When? Where?"

"We'll figure something out. But there's one more thing."

"There's more?"

"Seriously, Sondra, I haven't told this to anyone. Trina has asked me to be willing to contact Derek, if we need him to help us."

"Derek Northrup? Are you out of your mind? Does he even know she exists? I thought that whole episode of your life was closed almost thirty years ago?"

"Twenty-eight. And he never knew I had the baby."

"But he could have asked. Did he ever contact you?"

"No. Thank goodness."

"How did she know he was her father?"

"I told her. She asked, and I'm not starting this relationship with lies, even by omission."

"Well, you're right there. But what could he do?"

"I don't know. He has connections. If all else fails, he might be willing to help us."

"Well, let's hope it doesn't come to that."

"There is one more thing."

"You're beginning to sound like Lt. Columbo. Remember that show? It was one of my favorites."

"Yeah, I do. This is a weird twist and has nothing to do with our search but it's interesting. Remember my brother Troy and his wife Suzanne? Their daughter Lindsey went to Europe with Tess. Well, Troy and Suzanne divorced and Suzanne married Derek."

"That's creepy. So let me get this straight. The father of your love-child Trina is now the stepfather of your niece Lindsey. He's in your family. Right?"

"Technically you're right, although I've never put it together quite that way. They're more out of the family. We never see them. Suzanne fell from in-law to outlaw status when she divorced my brother. They're not exactly asked to Thanksgiving dinner, if you get my drift. I'm sure he doesn't know that I'm Lindsey's aunt ... different last names, you know. It doesn't matter."

"It's just so bizarre," responded Sondra.

"I agree. This whole deal has been spun by some master weaver in the sky, I swear. The web seems to be expanding by the day. Does it ever stop?"

"Not until the spider's destroyed."

They exchanged intense stares, and then were interrupted by the front door opening.

"Honey, I'm home. Where's this Katie I've heard so much about?"

There stood Mr. Wonderful, Joe Mahr, as handsome as his photos.

CHAPTER THIRTEEN

It is amazing how complete is the delusion
that beauty is goodness.
—Leo Tolstoy

In late January, Rudolpho took his last breath. Knowing that his health was inexplicably failing, he participated in the writing of his eulogy and obituary like a master screenwriter, having the final say with each edit. He created the guest list for his eventual funeral, as if planning a festive extravaganza. It just so happened that on the evening of his passing, Nico was in Lucerne so he could be in the company of people who could vouch for his whereabouts, and Sofia was at the stables with her horse Attila. In the end, Rudolpho passed peacefully, and alone, after his last drink of tea.

His funeral was scheduled for nine days later so that his friends and family members had time to make the journey. They came from all over Europe to attend Mass under the dome of the town's magnificent gothic cathedral. The service, exceptionally long; the flowers, lavish; the music, baroque; the air inside, infused with incense; the air outside, heavy as if expecting rain. The inauspicious circumstances of his death did not ignite the wrath of God by earthquake, rain, wind, or fire in the cathedral, but was simply noted on a celestial list of evil doings. Sofia played the part of the despondent widow, and Nico, the grieving son. The family physician was baffled by his inability to diagnose a specific cause of death and the staff of the estate was heartbroken. A grieving Chinzia, who had been the head cook at the estate for over twenty years, held herself together and provided an elaborate and sumptuous buffet that would have made her master proud. Lucia, the housekeeper in the strictest sense of the word, arranged for those staying the night to be shown to their rooms to freshen up. Flaviano hired extra help to park and care for the cars, as well as provide transportation to and from train stations and airports. Cyrano, the groundskeeper, planted fresh flowers along the driveway while the household staff prayed that severe weather would not decimate his floral pathway before the guests arrived.

After the service, immediate family members attended the interment while Rudolpho's closest friends and out-of-town visitors convened at the estate for food, drink, and a time to commiserate and comfort one another. By the time the family returned home from the burial, the atmosphere had lightened.

Among the foreign guests paying respects was Rudolpho's dear friend Clement Germond, the host of the party where Sofia and Rudolpho had met four years earlier. Sofia was relieved to have seen him in the church as he was one of the few people she recognized. At one point in the evening, she waved to him from across the room, signaling with a nod of her head that indicated she would circumvent the guests to get to him, as soon as she could unwind from a conversation with a boorish Armenian who insisted on giving her a chronology of his dealings with her late husband. Eventually, she squeezed through the crowd, feeling like an earthworm pushing through dirt, with no promise of air. Nico was attending the guests in the ballroom, as they had decided they would not be seen together after leaving the cathedral.

When she caught up with Clement, she threw her arms around him and whispered in his ear, "Take me away from here ... I need air ... to the terrace, please."

Clement Germond was as gallant a man as Sofia had ever met. In her mind, he exuded a European chivalry that put Sir Lancelot to shame.

"Come with me, my dear," he responded, putting his arm around her waist and sifting through the crowd as if rescuing her from an agonizing fate. She lowered her eyes and head toward his shoulder as he held out his hand to part the Red Sea of guests, whereupon a path materialized in front of them, with no questions asked. It was apparent that Rudolpho's widow was in pain and needing his attention.

"Wouldn't you rather be inside, where it's warm?" he asked as they approached the terrace door.

"No, no. Please. We won't stay out here long. I just need to breathe."

He opened the door and a waft of cool air entered the room like an unwelcomed intruder.

"Thank you," she cooed. "I was suffocating in there. Thank you so much for being here, Clement."

"Of course, Sofia. Rudolpho was my friend, my dear friend."

"How did you come to know him, Clement?" she inquired as she folded her arms to warm herself. Clement instinctively wrapped his arm around her.

"I met him through a fellow attorney who handles your estate, Santino Scardina. Have you met him?"

"Oh, many times," she answered, quickly recalling the hours of fine-tuning Rudolpho's will and trust.

"I am devastated that Rudolpho has died so young," Clement continued. "As you know, he was shattered when he lost his first wife years ago in a car accident near the villa. But I know through our correspondence, that the happiest years of his life, although brief, have been spent with you. You were the love of his life, Sofia."

"And he, mine," she replied, looking through tear-filled eyes, then melting into his shoulder for solace, obliging him to hold her tighter.

"And they never determined his illness? One would think that the wonders of western medicine could have diagnosed his condition. How terribly frustrating these past two years must have been for you, my dear."

"Clement, you have no idea. Life without him will feel so empty."

"When things settle, why don't you get away on holiday? Come and stay with Fiona and me. Bring Luca. Our oldest daughter Celine is having her first child this week. And our youngest, our son Gabriel, is only six so she has her hands full. Otherwise, Fiona would be here with me. She sends her sincere regards."

"Thank her for me, Clement. A child coming into the world? There's never better news. Motherhood is my greatest joy. I appreciate your offer, Clement, but I won't be traveling for a while, a long while. A very long while. There are so many loose ends here, and beside which, I just want to be alone, to cry, to sleep, and not have to see anyone. I feel closer to Rudolpho here."

"I understand completely, sweet girl. Just know that you always have an oasis at our home ... when you're ready. Oh, and by the way, in the madness of this sad occasion, I almost forgot to mention something. Two Americans were in Lucerne recently, looking for you. Your aunt and cousin, I believe. It was a surprise to us because we didn't know you had an American branch of your family tree."

"What?" Sofia's heart thudded so hard, she thought it might stop.

"Yes, they didn't know you'd left Switzerland, that you'd married Rudolpho..."

"Did you tell them where I was?"

"No. I didn't."

"Thank you." Sofia collected her thoughts as they sifted through the sieve of her shock. She spoke slowly as if grasping for the words, but delivered them with deliberation as she now faced him directly. "You see ... I had ... a falling out ... with them ... years ago."

"I'm sorry, my dear. But please, don't misunderstand me. I didn't tell them, but Fiona did. Not directly, of course, but through Klara Zutter, the woman who hosted your art showing before we first met? I presume Klara has been in touch with them, as they seemed quite insistent to reach you, probably to make amends. They were on holiday in Switzerland, hoping to see you, and connected with Klara."

"How long ago did this happen?"

"Well, let's see. We've been in Austria for the past month and returned less than two weeks ago. Klara called Fiona a couple days after we returned, I believe. Before we knew that Rudolpho had died."

Sofia panicked, hoping she was not reacting transparently. After all, her husband's death should seem more disturbing than family members wanting to see her. Her peripheral vision became fuzzy and as she stared at Clement, he looked like a photo negative, black, gray, and two-dimensional.

"If you don't want to be in touch with them, you might call Klara and ask her not to convey the message, my dear."

"Thank you. Do you have her number?"

"No. But Fiona would. I'll have her call you when I return."

"Thank you, Clement. Thank you for coming. Now if you'll excuse me, I need to lie down."

"Of course, Sofia. Are you all right?" asked Clement, the bearer of horrifying news.

"Yes. Just suddenly overwhelmed by the day. Goodnight, Clement. Thank you."

Sofia didn't re-enter the house through the terrace door but abruptly turned her back and walked to a separate entrance leading to a private room from where she could place the call to Switzerland. She entered the room, then watched her hands quiver as she opened her address book. The lamp on the desk appeared to flicker and even the furniture trembled. Klara Zutter's number was not registered. She looked under Germond, and thank God, it was there. She dialed Fiona and after what seemed like an interminable succession of rings, Fiona picked up the receiver.

"*Guten abend*, Fiona. This is Sofia Gherardini."

"*Guten abend*, Sofia. It's so good to hear from you. My apologies for not being with you. Wasn't Rudolpho's funeral today?"

"Yes, yes, it was. I've spoken to Clement. He is so good to have come. Has your daughter had her baby yet?"

"No, but at any hour now. We're very excited to greet our first grandchild. It's so unselfish and kind of you to call me on this difficult day to ask about the baby, Sofia. Thank you."

"Not at all, Fiona. Congratulations on the upcoming event. By the way, Clement mentioned that two of my relatives from America were in Lucerne this past month, and Klara was inquiring, on their behalf, about my whereabouts." Sofia tapped her middle finger on the desk, exhibiting and escalating her runaway tension

"Yes dear, I told her where you were ... no address, mind you, but the town and your husband's, excuse me, late husband's surname. I hope that was all right, Sofia. And let me take this opportunity to say how much I like your name change. When in Rome ... as the saying goes. I'm sure Rudolpho loved it."

"Yes, thank you. Fiona, do you have Klara's number handy? I presume she's not listed but I'd like to speak to her." *Fiona had to have her number handy.* Sofia bit her lower lip until she tasted blood.

"Yes ... let's see. I have it here somewhere. Oh, here it is. I hope I didn't misstep. I was just trying to help." Fiona gave her the number.

"No, Fiona. No harm done. Thank you so much. *Auf wiedersehen.*"

Within seconds, as if by sleight of hand, Sofia terminated her call and Klara's number was entered. Eventually her answering machine activated and Sofia resorted to leaving a message. She tried not to sound urgent, but firm, as if she needed a return phone call as soon as possible. She hung up, then panicking, redialed, and left a message asking her to hold off communicating with the Americans. Sofia's logic being that if Klara heard the first message, she might communicate with them before returning Sofia's call, and be able to report that she had followed up on the request.

How could anyone know she was alive? She had meticulously covered her tracks. How could they have trailed her? Who were "they"? Which of Monson women were on to her?

Sofia's mind went into maniacal overdrive as she calculated her next move. If Klara had been in touch with them, Sofia would have to leave the world she had so deftly orchestrated. She would have to leave the estate, the luxury, and Nico. She prayed to a God she didn't believe in, that Klara had not and would not contact the Americans and their track would run dry. *Unless they were persistent. They'd found Klara. Who else could they contact? What if they re-contacted Klara and incriminated her with their suspicions? Then Klara would tell Fiona who would convey the accusations to Clement and ... what if they already had?*

She didn't have the stamina to face the crowds in her home. She needed to be alone. She would feign exhaustion and refuse to talk to anyone but Nico. She called housekeeping and asked for Pia to come to her room. She headed up the servants' stairway, running into no one, and dashed to her room, locking the door behind her. *Now she could think.*

Within minutes, Pia knocked. "Signora Sofia, what can I do for you?"

Without opening the door, Sofia said, "Please tell Signor Gherardini that the stress of the day has worn me down. I must rest. Beg him to make an apology to our guests on my behalf. I will not be coming down again this evening. Thank you, Pia."

Knowing that they were to meet privately that night at his lake home, she figured that Nico would conclude that her sudden disappearance from the reception was a dramatic demonstration of a grieving widow.

Pia presumably set off to relay the message.

Back in her room, Sofia saw snapshots of what she might be leaving: the huge white cups of magnolia blossoms in the tree outside her window in the spring; the sound of the cascading flumes in the pool below; the topiaries that she imagined prowled the grounds of the estate at night; the teal awnings of her greenhouse that fluttered like freshly drying sheets when a breeze would announce itself. Then bam! It hit her. Misfortune was evicting her with far too little notice. *She was to leave all of this?* She had finally landed in a place she hadn't intended to leave, at least for a long while. Her anxiety was only outmatched by her anger. She picked up her pillow, smashed her face into it and screamed, unleashing her fury while attempting to muffle its terrifying sound.

The house phone rang and she at once realized her mistake. She snatched the phone off the cradle before a servant could answer.

"Klara?" she started, trying not to sound apprehensive. "Thank you for calling so promptly."

"You sounded troubled," Klara said in her stoic German accent.

"No, I'm fine. But may I call you back using my cell phone? I don't want to tie up the main line as our house is full of people."

"Certainly. I'll wait for your call."

Sofia couldn't risk someone else picking up the landline and hearing her conversation. She dialed Klara's number on her cell phone, and standing with her bare feet clawed into the floor, she braced for the moment of reckoning.

"Hello, Klara."

"What can I do for you, Yvette? Oh pardon me, Fiona tells me you have taken an Italian name ... Sofia. I like it."

"Thank you, Klara. Let me get straight to the point. Have you told my relatives where I am?"

"Why yes, just last night. I emailed your Aunt Tess."

Suddenly Sofia knew that she would be leaving Bellaterra the following day. The silence prompted Klara to continue. "I hope that was acceptable."

Sofia regrouped in order to glean as much information as possible because a second call to Klara would appear unusual, and magnify a situation she wanted to minimize as insignificant. "Who was with my Aunt Tess?"

"Let's see, a young girl, your cousin? Kinsey? Lizzie? Ah, no .... Lindsey, that's it. She didn't talk much so I'm afraid she didn't make much of an impression, other than the excess of lavender-scented cologne she wore. My apologies if I overstepped my bounds."

"That's all right. I just had a falling out a few years ago. I'm surprised they wanted to see me."

"Well, they must be over it because they went to great lengths trying to find you, even headed to the publishing house in Lausanne that apparently printed one of your paintings. Congratulations, by the way."

"Thank you. You've been a great help. I really must go now. Goodbye, Klara."

Sofia realized her call had ended too abruptly but she couldn't risk saying anything that might betray her. *So that's how they had tracked her. That damned painting publication.*

As she packed, she watched the cars intermittently disappear from the driveway until she thought she could account for the six houseguests who were still in the residence. She had to see Nico. He needed to be privy to her plan so she called her co-conspirator.

"Sofia, where are you? I've been waiting for you. Exhausted, incommunicado for hours? You left me holding the bag, my sweet. But it was convincing. I'll hand you that." She could hear him smile through the intonation of his words.

"Nico, I'm in trouble. Something has happened and I need your help. I don't want to talk about this over the phone. I've been waiting for Jonas to leave. I'll be there in a half hour."

She hung up, leaving him alone to ponder her cryptic, frantic-sounding declaration.

Flaviano had retired, so her backing out the Ferrari without detection went smoothly. She couldn't see the guard gate from the main house but knew when Jonas was scheduled to be off duty. When she reached the gate, Jonas was still on duty.

"Don't you ever go home, Jonas?" She'd grown accustomed to flirting with Jonas to stay on his good side, his loyal side, but heard the irritation in her voice.

"Two of your houseguests left a few hours ago and haven't returned so I thought I'd stay until they did. How are you, Signora?"

"It has been a dreadful day, Jonas. I'm relieved it's over. I need to clear my aching head and driving is the perfect antidote. I'm not sure when I'll be back but I have the gate code so you needn't stay for me. *Buonasera*, Jonas."

"*Buonasera*, Signora."

The moon was almost full, a bright lemon-colored ball perched high and peeking through the leafless trees of winter. When she reached the vineyard, the vines were low and the eye in the sky could, without interruption, watch her slither through the vineyard like an eel, searching for a reef in which to hide.

Nico was waiting at his door. She slammed the car door and ran to him, and for the first time in years, she burst into tears.

"Sofia, what on earth?"

"I'm trapped. I need your help. My world is falling apart."

"Come into the house. Did anyone see you leave?"

"No, only Jonas, but he sees me take evening drives all the time so this was routine."

Nico poured her a Frangelica which she downed in one swallow. She then began to pace like a caged panther.

"Sit down and talk to me," he demanded.

She involuntarily gasped like a drowning victim reaching the surface. "I need to keep moving. Don't ask me to sit down."

With her eyes incessantly blinking, her trembling hands maniacally rubbed her temples as if trying to elicit an answer from a prisoner in her mind.

"Nico, my love, I told you that your father helped me start over, gave me a new name, so I could escape my tortured past. Well, it seems to have caught up with me. I've been thinking it through for hours. I need to leave Bellaterra ... in the morning."

"What? Are you crazy? What about us? Our plans? You can't be serious."

"I'm perfectly serious. There is no other way. We can still be together, Nico, but not here."

"I can't leave Bellaterra. This is my family's estate." He now stood and grabbed her arms, forcing her to look at him. "I won't leave Bellaterra."

"You can keep the estate. We just won't be here together. I'll settle somewhere else and we can be together there, just not always together, and not here. Believe me, there is no other way."

"This is madness! What do I tell the staff, and guests who are staying at the house?"

"You can tell them that I was distraught about your father's death and needed to get away, to be alone. I have to lose myself again. I can't believe this. I have to reinvent myself all over again. I thought I was finally free."

"What did you do, Sofia?"

She wrestled out of his grip. "Nothing that we haven't done together."

"You've killed before?" he asked incredulously.

"How do you think I know so much about toxic plants? Don't act so surprised. And you can't turn me in and we both know why." Her condemning eyes shot daggers.

"Tell me what you've done, Sofia." Nico's voice sounded agitated and demanding.

"No. I buried my past. I don't want to talk about it," she responded as she fiercely shook her head.

"It sounds like your past has been exhumed. So I want to know," he insisted.

"All right, if you must know … I killed a man who beat me and his family suspects where I am." A simple lie was always easier than a complicated truth.

"How do you know they've found you?"

"They contacted me, okay? Leave it alone. I need your help, Nico. Please. We're in this together, right?"

Nico looked dazed and dumfounded. He took a moment to digest the meaning of her insinuation. She was right. She held all of the cards.

"What do we need to do?" he asked with an acquiescent tone coming from the knot at the back of his throat.

"First of all, I'm going to need money and a new passport under a different name … in an English-speaking country! Do you know who your father used?"

"Yes. It's very expensive."

"You've got to be kidding."

"Never mind. I'll handle it but it may take a couple of weeks."

"I need to leave tomorrow. Where can I go to hide until the passport is ready?"

"I'll ask my cousin Mia. You met her this morning. She and her husband live in Capri. She'll do us this favor. They left a couple of hours ago. She'll be surprised I didn't mention it this afternoon but …"

"But what?"

"I'll just tell her my father's death hit you hard after the finality of the funeral, and you had to get away. You can grieve together."

Sofia shot him a cold, incriminating stare. "Let's not get melodramatic." Then she went on. "I need you to destroy the plants in the greenhouse … tomorrow."

"No. That would be too suspicious. I've never in my life spent time in your forbidden greenhouse … remember, no one was allowed."

"You're right. I'll do it tonight. I can't imagine the plants becoming an issue, but I never imagined Tess seeing the painting in that fucking Swiss magazine."

"What magazine? Who's Tess?"

Sofia instantly knew she was talking too much.

"It doesn't matter. Nico, if anyone shows up asking questions about my whereabouts, be careful. As long as they don't find me, we're safe. Guard your words. People who talk too much get in trouble. Listen to me. I was overwhelmed with the grief of your father's death. You had never seen two people so in love. I'm on sabbatical from my life at Bellaterra, healing. Incommunicado. You don't know where I've gone. But I've left a note saying that I'll contact you when I'm ready to come home. Flaviano will drive me to the train station. We have to stage this as if you believe I'm coming back, Nico. Got it?"

"Yes." Nico appeared somber, sullen with the news that their life, as they had planned it, was over before it ever really started.

Sofia took a deep breath, sat next to him, and whispered, "I'll have another drink, my darling."

Nico poured two stiff scotches, no rocks, and handed her one.

"What about your son?"

"Luca? I'll leave him here until we can figure out what to do with him. I'm going to need some time to process. I need to calculate every move I make, we make, from now on. Once I'm out of sight, Nico, once I'm gone, you need to appear normal, not worried about me. Okay?"

"Yes, got it. Sofia, we need to be together. You do realize that?"

She nodded furiously to comply and reassure him. "I love you. You believe me, don't you?"

He continued, "We'll just need to be careful, as you say. I love that you are so smart ... so calculating ... so incredibly beautiful ... so sexy."

His hand reached between her legs until she put her glass down, kneading her hands through his dark, curly Italian hair, and allowing him to ravage her, more passionately, violently, than he ever had before.

That night when she left the lake house, the sky was still clear; she closed the top of the convertible so the eye of the moon could no longer stare at her. Nico was her ally. Now if only time would grace her with alliance, even if only for a few more hours. A quarter mile from the main house, she gazed out her side widow to see the constellation and her astrological sign, Scorpio, on the horizon, following her from light-years away. How she hated feeling followed.

When she'd returned from Nico's, Jonas was no longer at the gate. She quietly drove the car up the driveway and into the garage, replaced the key, and lowered the garage door. She then crept through a back entrance, removed her shoes, stealing steps on tiptoes up the stairway and into her room. She changed clothes and stealthily made her way to the greenhouse. Finding two trash containers she quietly disposed of the plants in one and the containers in another, leaving nothing but a dusting of soil on the ground and on the tables. In less than two hours, the evidence had disappeared, and the trash bins returned to the trash disposal area behind the garages. No one had seen her.

As Sofia went to sleep, she thought of each necessary step of her plan. Then it hit her. *What about her inheritance? How could she collect her inheritance if she were missing? There must be a way, a loophole, a crack in the wall of the legal system that she could slip through. But she was getting ahead of herself. In the morning, she would leave Bellaterra. How did Tess know where she was? What else did she know? Conceivably, worst case scenario, a Monson woman could show up the following day.*

But Sofia would be gone once again, without a trace.

CHAPTER FOURTEEN

We are oft to blame in this,
'Tis too much proved,—that with devotion's visage
And pious action we do sugar o'er
The devil himself.
—William Shakespeare

By late morning, Sofia was en route to Capri via train. Nico had made her arrangements, as well as informing his cousin Mia that Sofia was coming for a visit. His instructions to Mia were definitive. Under no circumstances was Mia to call the main phone at Bellaterra, but rather call him directly. This was a family matter, a private family matter, and no one else's business, least of all the staff's. He explained that it was sudden because even Sofia had not realized how badly she needed to decompress and be with family. Family was everything to her. Mia cordially complied.

The staff was shocked by Sofia's sudden departure but politely supported her decision in Nico's presence. He was now the master in charge of running the estate and held the keys to their job security in his inexperienced hands. Mid-morning, he met with the staff. Auriane would have full care of Luca and be paid commensurately. He suggested that Pia, Sofia's personal attendant, take a couple of weeks off while the signora was away. The groundskeeper, Cyrano, was instructed to continue tending the flower garden in her absence but not bother with the greenhouse. After all, the signora wouldn't be gone long. Nico thanked them for their support, their performance the day before, and their kind words, adding that he knew that in their hearts his father would be missed, but life must go on.

After his exit from the room, Auriane was the first to speak.

"I didn't sign up for Luca's full-time care. He's not a baby anymore, you know. He's an active three-year-old. It's hard work and ..."

Pia interrupted. "You're full time already. She hardly ever sees him. At least you have a job. It sounds like I should start job hunting on my *vacation*."

Chinzia chimed in. "At least we're free of her for a little while. Good riddance. I hope she never comes back."

"Chinzia!" Lucia exclaimed, obviously overhearing the remark as she entered the room. "Everyone, go back to work! Your break is over, business as usual." She clapped her hands like a boarding school headmistress.

Flaviano and Jonas said nothing but exchanged glances and walked out the servants' door. The other men took the cue and followed.

Lucia continued, "Pia, please finish the day before you leave. Do a thorough cleaning of the signora's room. Her last-minute decision may have mussed things up more than usual. Besides which, this is an excellent opportunity to make it perfect for her return." Then she added, "Don't worry about your job. She'll be back. She wouldn't leave all of this."

Pia shrugged her shoulders and followed Auriane to the nursery where Luca was playing.

"I can't believe this!" Pia continued.

"Shh. Don't upset him," whispered Auriane.

"Nico ... I can't call him Signor Gherardini ... Nico-boy doesn't seem to know when she'll be back. What if she's gone for months? I'll need a job. I have bills to pay."

"He said she'll be home in a couple of weeks. If she's not here by then, you'll need to talk to him again. Don't borrow trouble, Pia. Have fun. I wish I had some time off." Auriane complained with a disgruntled shake of her head.

"You're right. Maybe Vinnie can take some time. He's on a big case though. Chances are he can't just pick up and leave with me. And I don't have the money to travel on my own."

"Ask him. You're lucky to have a boyfriend like Vinnie, Pia. That sounds like fun."

Luca started to cry. He wasn't a happy child but Auriane was expert in comforting him, directing his attention to something intriguing, changing the subject. Pia thanked her for being a friend and headed for Sofia's bedroom.

She opened the door to a perfectly undisturbed room, no piles of clothes on the floor, no empty hangers on the bed, nothing indicating a sudden departure, only an unmade bed. Status quo. It was disappointing. The only drama in her life was her possible unemployment. She opened the closet and examined the contents. Being familiar with the signora's clothes and their meticulous organization, she couldn't put her pulse on any garments missing. She opened the dresser drawers, and likewise, nothing seemed to be missing or disturbed. She resolved that her mistress had taken very little with her and was indeed planning on returning which put her mind somewhat to rest.

She opened the windows to fill the room with fresh air. The birds chirped, without a care, oblivious to the impending chaos inside the walls of the villa. She stripped the bed, dusted the shutters, and buffed the furniture with a strange-scented polish that always reminded her of some weed she'd shared with Vinnie. She removed everything on the desk, except the house phone, and polished its gorgeous cherry wood surface, while thinking how incredible it would be to own such a piece of furniture some day. She knew she was privileged with her job, to be surrounded by such beautiful objects like furniture and artwork, if not its people. Picking up the phone to shine the area beneath it, she discovered a ripped paper with a phone number on it, an international number. She put it back under the phone and continued her work. She remembered how Sofia had talked to her the afternoon before, through the door, asking not to be disturbed. She'd sensed that her mistress was distressed but thought little of it at the time. After all, the woman had just buried her husband.

Before she left the room, Pia did the unthinkable, almost as if she were watching someone else. She walked to the phone and grabbed the paper with the phone number on it, stuffing it in her apron. She was stealing and she didn't know why.

****

Marco and Mia D'Alessio lived on the island of Capri where he was a restaurant owner, and she, a shop manager. Due to her family's wealth, they lived in a commodious home overlooking the Tyrrhenian Sea. Although unanticipated until that morning, Sofia's arrival would provide Mia with time to acquaint herself with her deceased uncle's young wife, as she'd only met her once before the funeral, at a baptism in Rome. Mia was in her mid-thirties and childless, much to the disappointment of both Marco and herself. But their life was full, as they were unusually congenial people who had accumulated address books of friends and calendars of activities.

Sofia's trip to Capri took over seven hours, as there was no direct train service to Sorrento, the port from which she would take a ferry to the island of Capri. The closest city to Sorrento was Napoli. From the train station in Napoli, she took a taxi to Sorrento, then the ferry to Capri, a circuitous but necessary route and means to an end. She was to take the funicular to Capri Town where Mia would meet her. The train was uncomfortable; the taxi, dirty and hot; the ferry, crowded; and the funicular, stuffy; so meeting Mia was the sign that her trip had come to an end—at least for a couple weeks.

Sofia didn't recognize the woman but Mia's obvious recognition of her broke the ice.

"Welcome to Capri, Sofia. You must be starving," Mia said as she took Sofia's suitcase like an obsequious hostess. "Let's go to the restaurant for a home-cooked meal, no?"

"Oh yes," Sofia agreed. "Mia, thank you for this. I am hungry. That would be lovely, thank you."

"Well, it's been a tough week, no?"

"Yes, it has."

These were the last words Sofia would say for a while. She took a deep breath while Mia chirped like a parakeet about the weather, the state of the tourist industry, and the pregnancy of her friend at the hat shop. For the first kilometer, Sofia was astonished that someone could deliver such a lengthy monologue about nothing; unbeknownst to Mia, Sofia tuned her out. Somewhere during the third kilometer of the ride, the chatter became annoying, and by the time they reached the restaurant, Sofia wished she were back on the stuffy, uncomfortable train, alone. However was she going to survive two weeks of frivolous chatter?

The restaurant had a stunning view of the sea, cypress and olive trees in the garden for shade, and Puccini playing in the background. Marco was there to greet them and proved to be a charming man who spoke slowly and considerately, a welcome relief from his wife's unremitting prattle. First, a glass of Santa Margherita pinot grigio, then a dinner of antipasto salad, hot Italian bread with balsamic vinegar, halibut à la vodka with angel-hair pasta and lemon sauce with capers, chased by a rich spumoni that made Sofia's personal Best-Tastes-in-a-Lifetime list. She thought to herself that she could weather Mia's storytelling if she could eat at D'Alessio's Restaurante every night. There were, after all, trade-offs in life.

That night after a picturesque drive through narrow Caprian streets, lined with enticing shops and private homes, having meandered past cemeteries, orchards, vineyards and gardens, they arrived at her retreat. When her head met her pillow, it was the safest she'd felt in two days. She'd made her escape and only Nico knew where she was and what her intentions were. She would wait for her new passport … and then … disappear.

For the first few days, Sofia made it clear to Mia that she needed privacy. She had a garden outside her bedroom with a dramatic view of the azure sea so what more could she want? She was mourning her husband's death and needed the downtime. Mia complied, knocking on her door only in the evening to inform her when dinner was served in the house or to invite her to dine in town at the restaurant. Because Marco and Mia worked long hours, it was the perfect retreat. Sofia had time to think, talk with Nico, and not be concerned with being discovered.

Her mind was on overdrive. It was true that if any of the Monson women made it to Bellaterra, they would find nothing. No one knew when she'd return, and for a while, no one would think it unusual. One glitch however was the child. What mother would not return for her child, no matter how distraught she was? She knew she'd never go back for him. She would disappear into the world, and that world would proclaim her a missing person. The estate would raise her son. It couldn't be helped. Collateral damage.

She spent the morning trying to locate a boarding school that would take a child his age, and came up with nothing. She could most likely leave him with Auriane for a few months, but after that, when she'd been pronounced missing, a home with friends or relatives would be a more sympathetic and less pathetic scenario … at least until he came of age to go to boarding school. The world would look more kindly on that.

That afternoon when Mia returned from work, Sofia was dressed and singing softly while she prepared some appetizers. Mia entered the house through a side door, gabled with future wisteria blossoms, and followed her ear to the kitchen.

Sofia had risen and joined the land of the living. Smiling with a kind and gentle look on her face, she welcomed Mia home and announced that she was feeling much stronger.

"And I want to apologize for not being more sociable this past week, Mia. Marco and you have opened your beautiful home to me and I will be forever indebted to both of you for your generous hospitality. Would you like a snack?" she offered, while extending a silver tray with cheeses and crackers. "I didn't want to snoop in your kitchen but this was an obvious option."

"Thank you. I'm glad you're feeling so much better. Marco and I realize what a difficult time this must be for you," she remarked in a compassionate tone.

"Thank you for understanding. Is there anything I can do for you during the day when you're both working? I'll be happy to earn my keep until I return home."

"No, we want you to relax, but I must say, it is good to see you up and around, no?"

That night after a boring evening with Mia but a delicious dining experience at Marco's restaurant, Sofia set the stage for the next chapter of her plan, to be executed the following night.

It was a Monday evening, the restaurant was closed, and the three of them were in the living room with the windows open so the sound and salty smell of the sea would accompany her compelling entreaty. They were laughing and seemingly enjoying each other's company, when Sofia began to cry, gradually, but not dramatically.

"What's wrong?" Mia asked.

"I'm sorry," she responded. "I miss my little boy."

"Of course you do," Mia said compassionately, as she moved to the sofa and reached for her guest's hand which Sofia willingly extended. "He's a beautiful child. I can't imagine how much you miss him. If we had a little one like Luca, I'd be devastated to be apart from him for merely a day, no?"

Now sobbing, Sofia buried her head into Mia's shoulder while Mia stared aghast at her husband whose eyes welled with tears.

Sofia sat up with hands clenched in her lap, and without looking at them started to talk.

"He's such a little man. He has his father's intelligence and curiosity. I can tell already. He's so sweet and talking more every day, making those adorable mistakes that three-year-olds make. I need to go home to him this week, even though the house will feel so empty without Rudolpho."

Marco spoke as he used exclamatory Italian gestures. "By all means, you do. We'll help you make your travel arrangements as soon as you decide it's time to leave."

"You'd prefer to fly, no?" asked Mia

"No, I like to travel by train. I'm fearful of air travel," Sofia submitted, duplicitously.

"Anything you say, Sofia," Mia acquiesced.

"Marco and Mia," she said while looking at each of them individually, "you are the finest people I've ever met. May I ask you a question?"

"Please," replied Mia, appearing valued and bewildered.

"This is so difficult for me to say." Sofia swallowed and exhaled an anxious, audible breath. "If anything ever happens to me, will you take care of my Luca? I have no one else to ask. Nico will marry and have a life of his own, and I have no family. I'm awake every night thinking about Luca's safety, his future. It haunts me that now that Rudolpho is gone, I have no one."

Marco and Mia looked intently at one another. Mia started to cry. Marco spoke for both of them.

"Sofia, it would be the greatest honor of our lives to be the guardians of your son if anything were to befall you. We know it won't happen but the mere fact that you have asked us is a supreme compliment and sacred responsibility that my wife and I gratefully accept."

Mia decisively nodded her head.

The couple stood, and Sofia stood to hug them. Then a solemn Marco D'Alessio made a toast to the joy of their coming together under such extraordinary circumstances.

That evening, Sofia heard from Nico. Her passport and driver's license would arrive the following day before noon. They had been purchased from a homeless woman in Canada who needed the money more than an identity. Her new name was Madison Thomas, which she rather liked. Sofia would travel the day after tomorrow, presumably to Perugia, en route to Bellaterra. But she'd never arrive because Madison Thomas would be on a plane to the province of British Columbia and only Nico would know where she was.

And then there was Nico. What to do about Nico? She needed him to believe that she loved him and couldn't love another. It would be easier, long-term, to pull it off from abroad. He was madly in love with her and couldn't afford to deceive her, as she had evidence that tied him to his father's death, despite his alibi. After the estate was settled, her half would merely disappear into an untraceable account. Besides, how do you arrest a missing person? If Nico caused her any trouble, she could implicate him by revealing evidence that his motive of financial gain was traceable, that his forcing her out of the country and providing her with a false passport to rid himself of her was traceable. She could reveal to the authorities through planted evidence that he'd threatened to kill her if she didn't disappear, so out of fear for her life, she complied. He would most likely be sent to prison, and she would have access to his money, through Luca, his beneficiary. She would need the help of the accountant, Scardina, but she was good with men, and he was loyal to Rudolpho's memory. Of course, none of this would ever come to pass because Nico loved her. But every resourceful woman needed a back-up plan.

The night was long. There were so many logistics to consider. She thought through the benefit of having multiple passports, including the ability to draw on her off-shore bank accounts using the alias associated with each account. She could continue to draw from her account under Sofia Gherardini, and set up another under Madison Thomas, if necessary. Within a few weeks, Sofia would be declared missing, and within a few years, she would be declared dead and her beneficiary, her son Luca, would be entitled to the money. But Luca was underage, Nico his trustee, and Nico would do as she wished. At some point, she'd need to resurface to Rudolpho's trusted accountant to assure her access to all of it. But before that point in the game, there were other pawns that needed to be put into place.

In the morning, she informed Marco and Mia that she'd spoken to Nico the night before and he was sending a train ticket to Perugia, where he'd pick her up, and take her home to see her little boy. She couldn't wait any longer. The ticket would arrive by special delivery before noon and she'd be gone the following day. She thanked them again for their hospitality and restated that she would never forget their generosity and kindness. They were suckers, pathetic puppets, she thought as she spoke otherwise. But they believed they were everything she told them they were, and everyone was content.

When the doorbell rang and Sofia answered, she signed for the package, then slammed the door in the face of the messenger, never having looked at his face. She ripped open the parcel, to find cash, a passport with her photo and the name Madison Thomas, a driver's license, and an insurance identification number which the real Madison had given up for a generous sum. Just as planned, there was a one-way train ticket from Napoli to Perugia for Sofia, and a one-way plane ticket from Napoli to Vancouver, British Columbia, for Madison. A perfect plan had come together. Her silken strands of deceit were tight and strong, showing no loose ends or identifiable patterns.

After confirming with Nico that she had received the documents, she packed her few belongings: clothing, vital personal information, and a photo of Nico that she would display when he eventually visited her. She liked to travel light, with only the bare essentials.

The following morning, Mia drove her to the ferry in Capri, bound for Sorrento, where she took a taxi to Napoli, not to the train station, but rather, to the airport. She made it through security, boarded her plane, and by the time Nico didn't meet her in Perugia, she was approaching Toronto, Ontario, a gateway to Canada, her new country.

CHAPTER FIFTEEN

The real voyage of discovery consists not in seeking new landscapes,
but in having new eyes.
—Marcel Proust

In mid-February, Tia arrived in the flourish of Florence (Firenze, to the Italians.) The air was frosty, cooler than it had been when she left D.C. The city had classic elegance, a mix of architectural classicism in its buildings and a look of simple provincialism in its inhabitants. She rented a car and headed south, but not before taking a detour through the difficult-to-drive Florentine streets, confusing for a foreigner to navigate in that the founding fathers hadn't planned for its expansion through countless committees. It had emerged naturally according to its needs and was as unpredictable as any other European city, which contributed to its endemic charm. She viewed piazzas with fountains gilded with mythological heroes, entangling and overpowering savage, preying beasts. Lines queued at each gelato stand, and posters of upcoming concerts were nailed to every available telephone pole, stop sign, and building surface. The light of dusk cast shadows of twelve-foot statues, randomly sprouting from cobblestone street corners, which delightfully took one by surprise. Spears of golden rouge, splintered and splayed onto terracotta buildings that backed up to alleys, used most assuredly for concealing secrets and ignoble escapes. Yes, she would come back to Firenze and explore when her mission was completed.

She headed for the city of Orvieto, far enough south of Castiglione to be inconspicuous, but close enough for a daily drive to start her skulking. *Skulking, what a delicious word*, she thought. In the past, she may have thought to sulk or to hulk, but never to skulk. She liked how it sounded.

The sun was setting so the variety of resting orchards, rippling vineyards, and rambling farmlands were lit by solar slants upon the earthen upholstery that burrowed and rolled, appearing like an indiscriminately tossed cloak with ample material upon this land called Italia. Before the sun set, she could decipher lakes in the distance and the occasional graveyard with large sepulchers and tombstones in the foreground and, of course, the ever-present Etruscan eruptions of stone walls that appeared in random spots along the quiet roads that she seemed to own that evening.

Within an hour, a night shade had dropped from above, and the sky was clear and dark, presenting the constellations of winter she so loved. She felt herself almost succumbing to sleep at the wheel and it scared her. She was in a foreign country, going to a city she'd never visited. She had to stay awake, stay alert. She rolled down her window to a gust of cool air and decelerated to accommodate unexpected turns in the winding road. The benefit of slowing down was being able to hear cuckoos in the distance and to see fireflies in tree thickets. Despite the beauty, she dreamed of how good the bed would feel beneath her weary body.

The sight of the walled city of Orvieto, perched high on a plateau overlooking hills of Umbria, quickened her pulse; the shot of adrenalin she needed to stay awake. Just like a fairy tale, the road that entered the city led directly to the doorstep of the *duomo*. Breathtaking. Only in Europe could she drive up to a seventeenth-century cathedral without expecting to see one. She had learned from her travel in other European cities to lodge near an historical site to find one's bearings more easily. Taking a right at the front of the cathedral, she drove two blocks and took one more right. There it was, her home away from home, La Dolce.

The family-owned hotel looked exactly like the building pictured in the travel brochure which was a positive sign. She parked her car, grabbed her bags, and entered through a glass door with the inscription,

Benvenuto. Behind the counter sat an older lady, perhaps in her fifties, with pewter hair and a disturbing, single black hair growing out of the large mole on her chin. Tia handed a credit card to the woman who swiped it in exchange for a real key, the kind you could hold and insert into a keyhole—old school. The woman directed Tia down the hallway, speaking Italian so rapidly that Tia barely understood a word she said. But by interpreting the woman's finger-pointing and gesticulating, Tia deduced that she would be on the fourth floor, and there was no elevator.

Reaching the room, her heart pounding and her legs folding beneath her, she locked the door behind her and fell onto the bed. Her jetlag precluded any further expectations of the day. She needed sleep. Only sleep. The last thought she later remembered having was a desire to cut off the ungodly hair protruding from the mole of her hotelier, stuff nightmares were made of. Then she slipped away. Even the church bell that rang every hour on the hour went unnoticed and unappreciated by the city's most recent arrival.

The following morning, Tia awakened to the sound of a rooster crowing, instead of an alarm clock. For an instant, she didn't know where she was, confused by her unfamiliar surroundings, as if she were in a dream. As she lay in bed, still in her clothes from the night before, she gazed around the room to find a small, doily-covered table with a white Italian ceramic pitcher, and an off-kilter, silver-framed mirror over the wooden dresser. In the corner was a basket filled with dried sunflowers and a quilt holder with two hand-made quilts that her friend Traci from D.C. would have coveted. But the draw of the room was the window that overlooked the inner courtyard of the hotel. She walked to the window and smiled. In the middle of the area was a fountain. That was the sound she'd heard which had invaded her last dream. The window box outside her room, bordered with flaking aqua shutters, housed pruned purple sweet peas, and the wheelbarrow in the corner of the courtyard was used as a planter for bright yellow genista. The perimeter of the courtyard displayed unpruned gerania, leaning into the walkway as if trying to escape; fuchsia bougainvillea and ivy sprawled and smothered the whitewashed walls of the building, strangling each other and cascading in bunches. It was a lavish display, to be trumped only by what the summer months would bring to the party. Tia breathed the cool Umbrian air, suffused with garlic potatoes, frying, and Italian bread, baking. To the left, she could see the rooftops of broken tiles and hundred-year-old chimneys, and she wondered why she'd ever go home.

She took a shower with lukewarm water and homemade soap, dressed, and made her way to an outdoor café to sip a cup of the dark Italian coffee she loved so much. It was warm enough to sit outside which she always preferred to do when given the option. After she ordered, she looked at her surroundings, and reflected on the glory that was Italy. There were two doves cooing and mating on a telephone wire almost directly above her, an omen perhaps? No, she wasn't superstitious. In the corner was a rusty pergola with blackberry brambles vining its exterior, and two milk crates beneath it with a calico cat atop one of them. The exterior of the building was stucco, breaking away in layers of sienna and ochre paint. She had a friend in D.C. who had spent megabucks to have a muralist create that same effect in her kitchen.

The waiter brought her coffee and a plate of hard rolls and grey jelly. He was followed by a second gentleman who delivered her eggs soaked in olive oil and salt, which would take some getting used to, and a side of the most luscious, sliced tomatoes she'd ever tasted. While eating, she studied her map. Then realizing she wasn't sure where to begin, she asked the waiter if he knew on which side of Castiglione the Rudolpho Gherardinis lived. To her surprise, he did, and in his limited English, he asked if she were a friend of theirs. She replied that she wasn't but had met one of them once upon a time, thinking that was a suitably honest but vague statement. He replied that he hoped she would see the place and report back to him at a future meal, as he had heard it looked like a fairy-tale castle. She ironically had prejudged it as a house of horrors.

On her way to her black Fiat, in a shop window she eyed a Venetian-styled mask with an elongated nose and a face divided into symbols of the zodiac. Tia was a Pisces, and she remembered that Cristin-turned-Yvette had said she was a Scorpio. Probably a lie. She'd lied about so many things, who knew what the truth actually was?

She passed fields that would in months display golden bales of hay and ubiquitous nodding sunflowers, sumptuous vineyards dripping with grapes, and orchards heavy with olives. Considering the season, at least for the time being, she would have to imagine the ultimate beauty the summer would bring; regretfully, she wouldn't be there to see it.

Remnants of morning fog shrouded patches of trees that intermittently appeared on the side of the road like outcroppings. At one point she had to come to a complete stop as a small herd of sheep took their time crossing the road, ignoring her presence, oblivious to the potential danger of her automobile. As she approached the town, she reviewed her plan. For some illogical, but nevertheless compelling, reason she felt that she first needed a visual of where Yvette possibly lived. When she neared the town, she stopped to ask a local its exact whereabouts, confirming what the waiter had told her that morning. Within minutes, she had her scope set on the estate outside the east perimeter of the town. As she slowly approached the entrance, she noticed a guard shack, and the word Bellaterra in bronze above the elaborate baroque-style gate, bordered by two immense lions. She inadvertently made eye contact with the guard at the gate, then sped up. She could not do this again for a while, nothing conspicuous to alert the family that someone was watching them. It was a paranoid thought as she was certain that many cars slowed down to gawk at such a beautiful entrance, straining to see the grounds and mansion through the bronze-filigreed bars. While driving by, she'd tried to see how far from the entrance the main house was. It was not even in sight from the gate. It must truly be a mansion, she thought, and as isolated from the outside world as a prison.

The second step of her plan was to go to town and casually meet a few people. Eventually she would make informal inquiries about the Gherardinis. Then she would visit the local newspaper office in search of a photo that could provide identification. That was enough planning for the first day. She could hear the oscillating intonation of her father's voice saying, *Those who fail to plan, plan to fail*, followed by her mother's steady voice saying, *Don't expect miracles*.

On the road, there were signs pointing to the Tuscan vineyard towns of Montalcino and Montepulciano, which she'd read about. She was in Umbria where there were vineyards aplenty, and tasting rooms in which to nonchalantly inquire about the area's wealthy families. It was close to noon, too early for wine. She drove to the center of town and sat at a wrought-iron table for two, in a wrought-iron chair, crowned with a bower of vines above her head, which she guessed would be fragrant, trailing jasmine by mid-June. She bought a French newspaper and ordered a croissant and a strong cup of Italian coffee, which was strong but not as strong as the Turks made it. The air was cool, the clouds hung low, and the town was so sleepy, she was forced to remember the European culture. Towns didn't come alive until nighttime. People ate dinner after nine, sometimes at midnight; she'd come back in the evening, and find a bartender to talk to, or if all else failed, she'd find a place to get her hair cut. Who better to pump for information than bartenders and hairdressers?

She downed her coffee and headed for the local newspaper office where she asked to use their computer to scan social pages over the past four years. The receptionist was almost solicitously helpful, even offering to help expedite her search. Tia assured her that she was only getting a feel for *who was who in the zoo*, a colloquialism she'd picked up that made her smile every time she said it. Within the first half hour, she found a marriage announcement in 2001 of a Rudolpho Gherardini to a woman named Sofia. That couldn't be it because there was no mention of an Yvette Vandal. Frustrated, she wondered if Rudolpho Gherardini was as common a name as John Smith back in the states. Did she have the wrong Gherardini estate? Could there be more than one? There had to be an easier way, she thought. She was better with people than machines so she cut her search short and left the newspaper office.

Later in the day she chose Taverna Vingiano because she liked the sound of the seven vowels that tripped off her tongue when she said it aloud, as if she were making love to the language. She'd taken an opera class at the University of Grenoble and learned about the melismatic nature of the Italian language, which was based on the delicious sounding of vowels, lending itself to singing in Italian, and allowing the singer to improvise notes on the same vowel ... a fact she'd forgotten until then, but would share with Tess when she returned to the U.S. Her sister would be impressed.

The Italian tavernas didn't feel sleazy like they sometimes did back home. They felt more like neighborhood meeting places after a day's work, and they smelled so good, the air suffused with garlic and oregano. The man who welcomed her at the door introduced himself as Alberto Vingiano.

"Would you like to be seated at a table, *Signorina*?" he asked.

"No, thank you, at the bar please," she said in her best Italian.

"*De France*?" he asked as his arms motioned her to the bar.

"*Oui*."

"*Bienvenue, Mademoiselle*."

"*Grazie*," she responded with a smile, as she heard her heels clicking in time with the background score of the "Toreador Song" from *Carmen*.

She ordered a sangiovese from a local vineyard called Monte Vibiano and asked to see the menu.

"You're not from around here," said the handsome young bartender, setting down a napkin with a black and white sketch of Taverna Vingiano on it.

"I'm visiting a friend in Perugia for a month and am touring the area while she works."

"A night job. What does she do?"

"Oh ... she's involved with the import/export business and deals mostly with North America so her schedule is crazy, completely defined by phone calls to the U.S. and Canada. We sleep a lot during the day, but it's great for me because when I return, there won't be such a time adjustment." She surprised herself by how easily she was able to fabricate a story in French and understand his Italian. She'd almost embellished her phantom friend as a shopkeeper but was cautious enough to know that he may have asked the name of the shop.

"Hmmm. What is the time difference between here and France? An hour?" he asked, but didn't press her. She'd made her first mistake. "If you don't mind, I'd like to practice my French. Or English. I'm Dominic, Dom, by the way. What's your name?" he asked, as he delivered her Sangiovese and a complimentary plate of olives and select cheeses..

"Yvette," she blurted, and suddenly realized how brilliant using that name might be, in case Gherardini's wife's name would be mentioned. "French is perfect for me," she stated with confidence. "I was driving around the area today. There are some impressive estates here. Where do people get the money to live in one of these places?"

"Family money. We rarely have someone from out of the area buy the big ones because they're passed down through the generations. Excuse me, Yvette, let me serve these other people. I'll be right back." He winked, then walked away.

Tia nodded and continued to sip her wine slowly. She was close to asking about the Bellaterra property, but now she'd need to ease into her interrogation without sounding interrogatory. The place was filling up and she realized how critical it was that she'd claimed her barstool when she did.

Suddenly a large, hairy, sweaty man with a booming voice approached her, and without taking his eyes off her, addressed the bartender. "Dom, you gave my seat away. Who is this pretty young thing?"

"Serg, this is Yvette from France. She's staying in Perugia with a friend this month."

"Her friend ... male or female?" he inquired, still addressing Dom as if she was incapable of answering herself. With a lascivious smile and tongue wagging, he stared at her like the Big Bad Wolf spotting Little Red Riding Hood as his dinner. And there was no doubt about it ... he was hungry.

"Sergio, leave her alone. She's a customer and I want to keep it that way. Sit over here," he demanded, pointing at the opposite end of the bar and with his large Italian hands and wide brown eyes, the gallant bartender communicated an apology to Tia.

"You can't blame a guy for trying," bellowed Sergio.

In any language, in any country, men could be pigs, Tia thought to herself. Then again, men like Dominic were gentlemen.

After forty-five minutes, when everyone sitting at the bar had been served, Tia signaled that she'd like one more glass of wine.

"Would you care to order any food?" he asked, offering her a menu.

"No thank you. These olives and this soft white cheese are quite enough."

"Well, this one's on the house," he said as he accommodated her with a glass.

"Not necessary." She smiled, realizing she was flirting with the man.

"The pleasure is mine," he continued. "I've comped many a glass due to some of our locals, who on occasion can be rude, crude, and lewd, as they say in America."

Tia had never heard that phrase but found Dominic to be interesting, witty, and quite charming. After another half hour, she realized that she was not going to bend his ear because he was working so she asked for the bill.

"Tomorrow night is much quieter. If you're still in this area, come by and we can talk without interruptions." He smiled.

She paid her bill with cash and responded, "I might just do that."
She smiled back at him.

She left Taverna Vingiano, knowing full well that she'd return the
following evening. She needed to be patient.

Her trip back to her room in Orvieto was a nightmare she would live
to remember. Her fatigue, a by-product of her jetlag, plus the mistake of
drinking a second glass of Italian wine, made the last twenty kilometers
brutally harsh. She opened her windows, blared music on the radio, and
at the most terrifying moments, she screamed at the top of her lungs,
just to stay awake. Her drowsiness was much more intense than she'd
experienced the previous night.

Only once before had she felt her life was at stake while driving at
night. She'd returned from a rock concert in Marseilles and prayed at
deafening decibels for what had seemed like an eternity until she arrived
at her room in Grenoble.

But miles into this miserable drive, she had to close her windows
because rain began to fall. The world through her windshield became
darker and increasingly invisible from bucketing, blinding rain. She
didn't even have the intermittency of striking lightening to help her
focus on the unfamiliar, winding road. She wanted to turn off the road
and stop, but she couldn't see any side roads and didn't dare slow down
in fear of being rear-ended. Her windshield was fogged and she couldn't
find the defogger button, so she was forced to open the windows, the
mortaring rain drenching her. She trailed a set of distant, red taillights as
she blindly trusted the driver ahead of her, praying that he or she was
neither drunk, nor overtired, as she fought to stay on the right side of the
road. Her eyes stared widely, her voice grew hoarse, and her life was in
a stranger's hands.

When she arrived in Orvieto, Tia was exhausted; she turned off the
ignition, exited her car, stood in the rain on the flooded, uneven
cobblestones, and cried. She knew that her life had been spared. She
then slept for two days straight and vowed she would never tempt fate
again.

It was Thursday before she drove back to Taverna Vingiano, ready to again assume the role of a French woman named Yvette, and determined to scrape together a clue that would justify her trip. Tia entered the building.

"You came back," Dominic announced as she marched to the bar with renewed strength and resolve.

"Sorry about that. I was tied up with my friend, but she's working again tonight so I thought I'd take a drive," she said in her most casual manner.

"I was worried about you the other night. That was a devil of a storm. They come and go so unexpectedly that people here usually just wait them out. Your timing was bad. I'm glad to see you back, unharmed."

"Thank you, Dominic.'

"You can call me Dom."

"Okay ... Dom. It's kind that you gave me a second thought. I'd like to try a pinot grigio from Montepulciano, if you have one."

"Conducting a personal wine tasting?" he asked, followed by his gorgeous Italian smile.

"Among other things" she schmoozed, smiling coyly.

"Sorry it was so busy the other night. We don't have many tourists at our establishment, mostly regulars." He wiped the counter.

"So, what's the big news around these parts?" she asked.

"Nothing much. Well, one of our established land barons died a couple of weeks ago."

"Did he live in one of the big estates outside town?" she inquired, skirting the big question.

"He sure did. His son and his pretty little wife of a few years inherited a helluva lot of money, I imagine. Pardon my French. Can you say that to someone speaking French? Did that translate at all?" he asked, stifling his laugh. "Pardon me, I shouldn't laugh. It was very unexpected and sad. They say he was a good man."

Tia's mind stuck on the phrase "pretty little wife," so she asked. "What was his name?"

"Rudolpho Gherardini. He was only fifty-six. The entire town showed up for his funeral. Standing in the streets, they were. The closest we'll ever come to a Princess Diana-type funeral in this area, that's for sure."

Tia sensed the blood drain from her head, feeling like someone had just socked her in her gut.

"That's ... that's terrible. I'm so sorry. His wife must be devastated." She could hear her voice but it felt disconnected from her body, like a puppet mouthing the words.

"Who knows? They'd only been married about three or four years. She fell into a load of money though. I guess she's a real beauty. I've never seen her; she's not from around here."

"When did this happen?"

"On January 21. I remember it well because it was the anniversary of my grandfather's death, and we all went to the cemetery."

"My condolences. Was she Italian?" asked Tia.

"Who?"

"The widow."

"Oh. I've heard mixed reports. She has an Italian name. Sofia, I think. But rumor has it she was from Switzerland. Don't quote me on that. You know how rumors go."

All Tia could compute was that sometimes rumors existed for a reason. Her head spinning and throat pulsing, she asked for some bread to soak up her mounting indigestion.

"So you haven't seen her?"

"The widow? No. She's a private type. I didn't go to the funeral but in the photos, she wore a black veil, so she remains a mystery to me. Another drink?"

"No. Thank you, Dom. I'm actually not feeling well." She paid in cash and stood. "I think I'll head back tonight. I'll drop by later this week with my friend."

"Try Wednesday night if you like it quiet. The skies are clear. Drive carefully."

The drive back to Orvieto was beautiful that evening, a striking antithesis of her journey two nights before. The sky was poetically clear and the almost-full moon shone as if it were a bright hole burned into black velvet, lighting the landscape as in a Turner painting.

As she drove, Tia concentrated. Sofia ... that was the new name if her hunch was accurate. The newspaper article had mentioned a Sofia Gherardini but she was not Italian according to Dom. She was from Switzerland. Tia needed to identify Sofia, the recent heiress to an Italian fortune. The following morning she'd go back to the newspaper office to find the obituary and any follow-up articles regarding the ceremony and Gherardini's life; and should she be so lucky, there would be a photograph of Sofia Gherardini. As she followed the winding road to Orvieto, Tia let her mind wander. She rather liked the bartender, not only because he was her primary source of information, but there was something intangibly appealing about him. She was attracted to him, by his smile, by his caring. She could tell he liked her too. But that kind of thinking would lead nowhere. She was on a mission and would return to D.C. in a couple weeks. End of subject.

Before she drifted off to sleep that night, she envisioned Sofia Gherardini, the widow, dressed in black as Dom had described her. Dressed in black, the widow dressed in black, the widow ... the black widow. That's what she was; the black widow, who wove her web, then ensnared and killed her mate. She knew she was jumping to the conclusion that Yvette was Sofia, but she could feel it. She just needed to prove it. Was there no one else who was curious about the circumstances of Rudolpho Gherardini's death? Once she identified Sofia as their target, she'd find something to prompt an investigation regarding the cause of death, and if there wasn't an investigation, she would somehow stir up the natives. Sofia Gherardini, if she was Hunter/Cristin/Yvette incarnate, had no idea they were on her trail. That was their trump card. The heiress may have thought she was smarter than anyone, specifically the Monson women; but she was about to be strangled in her own web, caught in the creation of her own delusion, unable to see beyond the circumference of its dimensions. Yes, if they could establish motive and proof of foul play, they stood a chance of nailing the beast.

CHAPTER SIXTEEN

There is room in the halls of pleasure
For a long and lordly train,
But one by one we must all file on
Through the narrow aisles of pain.
—Ella Wheeler Wilcox

It had been one of the cruelest winters in Dori Shanihan's memory. Downed phone lines, power outages, blizzards, sleet storms, icy county highways. There were mornings when she'd look out their picture window and not be able to make out the neighbor's fence as the snow furiously plunged in sheets, and obstructed her vision. There were late afternoons that crept into evenings like a thief, stealing the light, shortening the day, and robbing her of another day's promise. And there were nights when the wolves howled on the edge of town, causing her to imagine scenes from the movie *Dr. Zhivago*, so she expected to wake up to icy furniture, coated with hoar frost, and doors, blocked by impenetrable snowdrifts. Winter was beautiful and cruel, like life.

On Sunday mornings, it was routine for Dori to call her daughter for a visit. But on this Sunday, with the lines down, she used her new cell phone, a gift from Trina and Bryan the past Christmas. Even though the whole world was apparently using cell phones, some to the exclusion of even installing a landline, as they now called the home phone, Dori hadn't experimented with the cell device, except to keep it charged. She felt like a dinosaur but this was as good a time as any to jump from the Jurassic Era into the twenty-first century. She did have a computer. She'd grown tired of not understanding phrases like dotcom and google so she'd taken a course at the community senior center and braved the new world, much to her eventual satisfaction.

She punched, not dialed, her daughter's phone number and waited.

"Mom, you're calling me on your cell phone!" exclaimed Trina, obviously surprised and pleased.

"Yes, dear. Have you been watching the news? We had a miserable ice storm last night ... lines are down, schools are closed tomorrow, and the roads are a mess. Car pile-ups everywhere. I haven't seen the latest because our electricity is out, but last night on the news, there was a dreadful picture of a car dangling from a bridge with a family trapped inside. I'm praying they're okay. I feel so isolated without the television."

"Wow. Aren't you glad you don't have to drive in it, Mom?"

"I am. We live a simple life, dear. We don't go out much, just to the store and back, really. I'm so grateful I never felt the pressures of having to work like so many women. I'll probably live to be a hundred." She laughed as she spotted the book *100 Places To Go Before You Die* on her coffee table and doubted that she'd see any of them

"I sure hope so. How is Dad?"

"I'm sure he's fine but frankly he hasn't been feeling well. He has an appointment with the doctor tomorrow."

"Dad's going to a doctor? That's a first, and about time, I might add. I hope you're going with him as his advocate, Mom. These days, doctors do seem to prescribe medication as a bandage rather than spend the time to find a proper diagnosis. I know it's all tied to insurance coverage and fear of malpractice litigation, but please make sure he gets a complete physical, Mom. He hasn't had one in years and this is his chance. You don't think it's anything serious, do you?"

"No, I'm not worried, dear. He's probably just run down. Tell me about your week."

"Well, I know you don't like to talk about this, but remember that I told you about trying to track down Hunter Cross? Well, we think we've located her ... in Italy. Katie's sister Tia is in Italy to make a positive identification."

"That's such an ugly business, Trina. Are you really going to pursue this?"

"Mom, we've discussed this before. Yes."

"Well, I can't talk about it. Just keep me posted if there are any big developments. I did want to mention one thing that's been on my mind, dear. I'm sorry we weren't able to give you more family, Trina. With me being an only child and your father's sister living in Australia and childless, we didn't provide you with much family, did we?

"Mom, I never knew that bothered you. I loved my life with you, Dad, and Cristin. We had wonderful friends when we moved to Iowa. Uncle Michael and Aunt Harlene, even though they're technically not relatives, are like family to me. I've never given it a second thought. And I don't want you to either."

"Well, when I hear you talk about these Monsons and their families, I realize how wonderful it is that you now have extended family."

"Yeah, it's fun. But Mom, no one will ever take your place. You do get that, don't you?"

"Of course, dear. I'm just ... a bit envious as I would have loved a large family. It just wasn't in the stars for your father and me. But we have you, Bryan, and the girls, and we feel truly blessed, I promise."

"You're the best, Mom. Here's a thought ... would you feel comfortable meeting them sometime? You can come with me on my next trip to see them ... whenever that is."

"That's sweet of you to offer, honey. I'll think about it."

"Just say yes, Mom."

"I'll think about it, Trina."

"That's one of those phrases that makes me crazy, like 'we'll see.' It means no. I look forward to introducing my wonderful mother Dori Shanihan to the lot of them. Mom, I'm so proud of you. And by the way, you used your cell phone today! Congrats! Listen, I have to go. We're taking the girls to the movies and Bryan is calling me. I hope your power is restored soon, and please call me after Dad has his once-in-a-decade physical. Promise?"

"I promise, dear. I love you."

"I love you too, Mom. Bye."

After hanging up, Dori unfolded the Monson family tree that Trina had considerately mapped out and sent to her. *Who was Tia? Ah, Tia was Katie and Tess's sister who had lived in France, and now resided in D.C., the translator whose friend Yvette Vandal had died, or had been murdered, according to Trina.* It all sounded possible but far-fetched compared to Dori's unsophisticated life in Iowa. Global intrigue. She hoped her daughter wasn't playing with fire.

There were times, although rare, when Dori Shanihan allowed herself to think about the circumstances of her daughter's death. Her reticence to reflect upon losing her child was a coping skill she had honed because the alternative was inevitably crippling. Her denial felt harmless enough and necessary in order to persevere. The fact of the matter was that she had never recovered from the death of her daughter but rather had learned to function in a different world, a world without Cristin.

But on this late winter morning, alone in her modest kitchen, staring through her small, yellow, gingham-curtained window at nothing, this was one of those times. The film in her head began to roll. The last time she saw Cristin had been at breakfast that Saturday morning—scrambled eggs, bacon, toasted homemade bread, and strawberry preserves she'd canned the year before. Trina was going to a play rehearsal at the high school, and Cristin, to the Cross farm, to listen to music with Hunter. It was a day like any other day. Dori baked and Daniel mowed the lawn and read the Muscatine Journal. It was strange how she could remember the details of that day, and yet when a week ago, her friend Marg had asked her the name of a book she'd recently read, she went blank. Selective memory, she guessed.

She remembered hearing an ambulance or a fire truck in the distance, and as she always did, blessed the person or family that was in trouble. She knew her girls were safe.

"What's the ruckus?" Daniel stood up from his recliner and walked out the front door.

She recalled hearing the screen door slam and wishing he wouldn't do that. Bad habits die hard, she thought.

"Dori, get out here! There's a fire, a big one," he yelled.

She'd quickly washed her hands, dried them on her apron, and joined him in the front yard.

"Isn't that out where the Cross farmhouse is?" he asked, his voice magnifying with every word as he stared directly at her.

"Cristin!" she screamed. "Cristin's there! Danny!"

They were in their truck within seconds. Where were the keys? In the house on the entry table. Daniel ran to retrieve them and Dori started to quake. Surely, the family had safely vacated a burning house.

When Dori reconstructed those moments, that terrible whooshing in her head and the thunderous pounding of her heart returned, as if she were back in the moment. She could smell the smoke. She could taste the ashes. She could feel her spirit sinking like an irretrievable stone into deep, deep water. She stopped and thought to herself, *this is why I don't allow myself to think about it*. She was shaking.

Suddenly the power was restored and she was back in real time. As in the movie *Close Encounters of the Third Kind*, simultaneously, the lights turned on, the television blared, and the refrigerator began humming again. The clocks and the computer would all need resetting. Dori placed her memories on the back-burner of her mind and checked to see if they had phone service. They did. Thank God for the conveniences of modern life and the unexpected detours when traveling down a dark memory.

That evening, as they ate dinner, Dori and Daniel talked about the day's events. Because Dori didn't have a job outside the home, she often wondered if her husband was bored with her conversation. She couldn't bring home stories of what happened at work or discuss a problem concerning an associate or a boss, or even a work project. She usually spoke of a guest on Oprah or the behavior of a game show contestant. She'd learned not to bring up an episode of *As the World Turns* or *The Guiding Light* as Daniel thought that soap operas were "a colossal waste of time." She still tuned in from time to time, but that was her little secret. She'd cut back watching them daily when she'd started dreaming about the characters as if they were real people. That was the danger sign she hadn't shared with anyone. Besides which, there was substantial drama in her extended family. She didn't need to watch other people's problems.

"Do you mind if I turn the news off while we eat?" Dori asked her husband.

"No, go ahead. There's nothing we can do about the world anyway. It's just depressing."

He sat at the table and she turned off the news.

"I guess that's what makes it news … it's out of the ordinary and sometimes bad," Dori reasoned, as she served him a slice of meatloaf, then passed the mashed potatoes.

"Well, I just know that as bad as it makes me feel that there's a genocide going on in Sudan, there's nothing I can do about it. I guess I could. I could join some humanitarian effort to restore peace among tribes that have been fighting for centuries, but I'm not going to. It just makes me feel bad that I'm part of a human race that kills each other. As soon as I turn off the news, even though I know what's happening outside Khartoum, I dismiss it. It didn't do me any good to hear it in the first place, and I feel bad that I acknowledge my fellow human beings' horror, and in the next sentence, have an inconsequential conversation about the price of corn."

Dori changed the subject.

"I called Trina on my new cell phone today," she said to Daniel, as he began eating his meatloaf.

"How are they doing? Are they coming to see us this summer?" he asked.

"I don't know. We didn't talk about that."

"What did you talk about?"

"I told her you had an appointment with the doctor tomorrow."

"Now why did you go and do that? She'll just worry, Dori. Pass the bread please."

"She's too busy to worry, Danny. Besides which, I'll call her tomorrow and tell her you're fine."

She paused and rearranged her potatoes around her meatloaf.

"She did mention something about this Hunter Cross business."

Daniel peered over the rim of his glasses with transparent displeasure.

Dori continued. "I know you think this is a wild goose chase, and I don't suppose anything will come of it but what if she really did murder our daughter, Danny? And she's still out there? Trina is positive she did, and frankly, with the information they've gathered on this person, so am I."

Daniel continued to eat without comment.

"They've tracked her to Italy, and Trina's biological aunt has gone there to identify her."

"Who are 'they'?" Daniel asked, after taking his time to chew and swallow his food.

"The Monson women. You know … Trina's birth mother Katie and her sisters. Trina has asked me to go with her the next time she sees them."

"She's met them?" he asked in disbelief.

"Yes, once, last November. I think it's wonderful, Danny. She has an extended family now." Dori paused to sigh, then continued, "The world is different than it was when we were kids. People discover their roots, and sometimes families come together. We have to remember, there can't be too much love."

"Pass the gravy … please," he responded, not looking at her.

Feeling her heart pounding, she asked, "Would you mind if I went?"

"Where?"

"To meet Trina's other family."

"Do you want to?" he mumbled.

"I don't know."

"I don't see how this is going to have a happy ending, but if you want to go, go."

"You don't sound very happy about it. Maybe I won't then," she acquiesced.

"What do you want me to say, Dori?" Daniel put down his knife and fork, put his elbows on the table, folded his hands, and began speaking slowly and deliberately.

"Ten years ago, our daughter died. Our lives will never be the same, and there isn't a day that goes by that I don't think of her and feel the hole in our lives. She's gone. Can't we be done with it?" His voice quivered and his eyes welled with tears. "I don't want to talk about it any more."

Daniel stood and walked into the backyard, which was always where he adjourned when he wanted to be alone. Dori honored her husband's retreat, cleared the table, and realized she would not be making the trip.

The following day, when Daniel went to town and her home once again became her sanctuary, Dori completed her morning chores, and rather than turn on the television, she sat down with the sole purpose of examining her thoughts about the hunting of Hunter Cross. Her rationale was that if she could resolve her conflicting feelings, she'd know where she stood and put it to rest. But in order to do that, she'd need to revisit the day of reckoning, hopefully for the last time.

The day of the fire was scorched into her memory, leaving an emotional scar, so painful, so ugly, and so deep, that she'd have to excoriate it, one layer at a time. She and Daniel had driven to the Cross farm and could see in the distance four fire trucks lined up like box cars of a train, with hoses spraying gallons of water on a ferocious fire where once a home had stood. The asphyxiating smell of dense, black smoke blew toward them, causing them to cover their eyes, noses, and mouths. A police line had been established so on-lookers could not get close to the blaze.

Daniel ran to the police officer in charge and screamed, "My daughter's in there! I need to get past."

He responded, "There's nothing you can do, sir. No one gets past. If your daughter was in there, the men have done their best to get her out, sir. Please stand back."

There wasn't a word in any language to adequately describe the horror and helplessness they felt that afternoon. They could only pray that no one had been home, that the girls had gone to town and were safe.

After the fire was extinguished, the area was too hot to investigate. With no bodies having been retrieved, Daniel and Dori drove home to check their answering machine, or find Cristin there. There was no sign of her. Dori stayed and Daniel went into town to find his daughter.

Trina walked in the door an hour later and yelled, "What's with the smoky air? Where was the fire?"

Stunned and drained of color, Dori appeared from the hallway.

"Mom, what going on?" Trina screamed.

"Where's your sister? Did you see her in town? She went to see Hunter this afternoon and hasn't come home."

"I just saw Hunter at Pokey's but Cristin wasn't with her. After rehearsal, Suz and I stopped for a burger. Hunter was there but Cristin wasn't. Why?"

"The Cross farm burned to the ground this afternoon, Trina. We have to find Cristin."

"Mom, if she went to the farm to see Hunter, she wouldn't have stayed to talk to the Crosses. She would have come to town to find Hunter."

"Well, where is she then?" Dori shrieked.

"You're scaring me, Mom. I'll go back to town and find her."

"Your father's already there."

"Well, two sets of eyes are better than one. You stay here in case she comes home."

Trina tore from the house and backed out of the driveway at break-neck speed. Three hours passed and the only phone calls placed to the Shanihan residence were from Trina and her father to check if Cristin had returned. When they later walked in the door, there was still no Cristin to be found.

The next day, after they tried to file a missing person report and told the police department they suspected that their daughter may have been at the home of the fire, the Shanihans were informed that three bodies had been recovered from the scene, purportedly, two women and a man. It would take a few days for the dental records to verify the identities of the victims. Although the hours that followed were the longest of their lives, they already knew the answer, but hope tormented their spirits, detaining them in a purgatory of dread.

When the call was received, identifying Cristin as one of the three victims, the torture the Shanihans endured as a family intensified so dramatically, that as if struck by emotional fission, they split into separate ellipses, needing to grieve in private worlds. Cristin became their sun. Their misery and despair encircled her in isolated orbits, each mourning a loss and extolling her memory in private eulogies. Daniel suffered by withdrawing to Neptunian remoteness. Dori sobbed inconsolably, wanting to be near her daughter in Mercurial proximity. And Trina exhibited a Martian fury at a God who could arbitrarily snuff out her sister's short life.

The investigation later determined that due to the fact that the victims had not run from the fire scene, they had probably succumbed to carbon monoxide poisoning from either an improperly vented heater or a gas leak from the kitchen stove. It was difficult to determine what caused the fire, but they speculated that a burning candle or stove burner that hadn't been successfully turned off was the accelerant. The theory suggested that her daughter hadn't suffered, one small blessing among the curses of the memory. Cristin and the Cross parents had most likely fallen asleep and hadn't felt the terror and pain of a fire burning their bodies beyond recognition. It also explained why they hadn't tried to flee. Her beautiful Cristin with the fair Irish skin and delicate features, burning with no chance to escape or say goodbye. These kinds of thoughts were excruciating, so Dori had to once again release the visual which had haunted her for years.

It was much later that Dori wondered how Hunter had been told. Months later, she'd even felt guilty that they hadn't reached out to the young girl who had lost her home, her parents, and her friend. But being consumed by their own hysterical, tortured grief, they didn't see past the collapsed walls of their own lives to even inquire about the neighbor girl. Dori remembered learning that Hunter had left town. People in town thought that the poor girl had suffered such a calamitous loss, she'd wanted to start over somewhere else. She had no other family, no reason to stay in the area. It was understandable. No one could blame her.

It wasn't until later in the year that Trina started to ask questions and share them with Dori. Why hadn't the Crosses fixed their faulty stove? Hunter had mentioned it to her a number of times which always struck Trina as strange, as if in retrospect, she wanted Trina to remember that the stove was a problem. Why had Cristin stayed to talk to Hunter's parents, when her perceived intention was to hang out with their daughter? What had kept her sister at the farm rather than going to town to find Hunter? Why hadn't Hunter come to their house after discovering that her home had burned to the ground and Cristin may have been in it? Where had she gone that night and the days that followed? Why did she leave town? Why did she cut her ties with Trina? And months after leaving town, why hadn't she bothered to at least let Trina know where she was? After all, Trina's sister had died in her family home. Was it grief? Was it guilt? What would she have felt guilty about?

Another year later when Trina discovered that the letter and locket from her biological mother were missing, she'd mentioned it to Dori, and had either one of them connected the two events? No. Trina's questions were bothersome but led to no conclusions. They were merely questions, like islands with a vague memory of a mother continent ... until Trina read Tess Monson Parker's book and recognized floating pieces of a puzzle that actually fit together.

Three years ago, Trina's trip to Minnetonka confirmed that the novel was autobiographical and the author, her bio aunt, was not only in possession of the locket but knew Hunter as Cristin Shanihan ... this was the revelation. Dori now knew that Trina's suspicions were warranted, that whether Hunter had masterminded the explosion or not, she had schemed to use their daughter's identity. But with the news of Hunter's death, there was no retribution to be paid. Trina no longer obsessed about it, and Dori slept through the night, knowing that the person who had violated her daughter was dead.

But now she had risen from the ashes, and Trina's new family planned to track down the wretched soul. The whole business was a crazy-maker, monopolizing her thoughts, and chewing Dori's insides like a ravenous animal. She was ready to discharge her nightmares, so she came to a decision. Hunter Cross had taken her daughter's life, even if only symbolically, and she must pay.

CHAPTER SEVENTEEN

Hope is the thing with feathers
That perches in the soul
And sings the tune without the words
And never stops at all.
—Emily Dickenson

On the afternoon of Sofia's scheduled arrival, Nico informed Flaviano which train he should meet to retrieve her and bring her home safely. The household staff prepared for her homecoming. Pia was summoned back from her leave of absence, Lucia prepared a special meal, and Auriane gave Luca an afternoon nap so he wouldn't be cranky when his mother reappeared. The staff was told that Sofia was returning to Bellaterra because despite her grief, she missed her child.

"Right!" said Auriane, under her breath. "That will be the day."

No one else said a word.

Pia looked refreshed, despite not taking a vacation. Her boyfriend Vinnie was working on a case and couldn't get away. Two years before, she'd met him in Firenze at a club, but he'd now moved down to the area to be near her and his family, although his detective work did keep him leaping around the country like a frog. He'd corrected her a number of times about the word detective. A detective worked for the police force. He was hired privately when the police were not involved so he was a private investigator. She preferred the word detective.

When Flaviano met the train from Napoli, Sofia was not on it. He called Nico and was instructed to wait for the last train from Napoli, due in three hours, and meanwhile Nico would try to find out why she'd been detained. Surely she'd left a message with someone. Three hours later, the train arrived and departed, and neither the train nor Flaviano had the designated passenger on board. By the time the chauffeur drove through the gates at Bellaterra, it was dark. Luca was sleeping, the posturing for the day had been for naught, and the household relaxed for a few hours longer.

By morning, the staff was clamoring with conjecture and innuendo. Where was the signora? Why hadn't she called? Had she been in an accident? Had she even boarded a train? The train from Napoli? What was she doing in the south? Who was she staying with? Had she been alone? Maybe she'd never come back. Maybe she was dead.

Pia appeared to be the most concerned. She went to Lucia because Lucia was in charge of the household and the liaison to Nico.

"Lucia, what do you want me to do? Do I have a job? If she doesn't come back, is there something else I can do in the house? I need to have a job."

Lucia responded. "I'll talk to Signor Gherardini this afternoon, Pia. I agree. You must know if you are employed or not."

"Thank you, Lucia. I appreciate anything you can do on my behalf. Today, right?"

"Yes, Pia. Today," Lucia responded impatiently to Pia's impatience.

Detached and unconcerned, Nico made bogus phone calls to locate his young stepmother, and by evening, reported back to the staff that he had called the police and filed a missing person report. They would be sending two officers to the house, and the staff was to cooperate with them. Before he left the house, Lucia asked him about Pia's future employment. Was her job secure, if heaven forbid, Signora Sofia was not located?

"No, let her go," he retorted. "Sofia doesn't want a personal attendant anymore anyway. She is more of an aggravation than a help. Give her two weeks' pay. Thank you for reminding me, Lucia."

"I can't very well tell her she's an aggravation, Signor Gherardini."

"Tell her anything you want. Her services are no longer required." Nico slammed the door as he left.

He was off in his black Porsche convertible, when he noticed that Flaviano was taking a smoking break and talking to Jonas at the gate. Of course they were acquainted. They had worked for his father for over a decade. He'd just never thought about the servants being friendly, let alone friends.

****

When Pia checked back with Lucia the following afternoon, she was stunned to hear that she'd been released from service. Lucia stoically gave the young girl her check and called Flaviano to take her home, or anywhere in town she wished to go. Frenzied with anger, and yelling so anyone within hearing range could hear her rage, Pia stormed out of the house through the main entrance, which she was not allowed to use except when servicing Sofia. Flaviano was there to accommodate her. Her destination: Taverna Vingiano.

Dom was tending bar when Pia blew through the door like an unleashed pit bull.

"Give me the strongest drink you make … fast!" she wailed.

"If I served you the strongest drink I make, you'd be on the floor in one minute flat. Let's start over. Do you like rum? Vodka? Scotch?"

"I don't know … just make it strong." Pia yelled with the force of an Atlantic Ocean hurricane.

"Hey, hey. Hey. Is it Vinnie? Did my brother treat you wrong?"

Pia looked up with small, red-rimmed brown eyes. "I just lost my job." Her hands were steepled, her fingers tapping together.

"Ouch. I think that calls for a Moscow Mule, the perfect antidote to job loss. It works every time." Dom started concocting the elixir.

Pia stared at him as if she couldn't believe what he'd just said, and almost smiled.

"Here you go, sweetheart," he said in a caring tone. "Tell me about it. Where did you work? Sorry, I don't think we've ever talked about it."

"At Bellaterra. I worked for old man Gherardini but nothing's been the same since he died. I was his wife's assistant," which sounded less demeaning than servant. "But after the funeral, she took off and they can't find her, so Sonny Boy fired me."

"Did he fire you or let you go?" Dom asked.

"Same difference."

"No, it's not. I bet they'll give you a terrific reference letter, if you didn't misbehave while exiting."

"I did. I couldn't help it. I don't have a job!" she bellowed.

"I tell you what. I'll put in a good word with Papa Al tomorrow afternoon. We have a waitress leaving at the end of the week. Have you ever waited tables?"

Her eyes lit up. "No, but I know I could. Would you really do that for me? Just until I find something ..." She stopped.

"Something better?"

I'm sorry. I didn't mean ..."

"Don't worry about it. No promises but I'll speak to him. I can even teach you a few bartending tips for a future job ... not this one, of course." He smiled.

"You're a life saver, Dominic."

She downed her drink and left her money on the bar. "Thanks. I'll see you tomorrow, around four?"

"Around four," he answered." Hey, how are you getting home?"

"I live a few blocks from here. I'll be all right. Oh, and tell Papa Al I'm dating his son, okay?"

"You got it."

Pia stood up, and feeling woozy, caught her balance by steadying herself with the barstool. She focused and headed for the door, and almost made it without incident, but not without bumping into Tia Monson who had come back to the tavern, without agenda this time, but merely to see Dom.

****

Tia looked fabulous and she knew it. She'd been shopping and wore a stunning Sandra Ferroni dress. Her makeup was subtle but enhancing, and she'd piled her hair on top of her head in the most seductive fashion she could manage. She wasn't quite sure what she was trying to prove other than she was ready to have some fun in Italy.

As she stepped up to the bar, Dom actually did a double take.

"Wow! Look at you, *Mademoiselle.*" He used his finest French accent.

"*Bonjour.* My friend couldn't make it but I thought I'd come anyway."

"I'm glad you did. Please sit down. I want to talk to you. A drink?"

"The usual," she said with the satisfaction that she'd always wanted to say that, but had never frequented any establishment long enough to pull it off.

"You look radiant, absolutely stunning," he said as he stared with obvious infatuation.

"Why, thank you," she responded, as she crossed her leg and dangled the heel of her shoe from her foot. "What did you want to talk to me about?"

He smiled, crossed his arms on the bar, leaned into her and whispered, "Where in the United States are you from, Yvette?"

Tia straightened. "What do you mean?"

"Exactly what I said. I like you. I'd like to know you better but you can't keep up this charade, if we're to be friends. You see, your French accent is exquisite, but you're literally translating American phrases into French and it doesn't work that way. The French don't say 'around these parts' or 'check you later.' And the comment about the time change was a big slip. There isn't a time change between France and Italy."

"How long have you known?" she asked with eyes downcast, not looking at him.

"Since the first time you came in."

"Why didn't you say anything?" She looked embarrassed, her tone aggravated.

"Because it was so entertaining. But I like you and I'd rather you were honest with me. And besides, I need to practice my English more than my French, *d'accord?*" He smiled.

"I'm sorry." She admitted her pretense with a contrite pout. "I thought it would be amusing and somewhat of a coup to pass myself off as French ... for the fun of it."

"Is that it?"

"Almost." She smiled, wondering whether she should be forthright.

"Well. Let's say we start over. My name is Dominic but you can call me Dom."

"How do you do? My name is Katia. But you can call me Tia."

"Russian?" He looked surprised, one eyebrow lifting in suspicion.

"Actually, Irish, but my mother loved Russian writers."

"Well, Katia, Tia, from the United States, you do look stunning."

"Thank you." She smiled and tilted her head.

"So are you staying in Perugia with a girlfriend?"

"No. In Orvieto, by myself."

"I thought so, at least the girlfriend part. Perugia is a long drive, but then again, so is Orvieto. There must be a reason you've hidden behind such an elaborate story. What brings you here?"

"Can I trust you, Dom? This has to remain between you and me or my cover that I've already blown with you will blow sky high."

"That's intriguing. Yes, your secret is safe with me ... unless it's immoral or illegal." He smiled.

"Neither." She leaned closer. "All right. I'm trying to find a woman who has hurt my family."

"And you think she's here?"

"Yes, but I need to make a positive ID and I've come to a standstill. I need to see a photo of the late Rudolpho Gherardini's wife Sofia, or have someone who knows her recognize a picture I have."

"Well, I have good news and bad news."

"Really? Tell me," she implored, squeezing her shoulders together as she leaned forward to hear more.

156

"We may be hiring a new waitress this week who just lost her job at Bellaterra, and she's generally pissed off so I don't imagine she'll mind helping you. She'd probably love to expose her former mistress whom she apparently didn't like in the first place. Now she has nothing to lose and only revenge to gain."

"That's amazing. What could possibly be the bad news?"

"According to young Pia, immediately following the funeral, Signora Sofia took off for a few days, and now almost three weeks later, she's still at large, as you would say."

"She's missing?"

"Precisely, Katia."

Tia was not used to hearing her formal name and wondered how long it would be before she asked Dom to call her Tia.

"I mean, Tia," he said.

She smiled, acknowledging his recovery.

"That's disappointing but frankly, not surprising. She has the habit of leaving after someone has died."

"Whoa. What are you insinuating?"

"Nothing yet but I would sure like to speak to this Pia. When do you think she's coming back?"

"You just missed her. But she didn't miss you. She was the girl who practically knocked you over when you walked in tonight."

"You're kidding me, right?"

"No kidding, I promise. She did say she'd be back tomorrow to inquire about the job so that would be your cue. I'll get a sense of her allegiance or lack thereof before I introduce her to you. After that, if it sounds like she'll cooperate without spilling her guts to anyone, I'd be happy to make the introduction. By the way, I think it best that you use your real name. She's a street-smart girl. She'll sniff out a phony if you try to pull off the French disguise. But after the intro, you're on your own. If she does have loyalty to this Sofia, and her mistress returns, Pia might tell her, and then you can be assured that your identity could be revealed. There could be consequences."

"It's worth a try. I can't thank you enough Dom."

"Okay. Be here around four. Enough business. I get off at eight tomorrow night, may I take you to dinner?"

"I would love that." Tia beamed, showing Dom her biggest, fullest, most sincere and flirtatious smile. She finished her drink, grabbed her purse, and walked out of the tavern, inflated with satisfaction.

The following afternoon, Tia arrived a few minutes after four o'clock. She saw Dom talking to his father, Alberto, and a young girl at the bar, and she presumed that there was a hiring in process. Tia sat at a table and was so intent on the trio that when the waitress suddenly materialized, Tia was startled, and jumped in her chair.

"You do want to order, don't you?" asked a caricature, with straight bangs, crooked teeth, and impatient rudeness written all over her face. It occurred to Tia that this was the waitress who was being replaced.

"Ah yes, I'm sorry. I'll have a pastrami sandwich on rye with extra mustard please."

"I've seen you in here before. Don't you usually sit at the bar?" she asked.

"Yes, but today I'm hungry."

"Are you French or American? I've heard you speaking to the bartender."

"My mother was French and my father, American, so I speak both languages. Dom likes to practice his English."

"Whatever you say. My name is Alexa. Do you want something from the bar?"

"No, I don't want to bother the bartender."

"It's no bother."

"No, no. Aquafina please…that's all." She wanted to say—*Leave me alone; I'm waiting for my cue.*

The interview lasted another ten minutes, at which time Alberto shook Pia's hand, and in Italian said the equivalent of welcome aboard.

Alberto disappeared into the kitchen, and Dom continued to talk to Pia, presumably about her feelings for the House of Gherardini. Pia glanced at Tia, then Dom came out from behind the bar and brought Pia to the table. He made quick introductions, mentioned that she spoke English, winked at Tia, and left them together, alone.

"Dom says you're one of his friends. I'm pleased to meet you," said Pia. "He's been wonderful. He got me a job working here, starting next weekend."

"Congratulations. Have you ever been a waitress?"

"Well, not this kind. I've been a personal assistant. Where are you from?" she inquired.

"Washington D.C."

"The capital of the United States?"

"Yes. But I'd prefer you not tell anyone that I'm from the states. Our secret?"

Pia nodded and grinned.

"It sounds like you just got hired. Can I buy you a celebratory drink?" Tia asked.

"Sure."

"What would you like?"

"How about a limóncello on ice," Pia suggested.

Tia smiled and placed the order with the rude waitress with the crooked teeth.

"So Dom tells me you have some questions about my old job?"

"Yes, if you don't mind."

"No problem. I liked the job. It was easy most of the time, but I couldn't stand the wife. She was so superior, always talking down to the staff. Nobody liked her except old Signor Gherardini, of course. But she had to be close to thirty years younger than he was. She could have been his daughter. You know what I think? I think she was after his money. So do the others."

Tia sensed the troops assembling. "Do you really think so?" she asked innocently, as if disbelieving.

"Yes!" Pia said indignantly. "And now she's disappeared—the day after his funeral, for God's sake. They say it's because she's grieving but we don't buy it. There has to be another reason. But even if she comes back, I don't have a job there. I'd love to stick it to them."

Enter Tia. "Are you serious?"

"Absolutely serious. Why?" Pia sipped her drink, her eyes not leaving Tia's, searching intently for her meaning.

"Pia, I am looking for a woman who has wronged my family. I have a picture of her in my purse. If I show you this photo, and it is your former employer, if she returns, will you tell her I was inquiring about her, or will you help me bring her down? I need to know up front."

Pia's look of curiosity turned to one of fiendish collusion. "If you want her knocked off her throne, you have found the right person, Miss Tia. And I'll go further than that. There are others who still work there who wouldn't lose a wink of sleep if they were guaranteed that she'd never come back."

Tia opened her purse, pulled out an envelope, and praying that she not be disappointed, slapped the photo on the table.

Pia stared at the picture, raised both eyebrows, and whispered, "We're in business."

Tia's heart practically stopped, as she acknowledged under her breath, *I've found her.* Then she looked at her new accomplice, saying, "Oh Pia, thank you. I'm going to need to regroup. At least we know where she's been. But where is she now? Where could she be?"

"I don't know but I know who could track her down if she's still in Italy."

"Who?"

"My boyfriend, Dom's brother Vinnie. He's a private investigator. And he's good." Pia beamed.

"That's outstanding. Do you think he'd take it on? It might get complicated because we only have circumstantial evidence. But we can pay him."

"That's a good start. I'll talk to him tonight. He's coming down from Firenze, not this weekend, but the next." Pia paused. "What exactly did she do to your family?"

Tia didn't have the energy, nor did she think it prudent to go into detail about Sofia Gherardini's past lives, but tossed Pia a conciliatory bone.

"Let's just say that we have reason to believe that she's taken vile advantage of other people as well."

"I knew it!" Pia exclaimed. "How long will you be in Italy?"

"I have to leave in a few days, but Pia, I prayed to God that I'd meet someone who could help us, and you are that person. We can be in touch by email. That will be the cheapest way but I'll also give you my cell phone number. Here," she said as she handed the girl her card. "It sounds like I'll be gone by the time Vinnie arrives. But if I could talk to him on the phone, I could explain the situation."

"Okay. This sounds like an adventure. I'm excited to help you. Can I talk to some of the people at the house? My friend Auriane is the nanny and we're really close."

"I think I better talk to Vinnie first, don't you? If we're going to employ him, we better play by his rules. He'll know what's best."

Tia knew she'd said the right thing as Pia grinned and nodded assuringly.

That night, feeling that she'd made considerable headway, Tia seized the most memorable, romantic night of her life with the handsome Dominic Vingiano as she relaxed into his arms, into his confidence, and into his bed.

CHAPTER EIGHTEEN

'Where are the people?' resumed the little prince at last. 'It's a little lonely in the desert ... It is lonely when you're among people, too,' said the snake.

—Antoine de Saint-Exupéry

The first thing Madison Thomas recognized when she landed in Toronto was the ease and subtle relief of speaking her native tongue. For the first time in her life, she was on foreign ground where English was the primary language. The airport was cosmopolitan with advertisements boasting cultural diversity, upcoming events, and historical must-sees, all accented with maple leafs. She had a four-hour layover in Toronto and time to think.

She'd slept most of the way from Italy and dreamed of a place of Gaelic/Celtic culture, a Brigadoon of sorts. When she woke up, she continued to obsess about the town, somewhere in eastern Canada, that had been described to her by a high school acquaintance. She hadn't thought of it for years but leave it to a dream to bring a memory to the surface. It had her full attention, and in her waking state, she felt compulsively drawn to see it. She figured she was close. She could feel it in her bones, as her father used to say.

Ten years ago, she'd killed her father, killed them all, her father, her mother, and Cristin Shanihan ... all poisoned from her garden plants. When they'd eventually died, like a movie producer, she'd positioned them on the floor near the yellow kitchen table on which sat a pitcher découpaged with rooster prints and a burning candle ... a vision, indelible in her mind. When the stage was set, she'd turned on the gas in three of the four stove burners, then ignited the fire on the fourth burner. She left the farmhouse and its deceased inhabitants to burn. No one had ever figured it out. Within five minutes, she was in town at Pokey's with Cristin's sister Trina and a few others from school, and she didn't hear the sirens for over a half hour. Who would suspect a seventeen-year-old girl of such treachery? No one ever asked her where she was the hour before the fire. Her reputation was spotless. No one had ever tied her to some of the heinous animal crimes that she had previously committed. She was untouchable. There was no funeral service for her parents, and she feigned being so distraught, she hadn't even attended Cristin's service. Poor Cristin. The town turned out for her funeral. Everyone loved Cristin.

And poor Hunter. She was a victim as well, a grieving young girl who could not bear to stay in a town reminding her of such personal tragedy, seeing it in the places and faces of its inhabitants. So she left. Who could blame her? What they didn't know was that she'd stolen the letter and locket from Trina to serve as an entrée to some random woman's life in Minnesota and resurfaced as a girl named Cristin Shanihan, a nobody from nowhere. Hunter Cross disappeared like a whisper in the wind.

But now she was Madison Thomas. As she walked through the concourse of moving walkways and beeping carts in the Toronto airport, the people were a blur, all intent on getting to their gate or baggage claim carousel, and ultimately their final destination, only to possibly repack and go somewhere else. *Madness.*

She continued to obsess about the place in her dream. She couldn't shake it. Where was that Celtic land of harps and shamrocks, blarney stones and magic? Was it an island? Yes, an island. To jar her memory, she bought a map of Canada from the airport bookstore and found a restaurant inside the terminal where she could sit and study it. It wasn't Newfoundland. Not Prince Edward Island ... she would've remembered that name. Nova Scotia ... that had a Gaelic ring but it wasn't an island. She stared at the map until it popped off the page. On the south coast of

Nova Scotia was an island called Cape Breton. That was it. That was where she would go, a place where she could hide for a while, lose herself far from the maddening crowd, to regroup, to make plans. She wasn't ready for anyone, including Nico, to find her. Maybe this magic land would be her haven instead of Vancouver. There had to be a reason she felt so driven to see it. She finished her martini and oysters Rockefeller, bought a cell phone, and purchased a one-way ticket to Halifax, Nova Scotia.

The flight was short, a little over two hours, and she was grateful she wasn't traveling to the other end of the continent that day. Greeting her in Halifax were ubiquitous posters of a lighthouse at a place called Peggy's Cove, with charming docks blanketed with lobster traps, fishermen mending nets, and colorful homes perched on craggy, fissured rocks. She was not in Italy anymore.

She thought about taking a train to Sydney, the far eastern city of Cape Breton, but decided to rent a car using her new Canadian driver's license for the first time. That way she had control and anonymity without being at the mercy of tedious fellow travelers. The coastline drive was magnificent. It took her only three hours to reach the island of Cape Breton. Scottish heritage had so accented her drive with names like MacDougal's Pub and MacInerny's Bonnie Seaside Inn, she might as well have been in Scotland. When she reached the island, she changed her mind again, cut through the middle on winding roads, over and past a string of lakes, and took the far eastern coast to Ingonish Beach where she found a cabin where she could crash for a few days. As Ren had once said, *It wasn't the end of the world but you could see it from there.* Never had she been more isolated. No one in the world, particularly the Monson women, knew where she was and it felt exhilarating.

The following morning, Nico picked up her call to Italy.

"Where have you been? I waited all day to hear from you," he scolded. "What area code are you calling from? I thought Vancouver was 604?"

"I bought the phone in the Toronto airport. I had a long layover."

His voice softened. "When can I see you?"

"Oh, Nico. I think we should wait a month or so. Nothing unusual for a while," she responded. "Have you ever been to Vancouver?"

"No, never."

"It would be a bit suspicious if you left now when you've not had business here before. Let me get settled first." She heard his reluctance, inferred from the long pause. But Nico agreed. He was so easy to manipulate. She needed time to figure out the timing of the inheritance transfer. Until she had a pulse on the money, he didn't need to know where she was or what she was doing. She was safer in Cape Breton, at least for a while.

They discussed Luca's placement with the D'Alessios, the estate, and ultimately the logistics of transferring her half of the inheritance funds to a Sofia Gherardini account in the Caymans while she was still missing. He shared the fact that her disappearance had been investigated, and she had been officially designated as missing. He was keeping up the front of an ongoing investigation but no one was pressing him. After all, he said, she had no close friends or family to insist that a search for her be ongoing. She thought how true it was. Tess and Lindsey had passed themselves off as family, but they weren't. She had no one, except a three-year-old. Who knew if she'd ever see him again?

"I miss you so much, Nico," she cried in a pathetic, amorous tone.

"Being apart is not what we'd planned, Sofia. I'm quite miserable. I will come to Vancouver, I promise. Very soon."

"Nico, I know it's hard, but you need to call me Madison, Maddie … no slip-ups, right?"

"No slip-ups, darling … Madison."

That night, Madison Thomas walked through the town, listening to the Gaelic accents of the highly Scottish-populated area. Even in a place she'd never been, at the end of the world, she stood out in a crowd. She wasn't one of them. She didn't belong to anyone, anywhere. She was alone.

She walked into a Scottish pub, took a seat at the back on a high stool, and ordered a scotch which seemed appropriate. A short stocky man with a full beard and out-of-control eyebrows took out a small accordion, and another skinnier man with a green plaid beret, fished out his harmonica, and before she knew it, the people who all appeared to know each other, began to sing...together. One sea shanty after another, they clinked their glasses of rye whiskey and mugs of ale, and sang their songs. These people had their own songs, and they knew all of the words. It was the quaintest, most charming experience she'd ever had. But she wasn't one of them. She was definitely alone.

She left the bar to take a walk under the stars overlooking Ingonish Beach. Being with those happy people had gotten under her skin, a skin she needed to slough in order to fashion her new self, which was a superior alternative to being lost among them. She looked into the sky and saw Scorpio staring at her and recalled his following her on the nights she'd driven to see Nico on the lake in Italy. Scorpio, her sign and reminder of the insect with the lethal sting. He just wouldn't go away. She tabled the thought and turned her attention to the lapping water. In the distance sat the Keltic Lodge, a white, red-roofed resort that looked like it was an island unto itself. Everywhere she looked, she saw snapshots of images, all meaning nothing to her, and whispering, *You're alone. Completely alone.*

She shook off her melancholy and began to think. Thinking, not feeling, was her strong suit anyway. She was smarter than the rest of them, and she was always in control. The Monson women; what was she going to do about them? Obviously Tess and little Lindsey, who was now about eighteen or nineteen, had gone to great lengths to find Klara. *How the hell did they know about Klara? And what did they know?*

What did they suspect? What if she hadn't spoken to Clement at Rudolpho's funeral? She would have been a sitting duck. The more she thought about it, the angrier she became. They had ruined her life in Italy, and who knew how far they would go to find her, to ruin her life anywhere. Katie and Tia were probably the other two involved ... the three sisters and the niece. She'd need to outsmart them though. Fortunately, Nico was the only link to her whereabouts, and Nico had too much to lose by speaking to the Americans or turning her over to the authorities. Besides, he loved her. She'd think about him later.

The next morning, she drove the Cabot Trail, one of the most picturesque drives in the world, to clear her head and quell her anxiety. She passed a sign directing her to Warren Lake and she thought of Ren again. What would life have been like had she stayed in Minnetonka, Minnesota? Certainly less complicated, but her road-less-taken choice had been so much fun. She drove the plunging cliff-line on the north side, wondering what it would feel like to sail off the edge, like in the movie *Thelma and Louise,* to a cold, dark, bottomless ocean below. She passed fishing villages, distilleries, forested valleys, sandy beaches, pubs, resorts, breathtakingly beautiful mountain vistas, and Celtic cemeteries, all in one day. Alone. And when she returned to Ingonish, she realized she would head for Halifax the following morning because she'd sensed an unnerving energy vortex in this Celtic cradle which frankly terrified her. It was magic all right, but not her kind of magic.

The Halifax waterfront, smelling of fish and salty air, bustled with bohemian activity by mid-afternoon. Century-old wharves and warehouses had been converted to shops, businesses, restaurants, pubs, and maritime museums. The downtown area wore a blend of soaring monoliths of glass and chrome, mixed with buildings of historic beauty and interest. Victorian homes lined arbored streets, and it wasn't odd at all to randomly see men in kilts from one hour to the next.

Although it was fascinating to experience Nova Scotia, Madison Thomas, now a Canadian, needed to figure out her next move. Of necessity, she had become a weary wanderer, with no rudder, no direction, no goal. She was hiding instead of masterminding, and she felt lost for the first time in her adult life. On the waterfront, she spied an outdoor café with a fleur-de-lis symbol on its banner, so she walked through its wood gate and sat down to sketch a map of her new life.

A waiter named Jean-Pierre greeted her.

"I thought this whole island was Scottish," she remarked, as she elegantly unwrapped her navy blue scarf, revealing her ample, deep cleavage.

"No, there's a French Acadian populace here too. You should go to Chéticamp ... our fishing village up north, very French," he responded in a modified French Canadian accent.

"I just drove by it the other day ... on the Cabot Trail?"

"That's it. You'll have to go back someday," he suggested.

"Oh, I don't think so. I don't know where I'm going, but not back, that's for sure."

She ordered a lobster cocktail and a glass of ale, and stared, without blinking, irritated by the crowds of people who impeded her view of the harbor.

"Excuse me?" A deep voice from the next table interrupted her privacy.

A handsome man with thick dark hair and kind brown eyes had spoken.

"I'm sorry. Do I know you?" she asked, knowing full well that she didn't.

"No, you don't. I just overheard you say that you didn't know where you were going. You sounded sad," he said in a caring tone of voice.

"No, not sad, just bored. I don't know anyone here."

"You're a very beautiful woman. May I ask what are you doing by yourself on a rare sunny day in Halifax?"

"You're kind. I'm just passing through."

"On your way to ...?" he asked.

"Vancouver." It just popped out.

"That's where I'm from. Do you live there?" he asked.

"No, but I probably will. I'm not sure yet."

"Well, you won't be lonely in Vancouver. It's a beautiful city with good people."

"Why are you in Nova Scotia?" she asked.

"I'm here with a friend who's a hockey scout. There's a lot of prime hockey talent in this province ... the home of Sydney Crosby and Brad Marchand, you know."

"No. I don't know, but if you say so," she replied dismissively.

"You're a Canadian and you don't follow hockey? It's the greatest sport in the world. Talent, speed, finesse, and toughness. Have you ever heard the phrase, 'I went to a fight and a hockey game broke out'?"

She looked puzzled and disapproving.

"You need a man in your life to show you the fine points of hockey," he continued, after taking a long swallow of golden ale.

"And I suppose you're just that man." She looked at him with the acquired disdain of a woman who knew she was the object of a pick-up and wished to distance herself.

"On the contrary. I'm a happily married man. Just throwing out some friendly advice."

He appeared annoyed, and as he stood to leave, she grabbed his arm to apologize.

"I'm sorry. I've become cynical about meeting men in public places."

"You prefer private places?" he responded. "Sorry, I couldn't help myself. You fed me the straight line and it was irresistible. No harm done." He nodded.

She laughed and extended her hand to the handsome, affable man. "Hello. My name is Madison Thomas. Maddie." It was the first time she'd introduced herself by her new name.

"I'm pleased to meet you, Madison Thomas." He shook her hand and said, "Joe Mahr. Have a good life." And he was gone.

CHAPTER NINETEEN

Judge a man by his questions, rather than by his answers.
—Voltaire

When Tia's plane touched down at Dulles, she landed with satisfaction that her trip had been successful and with hope that Vinnie Vingiano would discover the missing link that would lead to the arrest and justice. She knew it would take more than just finding Sofia. There needed to be proof of wrongdoing. If they could find her and charge her with stolen identities, they would at least have the chance to prove the murders of Cristin Shanihan, Yvette Vandal, Shep Shepard and the pilot, and most recently, Rudolpho Gherardini.

Tia stood in line, going through customs for what seemed like an interminable period of time, only to have a foreign-looking bald man with enormous ears compare her face with the passport picture and mechanically stamp her reentry to the U.S. At the baggage claim area, she stood with other tired, impatient passengers, before identifying her luggage, and grabbing it from the carousel. The last leg of her arduous journey lay before her ... the Metro ride, which fortunately passed quickly and delivered her less than two blocks from her final destination.

When she entered her home, the stuffiness detained her at the door like an unwelcoming butler. She barged in, dropped her luggage, and opened every window as fast as she could. After lighting a few candles, she turned on a Michael Bublé CD and found one local craft beer in her refrigerator. She hadn't had a cold beer for over two weeks and felt like one of Pavlov's dogs, salivating, as she popped the bottle cap. Oh, the taste of a cold, cold beer.

She fell onto the sofa, kicked her shoes off, and exercised her aching feet on the rim of the ottoman as she reflected on her trip. It was still only 10 p.m. She could call Tess, Trina, and then Katie, in the morning. It would probably be a few days until she heard from her Italian connection, but that was all right. She needed time to reenter her own world, go back to work, and pick up where she'd left off. In a way, it all felt like a dream, especially her few nights with Dominic Vingiano.

Five hours later she woke up to sirens on DuPont Circle. She hadn't made any calls, her luggage was still unpacked, and the candles were extinguished. The air in the townhome was cold, and her half bottle of beer, warm. She stumbled to her room and crashed onto her bed, four paws down, and remembered that she had one full day to revive before heading back to work.

At 8:10 a.m., her cell phone rang. It was Katie.

"You're home!" she yelled. "Tell me everything."

"I need to assimilate into the land of the living before I can tell you everything, but like I said in my text, her name is now Sofia. Or at least it was. No one seems to know where she is. But we figure she'll come back sooner or later because she has a three-year-old son."

"She's a mother? That's frightening. But what if she had an accident or someone abducted her?"

"You're watching too much CSI, big sister. Things like that don't happen to her … she instigates tragedies, rather than falls victim to them, remember? She'll be back. Besides, she doesn't know that we're on to her."

"So what can we do?" asked Katie.

"Just wait. But I do have a PI who will be looking for her in the meantime. And an inside friend, a girl who was fired from the residence and has a vendetta against Sofia. While her former mistress is gone, she's going to ask around to see if anyone has any dirt on her.

Apparently, my contact still has friends in the house so visits anytime she wants."

"Well, that's at least something. What else happened?"

Tia paused. "I met someone special." She knew Katie could hear the smile in her voice.

"A guy?"

"His name is Dominic Vingiano. He's a bartender, underemployed, I might add. He's wonderful, Katie. But so geographically undesirable. I'm afraid it was just a fling. But time will tell."

"Tia, that's terrific. You've been working so hard, and I don't remember the last time you sounded excited about a guy. And speaking of that, I have some news as well. Ingrid and Adam have set a date."

"The fiancé from Connecticut, right?"

"Yes. A November wedding. Can you come?"

"Oh, my God. I wouldn't miss it for the world. Ingrid is really getting married! You made my day."

"I knew you would be thrilled for her. Listen, honey, do you want me to call the others while you get some sleep? You have to be exhausted."

"Thank you. I need to catch up before going to work tomorrow. That would be great. Give my love to the girls. *Ciao*."

Two weeks passed with no word from Pia or Vinnie. Tia sent another email to both of them, asking for a progress report. *Surely had Sofia returned, they would have emailed her.* One night while she was mulling over possible scenarios, she thought back to what she'd said to Katie ... *She'll be back. She doesn't know that we're on to her. How could she?*

In an instant, other questions surfaced. *What if she had known they were tracking her? But how? What or who could have tipped her off? Then it hit her. What was the name of the woman Tess and Lindsey had contacted who knew her and gave them the lead of her whereabouts? Clarissa? Claire? What if, for some random reason, Sofia had called the woman, and this Clarissa/Claire person mentioned that Tess had been looking for her? That would certainly explain her sudden disappearance. And if this had happened, Sofia would be forced to lose herself again and would never go back to Bellaterra.*

But what about the child? Was she such a monster that she could leave a child? She certainly couldn't take her boy with her if she were on the lam. Not if she changed her name. Not if she left the country which she typically did. The potential situation read like a novel. Yes, that was it. Tia felt like a character in a complex novel; or like a chess piece, trying to figure out how to capture the evil queen.

Before her imagination went feral, she needed to determine if Sofia had called the Swiss woman. It was still early enough in Minnesota to place a call to Tess, so she did.

Tess answered the phone. "Tia, you're not sleeping? It's almost midnight there."

"I know. Sorry. It's late where you are too, but I know you're a night owl. I hope the ring didn't disturb Ren."

"No, he's on a business trip so I'm here by my lonesome. What's up?"

"Have you been in recent touch with that Swiss woman who gave you the breakthrough lead on Sofia?"

"Klara Zutter?"

"That's it. Klara. I knew it was something like that."

"No, I haven't. I don't have a phone number because the banker insisted upon making the appointment but I do have her email address. I'm sitting here by the computer. Do we need to ask her something specifically?"

Tia explained her theory and as they were speaking, Tess input a message asking Klara whether Sofia was aware that they had been looking for her, and pressed SEND.

"Done. Now we'll just wait for a response. I hope you're wrong about this, Tia, because if she disappears again, we may never find her."

"Never say never, big sister. We're going to find her. Call me when you hear back from Klara, okay? And isn't it wonderful to hear Ingrid's news?"

"Yes! So if not before, I'll see you at the wedding. Katie told me about your handsome bartender. Why don't you ask him to fly over for the big event so we can give him our stamp of approval?"

"Yeah, right," Tia responded.

After the call, Tia forgot about Klara Zutter and thought about Dominic, wondering if he would come, if asked. She'd see how the summer went.

****

The morning was drab with a low-lying ceiling of clouds that if labeled a feeling, would be called oppressive. Lucerne, Switzerland, was in dire need of sunshine, but its inhabitants, smothered by dull grayness, weren't holding their communal breath.

Fiona Germond looked out her window at the wet, gloomy air, deciphering ribbons of white smoke from local chimneys that subtly broke the monotony of the skyscape. The previous night, she had been to a local college where she'd viewed a collection of exquisite portraits painted by a young Swiss student who she believed needed a sponsor, or at least, a showing. She dialed her friend Klara's number in the hope of enlisting her support. Klara rarely turned her down, especially since her husband's death. She owned a reputation for responding charitably to a project concerning the arts. She loved social philanthropy, and festivity, and she certainly could afford the patronage.

After discussing the prospect of helping young Hermann Wichsteig, Fiona mentioned that Clement had seen Sofia at Rudolpho Gherardini's funeral.

"Your friend died? Wasn't he in his fifties?" Klara questioned, sounding shocked.

"Yes. It was tragic, to say the least. He'd been ill for a couple of years. Failing health is the diagnosis that was shared with Clement, which was a bit vague for this day and age. I was sure you knew about it because on the night of his funeral, I heard from Sofia, and she asked for your number. Clement had mentioned that her family was looking for her so that probably prompted the call. But... "

"She didn't mention her husband had died. Are you sure about the timing?" Klara questioned.

"I'm certain of it. Well, perhaps she just wanted to hear that her family still loved her. Apparently, there had been a serious misunderstanding. But frankly, I thought she may have been in touch with you recently, that you may have become friendly through the years, and that's why she needed to talk to you that night."

"No, she only inquired about her family. I haven't heard from her since. Why do you ask?"

"Well, something just doesn't add up. Clement called the residence to speak to her, extending his prior invitation to visit us. She had initially declined because she said that she couldn't imagine leaving Bellaterra, the name of the estate, because she felt closer to Rudolpho when she was there. She mentioned that there was so much legal work, that she couldn't imagine leaving for quite some time. She was apparently quite fervent about it."

"That's understandable," Klara replied.

"I agree. But when Clement called last night, he was told that she left town the day following the funeral service, and no one has heard from her since. That was over a month ago."

"She's missing?"

"Apparently so."

"I hope she hasn't come into harm's way. Their family doesn't need to mourn another death ... and doesn't she have a little boy?"

"Klara, I stayed awake last night thinking about the ramifications. What if she didn't want to be found? What if after hearing the news that these women were looking for her, she needed to lose herself, from fear of being discovered? The timing is just too eerie, too coincidental."

"Oh, my." Klara spoke through a sigh.

"If it is so, I wonder what she's running from. What did she do? ... or maybe, she didn't do anything. Maybe she's the one in danger. Maybe the Americans were 'the bad guys.'"

Klara's voice audibly trembled. "I don't want to be any part of this, Fiona. The first thing I'm doing after hanging up is changing my email address. That's the only connection I have with the Americans, except they know where I live. I don't want to be involved in a scandal. I thought I was being helpful."

"I didn't mean to upset you, Klara. I'm just trying to shed some light on what appears to be a mystery. I'm probably reading too much into the situation. But in the meantime, if you hear from anyone concerning Sofia, please let me know, and I'll do the same for you. And my friend, thank you for your help with Hermann. He'll be so grateful."

****

After hanging up her phone, Klara sat down at her computer, accessed her email account, and discovered Tess's inquiry. She promptly deleted it, then deleted her account. After creating a new account, she contacted only those people with whom she wanted communication. Tess was not on the list.

****

April dawned before Tia heard from Pia, and her email message was as welcome as flowers that bloom in the spring.

Dear Tia,
Sorry I haven't emailed you before this but Vinnie had to finish up his other case so there was nothing to tell. But I still have friends at the house. Servants talk more than you'd imagine (with the exception of Lucia the head housekeeper and the butler Mateo. They're loyal to the Gherardini name, tight-lipped and devoted to a fault, if you ask me). But anyway, Flaviano the driver is

my friend, and so is his girlfriend who's down at the stables. Flaviano was so good to me on the day I was fired ("let go," as Dom insists on saying). I asked him what train he was supposed to meet to pick her up, the day she was due to return. It was from Napoli. I told Vinnie and he suggested I find out who the Gherardinis could have trusted in Napoli. The name that was mentioned was his cousin Mia who lives in Capri, which isn't far from Napoli so Vinnie left this morning to scope it out. But he has to be careful because if she suspects he's a PI, she'll tell Nico and all bets are off.

And another thing. Auriane the nanny? She's been released from service too. Nico took off with Luca last week without Auriane. Nico said he'll be back in a few days but the kid would stay for the summer with friends. That's never happened before (Vinnie says we must be aware of anything unusual so that's why I'm bringing it up.). Auriane always accompanied Luca. She was more of a mother than the signora ever was. Something's not right there.

Oh, and one more thing. After the witch left, I did a deep cleaning of her bedroom. Almost all of her clothes and belongings were left behind, but nothing personal. No journals, notebooks, pictures ... only clothes and furnishings. Except I found a telephone number under her phone. I looked up the prefix. It belongs to someone in Switzerland. That's all for now, Let me know you received this, Tia. And I have to tell you, I like this spy stuff. Maybe if you ever lose your job, we could team up as Pia and Tia, International Private Investigators.

Ciao.

Tia shouted aloud, WE'RE GOING TO FIND HER! WE'RE GOING TO FIND HER!" She immediately responded to Pia.

I can't even put into words how happy I am to have heard from you, Pia. Please get back to me even if you have nothing to tell, just so I know you're still a player. Great job. And Vinnie going to Napoli? My fingers are crossed he'll find something, a clue, a lead, something. I agree that Luca going away without Auriane is unusual, but even more disturbing is that maybe he's not coming back, or why else would they have dismissed your friend?

And Pia, when Vinnie returns, please have him identify that telephone number. If it's who I think it is, we've discovered the reason she left so abruptly, and we can be sure she's not returning to Bellaterra.

Ciao.

CHAPTER TWENTY

Pay no attention to the man behind the curtain.
—L. Frank Baum

Vinnie Vingiano hadn't been in Napoli since his sister had married a Neapolitan eight years ago. One thing he remembered was that the drivers were maniacs, as one evening, when walking on a sidewalk by the port, a motorcyclist, going at least twenty-five kph, passed him on his right. Sheer insanity.

After he arrived, he revisited memorable landmarks, if only to reinforce his recollections of the city's pulse. The Spaccanapoli Quarter was less exciting, more plebeian, than he remembered. But busy and noisy, just as he remembered. The tenement buildings, revealing layers of sienna and ochre stucco and stone, crowded the neighborhood where laundry hung to dry from upper windows, absorbing the street smells of pizza from brick ovens and fish from the harbor. The narrow streets hosted the occasional opera singer, spontaneously exploding with a familiar Verdi or Rossini aria, in hopes that an appreciative passer-by would see fit to drop euros into the tip bucket on the pavement. Vinnie walked by the San Carlo Opera House and the Grand Hotel Vesuvio, knowing full well he hadn't the time to sightsee, but feeling ungrateful not to at least tacitly pay his respects to the home and haunts of the great Enrico Caruso.

Holding court over the city, the peak of Mount Vesuvius peeked through a bank of low-lying evening clouds. Vinnie would go to Capri in the morning, but tonight, he would eat at Bergalio's, a seaside outdoor restaurant near the Castle Nuovo. The name Castle Nuovo amused him, as he knew that it was over eight hundred years old. New was a relative word in Italy.

At Bergalio's, he ordered spaghetti *vongole,* with an antipasto salad, cheese, warm bread, and Italian red wine, and he wished Pia were there. Across from him sat a young boy with enormous blue eyes, either foreign or northern Italian, he surmised. The child stared at him without smiling, and even when Vinnie looked down, then reconnected with the boy, he was still staring. He must have been curious or mesmerized; if he'd been older, Vinnie would have labeled him rude but made an allowance for the boy's age and inexperience.

He reminisced about being that young and his first adventure with his sea captain grandfather who had taken him through the Straits of Messina beneath the heel of Italy's boot, showing him the land and the map and the land again, until Vinnie made the connection. He knew at a very young age that he would be a captain and an explorer. It was a stretch, but here he was in his thirties, a former police captain and a private investigator, exploring people's lives.

After dinner he walked into a shop where a man sold cameos he carved from shells. The proprietor claimed to have been commissioned to carve a cameo of Dwight D. Eisenhower and presented it to him in 1958. Sure enough, there was a photograph on the wall of him gifting his masterpiece to the American president, the commander-in-chief of the WWII Allied Forces. *Impressive.* Feeling generous, he bought Pia a cameo of a seahorse, remembering his grandfather telling him that the seahorse was a symbol of good luck for sailors.

The following morning, he took a taxi down the coast to Sorrento, then boarded a ferry to Capri. It was a gorgeous spring day, the red poppies ruptured on the hillside, and the blue sky was appliquéd with enormous cumulous clouds. He'd decided to go to D'Alessio' s Restaurante for dinner so his afternoon was free to take the funicular to Capri Town, then a bus ride to Anacapri. Within minutes, he discovered that he'd put his life in the hands of the bus driver, who through no fault of his own, had to navigate harrowingly steep, narrow streets and hairpin curves, at speeds necessary to adhere to his bus schedule. To think that this mode of transportation was Vinnie's only option for returning to Capri Town was disturbing, so he pigeonholed the thought into a *Do Not Consider for the Next Few Hours* file of his brain. He'd find another way back.

Anacapri was a slice of heaven. He'd been advised by the waitress at Bergalio's to take the cable lift to the top of the island to see the site of the famous faraglione, Capri's three signature rocks. The ride was quaint but stunning, traveling only meters above cemeteries, homes, gardens, lemon groves, shrines, and small private vineyards. In the distance, as far as one could see was the dalliance of aquamarine waters. When he arrived at the top, he saw the crown jewel of the island. The towering rocks, hundreds of meters high, jutted out of the brilliant waters of the Tyrrhenian Sea and offered the most divine vista Vinnie had ever seen. He decided that this would be his honeymoon destination if ever he were to marry.

By late afternoon, he found a taxi to return to the town of Capri, and although the road was the same, the driver was less hurried and unlike his ride up the island, Vinnie believed he would survive the journey. D'Alessio's was easy to find, and he asked to be seated by a window but with his chair positioned so he could watch the door and the activity. He determined in the first half hour who the owner was and decided to become friendly with the waitresses, perhaps on his subsequent visit. He'd have to be patient. No doubt about it, the food was delicious, rivaling his mother's cooking which was a supreme compliment. And there was no doubt that he would put on a few pounds eating there every day … collateral damage of a few hard days' work.

It was a tricky business. If he worked for the police department, he could investigate a missing person, but he was a PI. In order not to arouse suspicion, he'd have to remain anonymous, be sneakier, invisible, and get the same results. At all costs, his identity had to be kept from Nico Gherardini. Otherwise Vinnie would never be admitted to Bellaterra, which was a critical move in strategy. If he didn't find

Sofia, but found incriminating evidence of foul play at the estate, the police could then make her a target of their investigation, find her, and make the arrest.

The consensus was that Nico was probably protecting her whereabouts. But why? She was just his late father's wife. However, he was the only one who may have known where she went the day after the funeral, and now he'd taken her child somewhere for the summer. He'd fired household staff merely because she was missing? The more Vinnie thought about it, the more he realized he needed to gain entry to Bellaterra. He'd be introduced innocently as Pia's boyfriend and go to work. There was enough circumstantial evidence from Sofia's past, according to the American, that this could be a big case. His most pressing concern in Capri was to find out if Sofia had stayed with the D'Alessios and discover what they knew. In the meantime, he needed to be clever and opportunistic. It was a tough but intriguing case.

Later that night, he went to sleep thinking about his tactics, enumerating the possibilities, and strategizing how he'd proceed. As he slipped into sleep, he thought about the beauty of Anacapri, how it was always there. He could visit it in real time or also in his memory. He thought of his senile grandmother who had lost her memory. His sympathy altered to empathy in a split second, thinking how desperately sad it was that she couldn't call to mind visions of beauty she had seen, once upon a time. Then sleep stole his memory … but only until dawn.

Two days passed before Mia D'Alessio visited her husband's restaurant. She arrived at 4 p.m., and made her rounds greeting the employees and guests who patronized their establishment.

"Hello, Alicia, Tony, Cristina," she said as she approached the first table near the door. "Isn't it a beautiful day?"

"Mia, you look radiant."

"I've never been happier, Alicia. Oh, just a minute, I need to talk to the bartender about an order. To be continued, my friend."

In a wisp of a moment, Mia vanished to the back of the restaurant.

So maybe that was Mia D'Alessio, Vinnie thought to himself. *Yet to be confirmed.* She seemed approachable. He'd have to perceive his opening without appearing nosy. Finesse was a fickle skill to sustain, but on his menu of talents, it was the order of the day. He played the part of a tourist visiting his sister for the month or so, and having discovered D'Alessio's, would be eating there regularly. His waitresses Gianna and Bella were attentive to the point of being transparent, quietly arguing about who would serve him, which was flattering but also amusing, as neither of them was remotely attractive to him.

Bella won the draw and approached his table.

"And what can I bring you today, sir?" Her voice coquettishly played with each word as if auditioning for a part.

"I'll just have your *bruschetta* and a glass of Chianti to start. Thank you, Bella."

"Oh, you know my name," she replied with swelling satisfaction.

"Yes, you introduced yourself the other day. Is Bella shortened from another name?"

"Isabella." She blushed flirtatiously.

"I'm Vinnie. It's nice to meet you. Is that the owner's wife who just walked in, Bella?"

"Why, yes," she responded. "She's very nice. I'll get you your wine … Vinnie."

Bella turned away, making eye contact with Gianna, and subtly tossing her head as if she'd just scored.

Confirmation on the identity of Nico's cousin was accomplished.

Minutes later Mia returned to her friend's table. "So yes, I'm very happy. Marco and I have a houseguest for the summer. He'll be here shortly and I want you to meet him." As if on cue, the front door opened and a voluptuous, young Italian woman dressed plainly and with no makeup, entered the restaurant, holding the hand of a toddler.

"Here he is. Come, Luca, meet my friends, Alicia, Tony and Cristina."

The boy turned away and hid his head in what appeared to be his mother's skirt.

"He's shy. He's only been here a week, and he's only three." Mia turned to the woman and said, "Thank you for bringing him, Francesca. I'll see you tomorrow morning." So the woman was not the mother, thought Vinnie, as he witnessed Francesca hand over the child without kissing him or saying goodbye. Then it hit him. This was Sofia's child, the three-year-old Luca Gherardini. But where was Sofia? The questions mounted.

The following afternoon, Vinnie took a taxi to a location a block away from the D'Alessio home and waited on the grass beneath a large olive tree as he pretended to read, waxing inconspicuous. Some of the silvery leaves from the branches above, released their grip and drifted to the ground on a waft of breeze like dandelion spores, fragile and weightless. He rarely took time to notice the intricacies of nature in motion but at times like these, he was forced to slow down and admire her nuances.

At precisely 5 p.m., Francesca emerged from the home and started her walk toward town. Vinnie crossed to the opposite side of the street and then crossed to the corner where she had stopped. They walked together through the crosswalk before he addressed her.

"It's a beautiful day, isn't it?" he began, sounding nonchalant.

"Yes, it is. My job keeps me indoors during the day. It feels good to be out in the fresh air." Her voice was low but energetic.

"What do you do?" he gingerly inquired.

"Oh, I'm a housekeeper, turned au pair, it seems. What do you do?"

"I'm an architect from Firenze. I'm visiting my sister for a while. I love to walk. There are some beautiful homes in this area. Walking the neighborhoods gives me ideas for designs and how to integrate architecture with natural landscapes."

"That sounds so interesting. I've never met an architect up close." She smiled.

"I've never met an au pair up close. I'm Vinnie, by the way."

"I'm Francesca."

"I'm pleased to meet you. I don't really know anyone here. I'm taking a taxi to the center of town tonight for dinner. I found a charming restaurant ... D'Alessio's ... do you know it? "

She stopped in her tracks and looked directly at him. Her gorgeous, almond-shaped, green-amber eyes stared at him with the wonder of their correlated discovery.

"I work for the D'Alessios."

At that moment, Vinnie was face-to-face, not with Francesca, but with the aspect of his job he detested, deception.

"Really?" He paused. "That's bizarre."

"Vinnie, I'm going to a *taverna* that's only two blocks away. They serve food there. Would you like to join me?"

Vinnie tried to appear hesitant.

"I guess I could. I'll just have to call D'Alessio's to cancel my reservation ... unless you'd like to join me there."

"Thank you, but no. I practically live with the D'Alessios. I need time away from their family and their drama. Besides which, I'd like to hear more about what you do. I love houses."

"Well then, I'll join you, but just for a while. I'll need to get back to my sister's home."

Vinnie could tell that his reticence and timetable relaxed Francesca and that's what he needed, a relaxed housekeeper to give him the scoop.

After an hour of small talk and more lies and innuendoes about Vinnie's architectural background, he inquired about Francesca's au pair comment.

"It wasn't in my job description so I don't know why I'm doing it. But this little boy, Luca, was brought to us by a relative, some rich guy from Umbria. Luca's mom is missing and this Nico guy doesn't want him around so he dumped him on Mia and Marco. They're such nice people. They don't have any children of their own so they're excited to take care of him. Especially Mia. But I pull double duty because she still expects me to clean and cook, and take care of him ... sometimes. Does that sound selfish?"

"No, not at all. I think you're kind to take on the added responsibilities."

"Well, I do love children and he's pretty easy although he has his moments. Maybe he misses his nanny ... or his mommy, although I don't know why. But I guess all children love their mothers." Francesca sipped her drink and quickly looked up at Vinnie with her seductive, almond-shaped, green-amber eyes. "I'm sorry. I shouldn't have said that."

Vinnie saw his opening. "No problem, I don't know her, so your comment means nothing to me. Have you met her? His mother?"

"Yes, she stayed with them a while ago. Sofia was, how shall I say it? Difficult to like and I'm being charitable."

"Where did she go?"

"That's just it. Nobody knows. She was supposed to go back to her little boy but she never showed up. I'm actually not surprised. I feel sorry for the boy though. He's so young to be without a mother."

"That's sad," Vinnie sympathized, feeling closer and closer to pay dirt. "But she disappeared? That's strange and a bit intriguing. There must have been some clues as to where she went. Something she said? Somewhere she talked about?"

"I don't think so. I guess the family, presumably this Nico guy, filed a missing person report so they sent out a couple of officers to the house, but I was in the next room when they questioned Mia and Marco, and they were as shocked as anyone that she didn't go back for her child. They did mention however, that she'd asked them to be guardians if anything ever happened to her, so Sofia may have been scared of something or running from someone and maybe had to lose herself for a while."

"What do you think?" Vinnie asked.

"I don't think she was scared, if that's what you're asking."

"That's quite the story. I wish it had a better ending, especially for you."

"That's so nice of you to say. You're a really good guy, Vinnie. How long are you staying in Capri?"

"Not much longer. It's probably time for me to head back. I've taken up enough of your evening."

"Not at all. I've met my first architect tonight."

Vinnie stared at the beautiful Francesca and realized if he stayed any longer, he might forget Pia, and such a lapse would have an unfortunate ending, if only in his heart. He'd already taken advantage of Francesca. To betray Pia would label him a scumbag. He stood to leave when Francesca grabbed his arm.

"Now that I think of it, there was one thing I didn't tell the police or the D'Alessios because no one ever questioned me, and I didn't think it mattered."

Francesca's eyes blinked rapidly as she thought out loud.

"What?" His eyes widened with expectant interest.

"The morning after she left, I emptied the trash and there was an empty envelope at the bottom of the waste basket."

"And?"

"The return address was Air Canada. Do you think she went to Canada?"

Vinnie looked into her gorgeous, almond-shaped, green-amber eyes and heard himself say, "I guess we'll never know. Thank you for the pleasure of your company, Francesca." He leaned over, kissed her on the forehead, and thought, *there is karma after all.*

CHAPTER TWENTY-ONE

There is a crack in everything.
That's how the light gets in.
—Leonard Cohen

Before Vinnie returned to Castiglione, he checked the flight schedules from Napoli to Canada, finding Air Canada flights to Montréal, Toronto, and Vancouver, three major metropolitan cities, thousands of miles apart. She could be in any of those cities or anywhere in between. She could have flown to Canada, then taken another carrier to anywhere in the world. But chances were if the envelope Francesca found was marked Air Canada, Canada was her first destination. It was nothing solid to follow, but he was satisfied that Sofia Gherardini was no longer in Italy, and wasn't returning for a long while. As he saw it, his mission was less to track her than to find evidence, clues left behind at Bellaterra that could implicate her of a crime. The most obvious, of course, was the death of her husband. Vinnie knew he might have to leave the locating of the malevolent signora to an investigation team with longer arms, wider reach, and deeper pockets.

Pia was waiting at his apartment when he returned. She looked fabulous, standing with her hands on her hips, sporting a new dress, heels, and makeup, and posturing like a fashion model from Roma.

"Oh baby, baby, baby. I'm so glad to see you!" She seductively changed her pose, tilting her hips in the opposite direction.

"You look beautiful," said Vinnie as he dropped his duffle bag.

"Come here and give your girlfriend a kiss." She accentuated each word with deliberation and pouted with an alluring invitation.

After a long, lingering welcome-home kiss, he pulled away. "Pia, we need to go to the house. It's time to do some digging. Can we go tomorrow?"

"Wow. Thanks for the romance."

"Sorry. You really look gorgeous. Gorgeous. But I am a little pre-occupied. She was in Napoli with Nico's cousin but I don't think she's in Italy anymore, Pia, so I need to hunt for details, any clues that might congeal into evidence against her. I feel like a dog on a bone. Who can we trust over there?"

"Well, Flaviano and Jonas, for sure. Not Lucia, but Cyrano the gardener is cool. And Elena from the stables. Auriane is gone but we could talk to her in town. We just have to make sure Nico isn't around."

"What time can we go?"

Pia laughed. "All right, Romeo, how about 10 a.m.? If that's settled, will you take me out to dinner and not bring up the Gherardinis for the rest of the night?"

"It's a deal."

He didn't discuss the case during their evening together, but his mind obsessed over the details, the possibilities, as well as a few thoughts about his encounter with the beautiful Francesca from Capri.

They were up at dawn and drove to Bellaterra under the auspices of needing to talk to her friend Elena. The day was radiantly gold and blue, a perfect Umbrian morning. The rolling fabric of the fields accented with buttons of baled hay was a reverie in any photographer's eye. The sunflowers strained to show their faces to the sun like children wanting to shine in their Father's eyes.

"Pia, did you know that every sunflower is a beautiful example of a spiraling pattern which suggests a fundamental characteristic of the Universe?"

"What are you talking about?"

"Have you heard of Fibonacci?"

"Is it a game?"

"No, it's a name and we can claim him as our own. Leonardo Fibonacci from Pisa, thirteenth-century mathematician. He discovered a sequencing code that is evidenced in nature. Pineapples, pine cones, artichokes, nautilus shells, hurricanes, fingers, DNA molecules, sunflowers, and more."

"You certainly are a wealth of information this morning."

"Let's hope you feel that way when we leave Bellaterra today." His fingers nervously tapped the steering wheel as if beating a drum rhythm from an internalized rock song. "Pia, let's agree upon our approach. You know, lay down some ground rules so we don't step on each other. You are the gatekeeper who gets us in. Then, just normal conversation. If I see an opening, let me ask the questions, all right?"

"All right. Except let me feel totally comfortable about trusting them so they'll open up without spilling their guts to the boss, okay?"

"I thought you already were," he exclaimed with obvious surprise.

"Well, I am but let me reinforce it and give you the high sign, okay?"

"Got it. You're initially the boss. But I will run the investigation. I know what I'm doing, baby."

"I know, Vinnie. You're the best. Thank you for taking the case."

"It's not a favor, Pia. I'm getting paid and I want to deliver the goods, if there are any. By the way, that telephone number that you wanted me to investigate? It belonged to a Klara Zutter."

They passed a stand of towering cypress trees as they approached the gate. The saw Jonas jump to his feet and out of the guard shack as they buzzed around the corner and onto the property. Pia reached across the steering wheel from the passenger seat.

"Hi, Jonas, this is my boyfriend Vinnie. We're here to see Elena out at the barn for a few minutes."

"No problem, little one. It's good to see you again."

Jonas shook Vinnie's hand and opened the gate.

"Hey, Jonas, is Nico around today? I don't want to run into him. I'm sure you understand."

"No, he's up in Firenze on business. Won't be back until tomorrow."

"Good. Is Flaviano here? I'd like to say hello." She smiled her brightest smile.

"He should be in the garage but if you don't find him, I'll tell him you were looking for him, honey."

"Thanks, Jonas. We shouldn't be long."

"No problem." He waved them through.

They followed the road to the barn to talk to Elena who was brushing a stallion about sixteen hands tall. The smell of manure was bitter, the air suffused with small particles of hay, visible in the slant of morning sun.

"You talk to her. I'll stay back here," Vinnie suggested.

"Why? Come with me."

"I don't care for horses. I'm a little phobic," he answered.

"You're kidding. Horses are magnificent animals," she urged.

"Trust me. Their strength and unpredictable nature is intimidating. I don't like them. I'll watch them at the horse track from afar, thank you."

"You're serious?"

"Perfectly serious. I had a close personal encounter with a horse in a barn when I was a kid. He backed me into a corner and reared up. If the farmhand hadn't walked in at that very minute, I'm sure the stallion would have killed me."

She shook her head with a dismissing smirky smile, then walked toward Elena.

Vinnie continued to tap out his nervousness on the steering wheel, his active legs bobbing to the beat in his head. After five minutes, Pia returned to the car.

"Well, she's on board. She says the entire staff, except for the two I mentioned, are not happy with Nico running the place. She suggested we talk to Flaviano. He might have something of interest to share with us. She dates him so I guess they talk. We can trust him, Vin. And Jonas."

They found Flaviano in the garage that reeked of gas, oil, grease, and sweat. He was doing an oil change on the Maserati among a stable of a half dozen other cars, all of them Italian, except for the 1955 Porsche speedster convertible, Nico's pet. Vinnie eyed them like a child in a candy shop.

"Whoa. These are hot cars!" he exclaimed as they entered the building.

"Hey, Flaviano, I just stopped by to see Elena, and she said you were here."

"For you, Pia, I'm always here," he said with an enormous grin on his face. "Okay, okay, who's this ... the boyfriend?"

"Sure is. This is Vinnie. Vinnie ... Flaviano."

After the handshakes, Pia continued.

"Hey, Flaviano, Elena said I can speak freely with you. My Vinnie here is a PI. He's investigating why Signora Sofia left in such a hurry."

"Okay, okay, but the police have already been here. She's now a 'missing person.' "

"I know, but this is different. We're looking a little deeper. I mean, we were wondering if the old man didn't die of natural causes, if you know what I mean. Do you remember anything suspicious when that whole thing went down?"

"Okay, okay, I don't want to lose my job, Pia."

"Don't worry. Nico does not know we're here, and no one's going to tell him, right? But old Mr. Gherardini was a good man. What if he was wronged? Who was his advocate?"

"He's dead, Pia," Flaviano said with finality.

"I know but does that make it right to ignore possible wrongdoing?"

"Okay, okay, what do you want?"

Vinnie stepped in. "We believe she's not coming back to the estate, Flaviano, which begs the question, why would she walk away from all of this? Suddenly, the day after her benefactor passes away? Sorry, that sounded indelicate."

"Okay, okay, it's all right. I've thought the same thoughts myself. You're sure Nico won't find out you asked me?"

Vinnie assured him. "Not unless you tell him."

"Okay, okay, let me just wash my hands." Flaviano walked to the sink and scrubbed his hands like Lady Macbeth, probably buying himself time to reconsider his agreement to share what he knew. He dried his hands thoroughly, appearing to stall, then turned to them.

"Okay, okay. Last year, Jonas, you know, the gatekeeper?"

They nodded.

"Well, about a year ago, he asked me to record the odometer readings on that little red Ferrari over there, before I left at night and first thing in the morning. No questions asked. So I did it. The readings were different almost every morning. At first, I thought someone was taking the car for a joy ride. But why would he want me to know that? It didn't make sense. So I asked him. It was Signora Sofia going for a ride, and most of the time, after he left to go home. He just witnessed her leaving a few times."

Flaviano took out a handkerchief and wiped his brow, wet with sweat, although the temperature was only mildly warm.

"Is that it?" Vinnie prodded.

"I wish it was," Flaviano responded. "There's more. It was always the same mileage difference ... every night ... never varied. I'm sorry, but people don't take car rides every night, number one, and number two, what are the chances of it being exactly the same distance. Exactly!" he stared at Vinnie with angry earnestness.

"So where do you think she went?" Pia couldn't help herself, glancing at Vinnie after realizing this was his part of the role playing. She winced.

Vinnie's attention was solely on the driver's anxious face.

"To Nico Gherardini's house on the lake. When he was in Firenze, I drove it there and back, in the same car, to make sure it was accurate. She was spending late nights with the son almost every night, long before Signor Gherardini passed away."

The sickening silence was eventually broken by an enormous collective sigh.

Vinnie spoke first. "How many people know this?"

"Okay, okay. Just me, Jonas, Elena, and Cyrano. He's the groundskeeper. He loved Rudolpho more than any of us. When I told him about the odometer readings, he shook his head and cried like a baby." Flaviano's voice had broken, and his eyes welled up so fast, he had to wipe them to clear his vision.

Vinnie continued. "So it's safe for us to talk to any of them, right?"

"Absolutely. I'll tell them that we spoke. If there's anything you can do, we'd all be so thankful."

"Well, this is a start, Flaviano. Thank you for trusting us. We are the good guys, you know," Vinnie assured him.

"I know. Okay, okay. Any friend of Pia's is a friend of mine. She got a bad rap after the old man died. We were all sorry to see her go." He nodded at her.

"And Flaviano, do you still have those odometer readings? We may need them for evidence."

"Yes, sir, but I keep them at home … safer that way, you know."

"You've been so helpful, Flaviano." Pia gave him a heartfelt hug.

As they drove up to the guard shack, the gate opened and Jonas waved.

Pia rolled down her window and yelled, "Jonas, you might want to talk to Flaviano. We're working together now. Thank you." She waved.

Vinnie glanced at his rearview mirror to see that Jonas with a bewildered look had come out of the shack, and was standing in the middle of the driveway, staring at their car, and still waving as if sorry to see them leave.

"That was huge, Vinnie. Huge! Oh my God, she was fucking the son. They were having an affair."

"Sure looks that way."

"Why aren't you more excited? That was huge!"

"I'm encouraged. Although having an affair with your husband's son may be poor form, it's not a crime."

"No, but it shows a possible motive for killing the old man, doesn't it?"

"Yes, and the operative word is 'possible.' "

"Okay. Okay."

"You're sounding like Flaviano," he teased.

She laughed. "Yes, he does say that a lot, doesn't he? He was nervous. Cut him some slack." She laughed again. "Well, I don't know about you, but I think that was a colossal breakthrough. Now what do we do?" Her legs nervously bobbed up and down.

"You remind me of that overly enthusiastic little dog in that American comic strip Garfield. What's his name?"

"Odie? Thanks a lot." She laughed.

"You're adorable and you know it." He put his hand on her bouncing knee and squeezed till it tickled. She knew they were going to the tavern for lunch when Vinnie took a left at the boulevard.

"Oh goodie, you're taking me to lunch—where I work? Vinnie, it's on my day off."

"You know it's the best lunch in town and you won't be serving, you'll be served. After all, we're celebrating a small victory. A mile in a marathon, mind you. And remember, you can talk to no one about this, Pia. No one."

"Except Tia, right?"

"Right, but I'll be giving her the full report. She hired me, remember?"

"And Dom, right? He knows we're investigating the Gherardinis," she stated, giddy as a schoolgirl.

Dom was working and raised his eyebrows with a smile when they walked in.

"Hey, bro." Dom waved them to the bar. "Can't stay away, can you?" he teased Pia. "Here, sit here so we can talk."

They climbed onto the bar stools.

"So do you hear anything from Tia?" she asked the bartender.

"Yes, as a matter of fact I do. We communicate by email a few times a week and we talk once a weekend when we're not working."

"She's so nice. I'm glad you're friends." Pia grinned.

Dom wiped the counter as he spoke. "I might even be going to the U.S. to see her this fall. Her niece is getting married in Massachusetts, in the capital city, Boston. I've never been to Boston before. I've never been to America before. We'll see how it goes."

"Why didn't you tell me this before?"

"She just mentioned it."

"Sounds serious, Dominic." Pia smiled, raising her shoulders and shooting him a cutesy look.

"No, no. We live too far away. I'm Italian. This is my home."

Suddenly from behind, Vinnie and Pia received a joint hug. It was Auriane.

"Hi, you two. How are you?" And before they could answer, she continued. "I guess you've heard that they fired me too."

Dom interjected. "Let go, not fired. There's a difference."

"Whatever you say, Dom. Anyway, I picked up a job as an au pair in Spoleto. I'm there five days a week and have my weekends off. But I miss my Luca something terrible. He left so suddenly and Nico wouldn't tell me where he was going. The jerk. He said it was for the summer but I don't believe it. I doubt he'll come back, or else, why would they have fired me? I mean, let me go." She glanced at Dom, in deference to his prior remark. "I wish I knew where he is. I'm the only one who ever really cared for him."

Vinnie pinched Pia's knee.

"What?" she yelled.

Auriane continued. "Can I join you? Just for a beer. A Heineken, Dom … please? That whole deal with you being fired, then me, and you know Lea and Marta are gone too. I'm almost glad I'm gone, except for Luca, of course. When his mom left, everything changed. And she never came home for her little boy. Imagine that. Sometimes I think about it at night and hope she's somewhere with Luca. But I know that didn't happen. She was as maternal as a scorpion." She paused to catch her breath. "Oh, I'm sorry, I haven't even asked. How are you two?"

Vinnie wanted to say *yes, you did ask but you didn't stop talking long enough to hear an answer*, but he didn't.

"We're fine," Pia answered.

Dom left the group to serve someone at the other end of the bar so Pia continued.

"Auriane, can we talk privately? I mean very privately?"

"Of course. Did you hear something juicy?" she whispered intently.

"I'm serious. This is for our ears only, okay?"

She nodded as if she were about to hear where the famous Jimmy Hoffa was buried.

"You know what Vinnie does for a living, right?"

She nodded and turned her attention to Vinnie.

"We're investigating a possible crime at Bellaterra so we need to ask you some questions." Vinnie stared at her long and hard, deciding if he trusted her discretion.

"She killed him, didn't she?"

"Why do you say that?" he asked, shocked at her response.

"Everybody talked about it after the funeral, and especially after she disappeared so suddenly. Everyone, except Lucia and Mateo, of course. Did you ever see the movie *The Sound of Music*? They're Frau Schmidt and the butler. Can't be trusted. If they'd heard us talk, we'd all have lost our jobs ... which I did anyway." She shrugged. "But the police came and questioned us. I thought the case was closed."

"First of all they were investigating a missing person, not a murder. Think, Auriane. Do you recall anything out of the ordinary that happened at the house in January? Or before? Any change of schedule? Any incident that was suspicious, any gossip among the servants? Anything unusual that happened the day of the funeral?"

She paused, her eyes staring down to her left as if she'd just spotted a spider in the corner. Then she looked up. "I don't think so. I wish I did. Sorry."

"Well, just know that we're searching for any clues that might lead us to the truth, if there is a truth to be found. If you think of anything, no matter how small, let me know. Here is my card with my cell phone on it, or you can usually locate me through Pia."

"What else can I do?" she questioned eagerly.

"Do you ever go back to the house to visit anyone?"

"Not really. Pia was my closest friend, so it would look strange if I visited anyone else."

"Then, just let us know if you remember anything that might be helpful ... even a small detail could be a clue."

Just as Auriane was leaving, she turned to face them and spoke. "There was one thing that I never told anyone because it was so random. The night of the funeral, the night before she disappeared, someone was moving trash bins in the middle of the night. Right below my window. I was so tired, I didn't get up to see who it was ... but it was creepy."

"Trash bins? At what time? Approximately."

"I actually do remember. That's weird. It was 2:27 a.m. I opened my eyes to see the clock, then fell back to sleep. It had been a rough day with the funeral and everything. But the reason I know it was 2:27 is that my Aunt Mona died at 2:27 in the afternoon, and my house number where I grew up was 227. It's just one of those random numbers that haunts me. I remember thinking how weird it was that I woke up for a second to see that number again."

Vinnie stood and gave Auriane a hug. "Thank you, thank you. If you think of anything else, promise to call me?"

Auriane nodded obediently.

Vinnie looked at Pia. "Baby, we need to go to Bellaterra."

CHAPTER TWENTY-TWO

There are poisons that blind you,
and poisons that open your eyes.
—August Strindberg

It was weeks before Vinnie and Pia gained access to the grounds of the villa. Nico had returned from Firenze and was spending time there and at his lake home, settling his father's estate, and delegating maintenance issues to his staff. Hedging the off-chance of running into him, Vinnie knew that their presence on the estate was potentially provocative in a negative way, so patience enforced her rules of discipline—they waited.

The summer had come and gone like the turning of a page, leaving the property littered with the season's footnotes of red poppies and Italian wildflowers. Pia would occasionally borrow Vinnie's car and stop by the guard shack to greet Jonas. She suspected that he knew she was asking if Nico was in residence because it was the first thing he told her, every time. She was grateful to have an ally at the gate, and depending on the time of day, brought him bruschetta or cannoli from the restaurant, to express her gratitude.

But waiting made Vinnie restless. He had sent an email to Tia, logging his progress and basically telling her that what he had found could not be admitted as evidence to the *polizia*. However, he was accruing a catalog of implicating details; but details were not facts and he knew the difference. It was frustrating because he knew it was premature to raise her hopes, but he was a paid employee who was required to report whatever he found. Until he could walk the grounds outside Auriane's window and talk to Cyrano, the groundskeeper, he hadn't another lead to follow. The only other prospective lead was that Flaviano had been alerted that if Nico left the country, Vinnie would like to be informed of the destination.

What Vinnie had gathered to date was incriminating, although circumstantial. He believed that Sofia had escaped to Canada, and that she and Nico were having an affair. He knew that Luca had been relocated to Capri, and the majority of the staff at the estate thought there was treachery involved in the death of Rudolpho Gherardini. Most of it was inferred, anecdotal, and conjectured, and none of it proved that this woman was the murderer Tia and her sisters believed her to be. There were times that Vinnie wanted to quit the case because proving it seemed hopeless, like trying to catch a bubble and hold on to it. What kept him dedicated was the fact that the telephone number that Pia had snatched from the room had turned out to belong to a woman who knew that Tia and her sisters were trailing Sofia. And that's all Sofia needed to know to abandon everything she had hunted and plundered.

The day they entered the grounds of Bellaterra was long awaited. They approached as if born out of the olive groves flanking the road and in the distance, saw Jonas open the bronze, filigreed gates. Steering into the driveway toward the house, they barely reduced their speed to greet him, but waved from the car windows as if they were on to something.

They drove to the side of the garage to park. There was no sign of Flaviano. The grounds near the back of the house displayed stanchions of cypress trees bordering the gardens, serving as decorative windbreakers. Vinnie was primarily interested in seeing where Auriane's room had been in relation to the yard. They exited the car onto the gravel driveway and Vinnie watched Pia struggle with her balance in her high-heeled shoes.

"Next to the nursery, on the second floor ... it would have to be that one." Pia paused as she pointed to a room with white shutters. "That one."

"I don't see any trash bins here. Where are they kept?" he asked.

"Back by the garages, I think."

"Okay. Well, from her window she could see the flower garden, and ... is that a greenhouse?"

Pia nodded, and in synch, they walked toward the structure.

Vinnie opened the door of the unlocked greenhouse to a stuffy stench of nitrate soil. The shelves were sticky with humidity but the structure was empty, housing no plants, no pots, no bags of fertilizer; no hoses, watering cans, shards of pottery, gardening tools, nothing ... except weeds growing between the stone pavers.

"How long ago was this place used, do you know?"

"I have no idea but why does it matter?"

"I don't know. But what could've been so important that it had to be dumped into trash bins at 2:27 in the morning before she left? If trash bins were involved, this seems to be the origin of the trash, don't you think? There's nothing else out here. What was she hiding? If I left town suddenly and for good, the last thing I'd think of doing would be to throw away plants in the middle of the night. Even people who sell their homes don't normally empty the premises this thoroughly. She didn't take her clothes but she destroyed the contents of the greenhouse. Doesn't that strike you as peculiar?"

"Yes, but there must be a logical explanation. Maybe Cyrano did it."

"In the middle of the night? I doubt it."

They heard a vehicle approaching and exited the greenhouse.

Cyrano was bringing annuals to autumnize the lower level window boxes. He saw the visitors and killed the motor. He was a friendly-looking older man with a broad squashed nose that defied his literary namesake.

"Cyrano, it's good to see you," said Pia. "This is my boyfriend Vinnie."

He shook Vinnie's hand and said, "I've talked to the others and I'm glad to see you here. Anything I can do to help, just ask me."

"I do have a few questions, sir."

"Fire away."

"Has this greenhouse been used in recent years?"

"Yes. But it's empty now. Signora Sofia used it. I wasn't responsible for any plants she kept there. As a matter of fact, she didn't want me to go near it. It was her greenhouse so I stayed away."

"What did she grow there?"

"I have no idea … maybe herbs, orchids, ferns, the plants that need protection from the elements and mist for moisture, I suppose. After she left, a few days after Rudolpho died, God rest his soul, I was curious. The door was unlocked … it had never before been unlocked … so I opened it. There was nothing there. I was shocked because she went inside to tend them every day. Then when she disappeared, so did the plants."

"You didn't throw them away?"

"No. Nobody went near the greenhouse except Signora Sofia, I tell you. It was a rule of the house. She kept them private. I never saw what they were."

"What about the bushes around the greenhouse?"

"Let me see. The fuchsia bushes are oleanders and the green leafy ones are spurge laurel. Aren't they pretty? I did plant those for her on the outside, at her request, of course. She wanted the greenhouse to blend with the garden. She called it the aesthetic transition between the garden and the building. I agree. It looks real nice."

"Yes, it does. Can you think of any reason, any reason at all, that Signora Sofia would want to dispose of the plants she coveted?"

"No, sir, I can't say that I can." He shrugged. "Do you have any more questions? I need to get these plants planted before the rain comes."

"It does smell like rain," Vinnie concurred. He thanked Cyrano, then went back into the greenhouse to have another look and take some photos, of nothing. Pia couldn't stand the stuffiness, so elected to stand guard outside the glass door.

Minutes later, Vinnie heard Pia say. "Oh … hi, Lucia."

"What are you doing out here? From the upstairs window I saw you and some man I don't know, talking to Cyrano," barked Lucia.

Vinnie emerged from the greenhouse. "Vinnie Vingiano. I'm pleased to meet you. Pia always wanted to show me the grounds, and it's a beautiful day, at least before the rain comes."

"So why were you inside the greenhouse instead of outside on this beautiful day?" she questioned like a drill sergeant.

"I'd just never seen the inside of a greenhouse before."

"Well, I don't think Signor Gherardini would approve of you two snooping around. We don't offer tours at Bellaterra, you know. I think it's time you leave."

"I apologize, Lucia. I should have made an appointment rather than stop by unannounced," said Pia.

"Yes, you should have. But now that you've seen it, you can go. Don't come back, Pia. You don't work here anymore." Lucia turned and walked straight-backed into the house like a soldier having delivered her terms to the enemy.

"I shouldn't have given her my name. I know better than that. Never offer information not requested. And sometimes not even then," Vinnie barked at himself.

"Oh, she won't remember," Pia replied.

Vinnie shrugged.

Flaviano had not returned from his errand so they silently got back into the car, both feeling defeated, having alienated the head housekeeper who forbid them to return. However, they had two new pieces of inconclusive information ... the greenhouse was empty and Cyrano had not dumped the plants. Every answer seemed to sprout more questions. When they arrived at the guard shack, they told Jonas that they were banned from the property by Lucia so they would be more reliant on his continued assistance.

"Jonas?" Vinnie asked. "Would you ask Flaviano what flight Nico took yesterday? Where he went? One of us will come by in a day or two to hear his answer. We appreciate your help. We truly do."

Jonas agreed and that chapter was closed.

That night when Vinnie regrouped, he mused that sometimes a question just begs to be answered. *What plants were grown in the greenhouse and why did she get rid of them? She didn't want anyone to see them? She didn't want anyone to know what was inside. What could be so dangerous about someone discovering her plants?* It seemed like an idiotic notion but Vinnie couldn't let go of it. Once again, he hypnotically stared at the pictures he'd taken outside the greenhouse. Cyrano had called them oleanders and spurge laurels, beautiful ornamental bushes. Vinnie nonchalantly googled them on his computer. An article entitled "Nine Most Toxic Plants for Humans" caught his eye.

> *Oleander is very possibly the deadliest plant on earth. It is often planted as a decorative shrub, & is so toxic that one single leaf could kill an adult human. It contain several lethal toxins, such as neroside, saponins, oleandroside, and cardiacglyosides. Upon ingestion these toxins shut down the cardio-vascular and nervous systems, after causing severe nausea and projectile vomiting.*

Vinnie's heart started pounding like engine pistons on a runaway train. He quickly brought up spurge laurel:

> *The Daphne copse or spurge laurel is a woodland planted profusely throughout Europe, as an ornamental shrub. Its gloriously scented flowers hold a dark secret. If you should eat either the leaves or red or yellow fruits, you will ingest the toxic mezerein, and nausea and violent vomiting will shortly be followed by severe internal bleeding, coma and death shortly thereafter.*

So the plants outside the greenhouse were lethally poisonous. So what? What was planted inside? He turned on his camera to look at the empty interior once again, having stared at the photos dozens of times since he'd taken them. There was nothing on the shelves, no pots, no planters, no hanging baskets. Only weeds growing between the stone blocks that had been laid as stepping stones. Then it occurred to him. *What if some of the weeds weren't weeds? What if, in her haste, deadly plants had spilled and seeds had taken root, finding life in the soil of the greenhouse floor?*

He took out a sheet of paper and composed a letter to Cyrano which he intended to pass through Jonas the following morning. He asked the groundskeeper to take samples of the different weeds in the cracks of soil between the stones and have them analyzed, and report back to him. Vinnie would cover any expenses. He folded the note into an envelope with Cyrano's name on the front of it.

Morning didn't come fast enough. He awakened in the middle of the night with aberrant thoughts. *Did Sofia poison her husband? If Rudolpho was poisoned over a long period of time in small doses, is that why there was no definitive cause of death? Nico would have to have known. Were they were working together? If so, Nico knew where she was and had helped her flee the country. Did he know about her history? Where was she?*

At 4 a.m., he talked himself out of thinking anymore. He didn't have any proof anyway. Yet. But he was possibly one step closer to the truth. Finally, he forced himself to relax by taking slow, deep breaths as if he was snorkeling and fell asleep in a sea of four short hours.

In the morning, he drove through the misty beauty of Umbria which despite his pre-occupation, reminded him of why he loved his homeland. On some mornings it was as if he was seeing the rolling hills of his country for the first time. His senses were heightened … this was one of those mornings. The guard shack was his destination before his waiting game began again. Jonas was there and surprised to see him so early.

"You're back! Good morning, Vincenzo."

"Good morning, Jonas. Will you make sure Cyrano gets this today? It's very important. I'd deliver it myself but Pia and I are *personae non gratae*, thanks to our run-in with the Wicked Witch of the West the other day."

"No problem. I'll see him this morning. Say hi to Olympia for me, please."

Vinnie nodded and was already driving away when he realized that Jonas had meant Pia. Her name was Olympia? He hadn't realized it. Olympia. He looked in his rear view mirror to see Jonas waving him back so he turned the car around.

"I'm sorry but I have a message for you from Flaviano."

"What is it?"

"All he said was, *Vancouver*."

CHAPTER TWENTY-THREE

The world is a mountain.
Whatever you say, good or bad, it will echo back to you,
Don't say I sang nicely
and the mountain echoed an ugly voice.
—Rumi

Within a month of arriving in British Columbia, Maddie had rented a brick bungalow in an old section of the city near Granville Street where she became a random piece of the vast jigsaw of identities in a reality puzzle called Vancouver. It was the perfect place to reinvent herself. No history, no men, no urgency. She could make time her ally, after having felt the pressure of time as her enemy for months. She almost dyed her hair, but didn't. She almost had cosmetic surgery, but didn't. The one small change she made was a small, almost indecipherable tattoo on the lower inside of her navel which she covered with a piece of rhinestone jewelry. She liked her look, and despite the danger of someone, someday recognizing her, she rather enjoyed playing with fire. She hadn't been burned yet. The rental property was furnished conservatively with overstuffed chairs with doilies on the arms; and an oak dining room table with chairs that had paisley seat covers that attached with ties to the back spindles. The kitchen was bright with colored, glass birds lined up behind the sink faucets and a refrigerator covered with magnets from places like The Grand Canyon in Arizona and The Badlands in South Dakota where the owners apparently had visited. But she didn't mind. No one was allowed in her temporary home, not even Nico. Her home was her domain. No one entered the interior, the backyard where she cultivated a garden, or the basement where she would grow other plants of convenience in the sunlight of the window wells during winter months.

September was the month in which more photos of the city were taken than in any other. The colors were as beautiful as any she'd ever seen, in kaleidoscopic shades of reds, yellows, oranges, and browns, accented by the ubiquitous evergreens, cedars, firs, and pines that populated the province like a magnificent unending Christmas tree lot.

She often drove to Stanley Park, to walk on the wooded peninsula that extended into the Burrand Inlet. One morning, she stopped near the totem poles to muse about her next chess move in her efforts to checkmate the mightiest of her opponents who at this point, were the Monson women. She'd deal with Nico later. Nico was easy. He'd visited her in late August and had assured her that the estate, except for the family home, would be settled by the following February. Until then, she would be compliant and continue the charade of them eventually having a life together. She could do that.

She sat by the water that idly pooled and stared at her reflection like a modern-day Narcissa, admiring not only her outer beauty, but her inner superior brain that outmatched any other she'd ever met. Anyone who didn't know her would be stunned by her extraordinary reflection, her transfixing beauty. Anyone who had known the truth about her would have seen the reflection of a demented spirit and deviant mind. But in her mind, she was above the world, believing a twisted cognition of the quote *in the world but not of the world.*

In Vancouver, she didn't want to stand out. She needed to fit in, without being one of them, and would have fun playing the game of life, proving to herself, time and time again, that she could outsmart the best of them. That was her *raison d'être.* It was all a game and she was damn good at it.

A couple with two cupie-doll little girls caught her eye, coming down the arbored path ahead of her. The older one squealed, "Look at all the Christmas trees!" The parents chuckled, then seeing that Maddie had heard the remark, they stopped and said, "We're from Arizona. She hasn't seen this many evergreens before. Could we bother you to take our picture?"

Maddie stood to her feet to oblige them, exchanged a few pleasantries, and took their photo. Then watching them walk away, she witnessed the husband turn around to smile at her, followed by his wife's punch to his shoulder. There were always two sides to a coin. Being strikingly beautiful made it possible to get what she wanted, but made her more memorable. Even though she had toyed with cutting her hair or wearing colored contact lenses when she first moved to Vancouver, she knew she would still be beautiful, and besides which, Maddie was confident that the Monsons would never find her so there was no reason to disguise herself. They also had no way to track her, and their apparent suspicions about her past were mere conjecture. Except for the stolen identities. They were true but the statute of limitations had run out on the identities of Cristin Shanihan and Yvette Vandal. Sofia Gherardini was simply a name she had chosen, and Maddie Thomas was legitimate in the sense that it had been purchased from a homeless druggie who willingly relinquished it. She was safe on those counts. Besides which, Nico was the only one who knew where she was, and Nico was in love. So it came full circle that being beautiful was more of an asset than a detriment.

She mused for a moment about the power she held over men. She had a mythical hold on the ones she invited into her web. However, none of them had yet seen the tattoo on her abdomen, the tiny hourglass.

The clock struck nine in the lobby of the Wedgewood Hotel on the drearily rainy night that Nico was expected to reappear in Vancouver. The Wedgewood was historic but not as flamboyantly magnificent as the Pan Pacific or the Fairmont. The last thing she needed to do was call attention to herself in a highly frequented and visible venue. Sometimes she asked herself if the hiding, the cloak and dagger, was worth it. What did she get out of it? Certainly, not fame, not in a conventional sense.

But she did get fortune, fortune after fortune, if she played the game well. Fortune and the immense satisfaction of duping the world. Like a serial killer, she continued to outsmart her opponents, gathering the spoils as she walked through a world of patsies, playing catch-me-if-you-can, knowing she'd never be found. All she had to do was stay a step ahead of anyone who followed her, and when comfortable and safe in another part of her big glorious, beautiful world, she'd hit on another wealthy man, and start over again.

Maddie picked up her key, tipped the elevator man and the porter who delivered her bags, and entered the posh suite that Nico had named their *Garden of Eden*, which set the stage for their romantic necessity. She was poignantly paranoid about their relationship in public, even thousands of miles from Italy. She implied that she only wanted to be with him in private, to make love, so he obliged her penchant for seclusion. One thing was certain: Maddie would make sure he would never be seen at her home on Oak Street.

She threw open the curtains to see the view of the Vancouver Art Gallery and Law Courts, one of the city's architectural jewels. The buildings were magnificent guardians of beauty and justice, and with the rain gently falling, they appeared as perhaps Claude Monet would paint them, as if seen through squinting eyes to fade their definition and soften the senses, reminding her of his parliament paintings.

Nico arrived by cab, shook off his rain coat, and asked the gray-eyed clerk named Taunya, spelled with a "u," if the other key had been picked up. When she responded affirmatively, he winked at her and spotted her a purple bill over the counter. The Canadian money was indeed beautiful, so uniquely identifiable.

Maddie was waiting with full, chilled champagne glasses at the door. Without saying a word and without unlocking his eyes from hers, he tossed his damp coat, took the glasses, set them down on the entry table, and backed her down onto the sofa. For the following hours, she wrapped her naked body around him. They promised each other they wouldn't leave the building that night or the following day. Nothing but the release of pent-up sexual frustration and room service; no worries, no concerns, no business, and the world went away. He had missed her and she had misled him.

Two days later, they emerged from the suite, walked into a glorious painting of an autumn day, and took a cab to Stanley Park's Sequoia Grill where they sat outdoors, under gorgeous deciduous trees, overlooking the Pacific Ocean and the skyline of a grand city. The air was steeped with the scent of pine, intoxicatingly fresh. It was there, in a very public place, that Nico broached the subject of Maddie's son, Luca.

"He's now been with Mia and Marco for almost five months, Maddie. Mia called me a couple of weeks ago. Apparently, he's exhibiting some rather violent behavior. I suggested it's just a stage but I felt resistance. Anyway, they're having a difficult time with him, and I'm not sure how much longer they'll be willing to care for him. So I've investigated boarding schools ... in Europe."

Maddie said nothing, staring at him as if she either didn't understand what he was intimating, or frankly, didn't care what he was saying.

He cocked his head and furrowed his brow. "Do you have anything to say about the idea?"

"How early can he be enrolled?" she asked in a cold, disconnected tone.

"Well, there is one in Switzerland that will accept children as young as three, as long as they are potty-trained, of course."

"Is he trained?"

"I don't know. I can ask Mia but is that what you would have me do until you resurface?"

Maddie sighed aloud. "I'm not certain I can ever resurface, as you call it."

Nico stared at her intently, with his elbow on the table, banging his knuckle against his bottom teeth while staring at her.

"Sofia, what are you saying?" he asked, appearing exasperated.

"Maddie. Always Maddie," she insisted.

"What are you saying … Maddie?"

"I'm saying that I have to be sure that these Monson sisters have given up looking for me; I don't know if I'll ever know that for sure."

"I thought you were running from a brother of a man you killed in self-defense … or something like that. Who are the Monson women? What are you talking about?"

Maddie remembered the lie she'd fabricated the night of Rudolpho's funeral and segued to embellish her story even further.

"The brother contacted me in Italy but it's the women in the family who are trying to nail me to the cross. They are my biggest liability. But thanks to you, my darling, I may have successfully eluded them."

"Is Tess one of the Monson women? You mentioned her name that night but you didn't want to talk about it."

"Yes, she's one of them. They're like raptors. They can never find me, Nico. Promise me they'll never find me."

"They won't," he blindly assured her. "But back to the issue of your coming home to Italy with me someday."

"It won't happen, as long as these women are alive. It won't happen as we'd planned."

"That doesn't work for me. There has to be another way," he insisted as he abruptly banged his water glass down on the table, causing neighboring tables to stare at them.

Just then, a tall, athletic younger man, bumped into Maddie's chair.

"I beg your pardon, miss," he said with a seductive, attentive smile.

"Get lost," Nico countered.

"Nico!" Maddie countered his counter. "I apologize for my husband, sir," she said adoringly as she took Nico's hand across the table.

The man abruptly turned his back and walked away.

Nico said nothing, then smiled with his eyes downturned. "Did you say husband?"

"Well, what do you want me to say to discourage him? I figured that would do it, and besides, you might as well be my husband, right?"

Maddie watched her handsome Italian playboy Nico Gherardini relax, and thought to herself, *a girl's got to do what a girl's got to do.* Fondling his hand in one hand, she took a sip of wine with the other, then placed her hand under the table to firmly rub him until she had his complete attention. She loved the control, and she knew for a fact that he loved other men desiring her, as long as he wasn't threatened. She thought of all the women he had most certainly chewed up and spat out. Now it was her turn.

"So, Nico, let's continue the serious part of this conversation when we get back to the hotel. We'll figure it out, lover. As far as Luca is concerned, I don't care, enroll him."

When they returned to the Wedgewood, they discovered that they'd absentmindedly left a cedarwood candle burning during their absence that day so the air was saturated with a woodsy scent. They opened the balcony door to let the burnt-leaved, cool autumn air waft into their room, to neutralize the pungent bouquet, and then sat in front of their fireplace to talk.

When Nico brought up the possibility of his buying a home in Germany or perhaps, southern Italy, far away from Bellaterra, she agreed that it may be the perfect solution. That decision paved the way to a discussion regarding the estate money.

She began. "I've done some preliminary research on my unfortunate situation, and it appears that because I am a missing person, I cannot collect my, our, part of the inheritance. We would need to wait five years until I could be declared dead, then it would go directly into an account for Luca, to be administered by the remaining beneficiary, which is you. But until then, neither of us can get to it. How are we going to get around the fact that we can't touch it?"

"Don't we have enough with my share? We can't spend what I have alone. So when five years passes, I'll have you declared dead, it will pass to Luca in trust, and I'll use it for us as we see fit."

Maddie knew there was a way around this theory but wanted him to believe that she was compliant with what seemed to be. She cooed, "Okay, I guess you're right. No need to be greedy." She climbed onto his lap, straddling him so she could look into his deep brown eyes as she admired his long, long black lashes. She kissed him and fucked him without changing her position on top, always in control.

Afterwards, a satisfied and confident Nico walked onto the balcony to smoke a cigarette. Maddie considered smoking a disgusting habit, but in Europe and Canada, it was a common habit, much more so than in the United States, a country theoretically obsessed with health and fitness. Nico however was from the old school, where he preferred to roll his own. His father and his grandfather had rolled their own cigarettes for decades, so he claimed he carried on the tradition to honor their memories. *Really?* she thought to herself, but she let it slide. He had some fancy-shmancy tobacco from Brazil that he enjoyed as one of his solitary pleasures.

"Will you teach me how to roll your smokes, Nicolai?" she asked.

He laughed. "Now why would you want to do that?"

"I pride myself in being a Renaissance woman, master of many trades," she replied, tossing her mane of dark hair and shaking it as she seductively smiled at him.

"Sure. Why not. But another time, all right?'

"It's a deal. By the way, this afternoon at lunch, you said you were allergic to shellfish. I never knew that. You're missing out on some tasty food," she mentioned.

"Yes, I hear you. I'm also allergic to bee pollen and penicillin, not very original, but true."

"Poor baby," she said with flirtatious sympathy while adding the newly-discovered facts to the reference section of her mental library.

Nico closed the door of the balcony after his smoke and sat down on the ottoman opposite Maddie.

"There's something else I need to tell you, sweetheart. We need to discuss it to cover all of our bases, right?" he stated with a serious tone.

Startled, she asked, "What?"

"Well ... the day before I left Bellaterra, Lucia, our head housekeeper, told me that last month while I was in Firenze, our former employee Pia came to the house with her boyfriend to show him where she'd worked."

"So?"

"They didn't go to the house. They went to the greenhouse."

Maddie's heart began to hammer.

"I emptied the greenhouse. There's nothing there. All plants, all pots were thrown into the trash bins the night before I left. There's no evidence, Nico. There's no evidence." Her head felt woozy like it was filled with minnows, swimming.

"Why do you think they were looking inside?" he continued.

"I have no idea. They couldn't have found anything!" she yelled emphatically.

Her voice had escalated to a much-too-fevered pitch for someone who wasn't worried so she lowered it and started searching for the answers.

"Did someone hear me out there that night? We've eliminated Lucia, and it couldn't have been Mateo ... maybe Auriane? She's the only one who lived there and her bedroom overlooked the gardens! ... except for all of the guests who stayed after the funeral. Okay, who is the boyfriend? Why would she show the boyfriend the greenhouse? No one went into the greenhouse, not even Cyrano."

"Lucia gave me his name ... I wrote it down. Vinnie, I think. He might be related to the Vingianos who own the tavern in town because that was the association I made with the name. I'll check it out when I return."

"Nico, you can't come to Vancouver anymore. I'll need to meet you in other cities. If they are snooping around in the greenhouse, where else are they snooping? What else could they possibly put together? You said you've never had business in Canada, right?"

"Right but ..."

"That's suspicious. They might try following you to find me. Did you tell Flaviano where you were going when he drove you to the airport?"

"I may have. I don't remember."

"You mustn't ever tell him where you're going again," she insisted.

"But sweetheart, they don't link me to you. They didn't know about us."

"We don't know that. We can't take anything for granted. Not this soon. They cannot find me, Nico. Damn those women."

Maddie stood. "I want to sleep alone tonight."

"But ..." Nico started to object.

"It's not open for discussion, Nico. Please, please, just tonight. I need to think. I love you."

Maddie exited to the second bedroom and closed the door. Her pulse, banging with adrenalin, her mind whirring. She took a succession of deep, labored breaths, and for a split second, thought of the family she'd seen in Stanley Park a few days before. They had no problems. They thought they were happy. Their lives were perfect. Their lives were boring.

She jerked back to the problem at hand. Her best-laid plans were possibly unraveling. Her objective: she had to remain undiscovered. But looking at the facts, it's true that the intruder would not have found anything in the greenhouse. She was safe there. But what was he looking for? Why was he probing on the estate? Everything had gone so smoothly until Clement Germond had informed her that "her family" was trying to find her. Had they contacted someone to investigate her? The root cause analysis revealed that the Monson women had confirmed that she was alive. After the estate was settled and she'd done what she needed to do, Maddie would need to disappear permanently. Meanwhile, if they really wanted to play the game, she would let them. But she'd play offense and her opponents wouldn't be allowed to win.

CHAPTER TWENTY-FOUR

A thousand fibers connect us with our fellow men:
and among those fibers, as sympathetic threads,
our actions run as causes,
and they come back to us as effects.
—Herman Melville

Nico Gherardini strode into Taverna Vingiano like he owned the place.

Forgetting that his finger had a fresh paper cut, Dom grabbed a lemon slice and winced. He stuck his finger in his mouth and sucked it. When he raised his head, Nico was standing at attention and tacitly demanding attention.

"What can I get for you, sir?" asked Dom, shaking his finger to dry it off.

"Some answers," barked Nico.

"Not on the menu but if I have some, you're welcome to them. What's on your mind?"

"Do you have a brother named Vinnie?" Nico asked.

"No."

"I know you do. You're Dominic, right?"

"Yes, sir. That's my name."

"Why are you lying, Dominic?"

"I'm not. I have a brother named Gianni. His friends call him Vinnie ... Vingiano? Get it?"

"Where is he?"

"I have no idea. What do you want with my brother, Signor Gherardini?"

"I want to know why he was trespassing on my property last month."

"I know nothing. I don't see him very often but I'll be happy to pass on a message to him."

"Tell him to stay the hell off my property. If he ever comes near my place, I'll have him arrested."

"Will do. Would you like a drink?"

"No!"

Nico did an about-face and marched out the door, slamming it behind him.

Like a frightened child, Pia peered from behind the kitchen door to make sure he was gone.

"What was that all about?" she asked in a whispered tone.

"Nico Boy is looking for my brother. Someone told him that Vinnie was on his property last month."

"Lucia. She's such a rat. You didn't tell him that Vinnie's a PI, did you?"

"Of course not. But it won't take him long to figure it out. The man's on a rampage. If I didn't know better, I'd say he's hiding something. I mean just last year, I found out that my ex's boyfriend was sniffing around my neighborhood, and it didn't bother me in the least. You know why? I have nothing to hide."

"I should tell Vinnie right away."

"Vinnie's fine. You were with him, right? He didn't go back unchaperoned, right?"

"Right," Pia responded.

"Don't worry. He's done nothing wrong. Back to work, Pia." Dom smiled his Dominic smile and winked at his brother's girlfriend like an older brother.

****

Three days later, Vinnie picked up an envelope from Jonas at the gate and sped from the property like a stealth missile. Coming from his lake home, Nico passed Vinnie from the opposite direction, swearing at whoever was speeding past his property. He stopped at the gate to speak to Jonas.

"Who was that maniac in the black Fiat?"

"I didn't see him, sir," replied Jonas.

"Well you sure as hell heard him!"

"Yes, sir."

Nico rolled up his window and proceeded to the garage. He then walked past the gardens and into the greenhouse to take a look for himself. It was empty, just as Maddie had said. No pots, no plants, just a few weeds growing in the soil between the pavers. There was nothing there to discover.

Meanwhile Vinnie, who had returned home, tore open the envelope that had been passed to Jonas, not from Flaviano this time, but from Cyrano. The envelope contained the results of the weed analysis for which they'd been waiting for almost a month. The plant samples were listed in one column as samples one, two, three, four, and five; the second column named them; the third column described them. It was third column that supplied his answers. Toxic, Toxic, Lethally toxic, Lethally Toxic, Lethally Toxic. His hunch had been spot-on. Sofia Gherardini had been harvesting poisons. That explained why she always locked the greenhouse, barring entrance to anyone, and why she tried to destroy the plants before disappearing.

Vinnie lit a cigarette and opened a beer. It was time to celebrate his victory, a small victory, but it did constitute another step toward building a case against the ghost no one could bust. More circumstantial evidence, yes. What they really needed was to find her and catch her making a critical mistake. Their window of time for identity theft charges had closed so they were definitely posturing for more serious counts, which would put her away for good.

He picked up the phone and dialed Tia's number in D.C. to inform her of the findings in the report. She answered, sounding sleepy.

"Tia, this is Vinnie. Did I wake you up?"

"No. I was reading in bed and must have fallen asleep. I'm awake now. What's happening over there?" She sat up and closed her book.

"I just read the breakdown of the plant analysis. I was right. All of the so-called weeds were poisonous at some level, three of them lethally toxic. We asked the analysts to specify how each affected humans, and the results are staggering. Two of them in small doses could eventually kill a person over an extended period of time; two of them in remarkably small doses would kill a person instantly; and one would take one to two hours to be absorbed into the bloodstream, so the death would be delayed, but imminent, and the poison would be undetectable."

"I knew it! Oh my God, Vinnie. Will you fax me the report? You have my fax number."

"You're the boss," he replied.

"So what do we do next?"

"Knowing that she was growing poisons is incriminating, but it's still circumstantial. We need to find her, Tia."

"Where do we start?"

"I wanted to get this report back before we continued, but as previously reported, she may be back in North America. Maybe Vancouver, British Columbia."

"Why Vancouver?"

"Nico Gherardini made a trip there recently, and remember, I learned that there was an Air Canada envelope found at Nico's cousin's home when the signora visited Capri. But we don't know her name now. I can practically guarantee you that she is no longer Sofia Gherardini. Our best bet is to follow Nico in hopes he'll lead us to her."

"Don't be too sure. If she knows we're looking for her, she'll cover her bases and his."

"But our odds of one of the two making a mistake have increased."

"I hope you're right. This feels like we're looking for a needle in a haystack." Tia sounded discouraged.

"But it looks like there is a haystack. Don't lose faith, Tia Monson. We're making progress."

"Okay, you're right. Thank you for the call. I'll relay the update to my sisters and Trina."

"Who's Trina?"

"It's a long story. She's the family member who actually started this hunt. She's the one who figured that his horrible human being was still alive ... through the publication of the painting. Remember?"

"Oh yes ... the painting."

"Vinnie, you do understand that we will pursue her like bloodhounds, right? Thanks again. Oh, and by the way, have you talked to your brother lately? He's coming to my niece's wedding in Boston next month. How amazing is that!"

The following afternoon, Vinnie paid his brother a visit at work.

"So I hear you're going to *pahk the cah in Hahvuhd Yahd,*" he teased in his best Bostonian American Italian accent.

"Hey Vinnie, good to see you. Yep, I'll be flying to the U.S. for Tia's niece's wedding next month. Must say, I'm looking forward to it, and seeing her, of course. Maybe take a ride to Cape Cod. You know, Nantucket, Martha's Vineyard."

"I don't know what you're talking about. Nantucket?"

"You gotta be kidding. You either need to read more or travel more, Vin. That's like coming to Italy and not knowing about the Leaning Tower or the Sistine Chapel."

"If you say so. Hey, while you're there, maybe you could take a trip to Canada and locate Signora Gherardini for me."

"She's in Canada? I thought she was missing or maybe even dead."

"That's what Signor Gherardini would have you believe but I don't think so. Of course, this is hush-hush. You'll get an earful from your girlfriend in the states but keep it under the radar, my man. *Capiche?*"

"Got it. By the way. Nico Gherardini was here looking for you. He was sufficiently pissed off that you were snooping around his yard a while back. Pia said the housekeeper probably snitched."

"Lucia? That could be. Does he know I'm a PI?" asked Vinnie.

"I don't think so but the man was irate so I doubt he'll let it go. Be careful, little brother. I wouldn't want to be on the bad side of Nico Gherardini," said Dom, as he started washing bar glasses.

"Don't worry. It's my job to be careful. Besides, the dangerous one is the signora." Vinnie grimaced and turned to leave.

"Hey, how do you like my new painting?" Dom asked as he pointed to a painting of a vineyard over the fireplace. "I've always liked the Montepulciano area. It's done by a local artist. I think she captured the light really well, don't you?"

"I didn't know you were a collector, Dominic."

"Only stuff I really like," he said as he smiled broadly.

"*Ciao.*" Vinnie turned his back, continued toward the door and with his hand high in the air, he waved goodbye.

Walking from the dark tavern to the white sun of the day was always a shock. Vinnie squinted as he fumbled for his sunglasses. The wind was strong. The cypress trees that bordered the property blew, like synchronized swimmers, swaying from side to side. He liked the wind. Cold wind woke him up. Hot wind wound him up, setting his senses on edge and sometimes giving him an edge to think creatively.

He felt exhilarated and suddenly aware of a gut feeling. And there was nothing as exhilarating as a gut feeling. It was like a relative of *déjà vu*, like a second cousin. With *déjà vu*, he'd get a feeling, then poof, it was gone. He couldn't grasp it. But a gut feeling lingered.

He sat in his car and tried to pinpoint it. Some of his best ideas came from connecting his day-to-day dots-to-dots. It had something to do with the painting Dom had shown him. Not the painting, but a painting.

Then it hit him—the conversation the night before when Tia mentioned the painting that Trina had discovered, the spark that had spontaneously combusted into what was now his case. Maybe he should visit the publishing house in hopes of finding the missing painter. Yes, that would be his next step.

****

Sometimes the universe aligned brilliantly. Maybe it always did but people didn't realize it. Only the beauty of retrospect and hindsight could reveal the degree of each person's connectedness, the magic of the oneness.

That night, Vinnie Vingiano in Italy called Tia Monson in the capital of the United States, to get her sister Tess Monson Parker's number in Minnetonka, Minnesota, to get the information and details regarding the publishing house in Lausanne, Switzerland.

That night, Dominic Vingiano purchased a ticket to Boston, Massachusetts, to visit his girlfriend and meet her family.

That night after her husband fell asleep, Dori Shanihan spent countless hours on her computer with her new best friend, the Internet.

That night, Nico Gherardini discovered that the man named Vinnie Vingiano, who had visited his greenhouse, was a private investigator, and Nico placed a call to a missing person in Vancouver, British Columbia.

That night Maddie Thomas, who had ordered subscriptions to the Boston Globe, the Minneapolis Star, and the Washington Post, noticed in the society section of the Globe, a wedding announcement of the upcoming marriage of an Ingrid Shepard to an Adam Lovett, along with an abbreviated list of expected out-of-town guests, including a Dominic Vingiano from Castiglione, Italy.

CHAPTER TWENTY-FIVE

The time will come
When, with elation,
You will greet yourself arriving,
At your own door, in your own mirror,
And each will smile at the other's welcome.
And say, sit here, Eat.
You will love again the stranger who was your self.
Give wine, Give bread, Give back your heart
To itself, to the stranger who has loved you.
—Derek Walcott

It was time. Time to make the dreaded phone call.

Dori Shanihan picked up the phone to call her daughter. How many times had she picked it up and placed it back on the cradle, deferring to another day? She'd even left a message the week before, saying that she was busy on Sunday so she couldn't keep her routine Sunday morning phone appointment with her daughter. But another week had passed so she couldn't stall any longer. She dialed the phone.

"Hi, Mom," said Trina.

"How did you know it was me?" Dori stalled.

"Caller ID? You really need to add this to your phone service, Mom. You can screen your calls and not answer the solicitors."

"That's okay. Sometimes the solicitors are the only people I talk to except your father."

"Oh, Mom," Trina acknowledged. "How is everything in Iowa? I missed our call last week."

"Sorry about that, dear. I do have some news though, Trina."

"Tell, tell."

Dori could hear commotion in the background like Trina was multi-tasking, perhaps unloading her dishwasher.

"I need your full attention, dear." The aberrant noise disappeared. "I don't know how else to tell you this, dear, but you know your father has been tired. His doctor put him on iron pills and prescribed rest. Well, he gave that a try for a while but he continued to feel more and more fatigued. So he went in for some bloodwork."

"Mom, you're scaring me. I don't like the sound of your voice. What's wrong with Dad?"

"We received the test results, Trina. Your father has leukemia."

There. She'd said it out loud for the first time. Her announcement was met with silence.

"Trina dear, are you there?"

She could hear her daughter's muffled cry from the other end of the receiver and listened to her stammer through a litany of questions.

"So what do we do? What needs to happen to make him well? Will he go through chemotherapy, radiation? When does his treatment start? How is he taking it? What are his chances?"

"Slow down, slow down. First of all, he's pretty steady. You know your dad. Of course, it's shocking news and the prognosis isn't good, Trina," Dori said, hearing her own voice tremor.

"What do you mean it's not good? He can go through treatment, be a survivor. He can do this, Mom," Trina insisted.

"He hasn't decided what he wants to do. Treatment might prolong his life a short while but he feels that going through the chemotherapy might be so stressful for you and me, that he's considering just riding it out."

"Dying? He's going to give up and die?" yelled Trina.

"Your father doesn't see it as giving up, dear. He's been told that a person his age doesn't gain much time by going through treatment. He feels strongly that he doesn't want to prolong his life for a short time and subject us to the pain of his treatment."

"Mother, put him on the phone. Please! Right now!"

"He's resting, dear. I waited until I knew he was sleeping to call you."

"Then I'm coming home to talk to him. I'll call you tomorrow with my travel details, Mom. I love you. Tell Dad how much I love him too. Bye."

Dori could hear her daughter's voice tremble as she hung up the phone. Then it was her turn to cry. She spilled her tears and allowed herself to sob, the sound making her pent-up feelings chillingly real. She'd tried to control herself in front of Daniel but sometimes she couldn't contain her sadness and they cried together in each other's arms. Strangely enough, she had noticed that she felt relieved after crying. She felt stronger and better able to cope.

Her path ahead was clear. She would become a full-time caregiver, guardian of her husband's health and spirit. This journey that she didn't want to take would test her courage, strength, and faith. She could now bear witness to the multitudinous emotions she could simultaneously feel: sadness, fear, anger, responsibility, burden, failure, mortality, threat, shock, denial, guilt, impatience, compassion, love. She'd spent countless hours on the Internet in quest of answers. She was angry at the doctors who gave them no hope due to his age and the advanced stage of his disease. She was angry at God for letting this happen to her husband at this time in their lives together. She was afraid that her caregiving skills would not be sufficient to comfort him. She felt guilty that she hadn't insisted that he see a doctor earlier about his chronic fatigue. And in her wildest imaginings, she couldn't bear the thought of not sharing her life with Daniel anymore. She was terrified of the journey and its aftermath ... the inevitability of being alone.

She quietly opened the bedroom door to confirm that he was still asleep, then walked into the living room where she took out photo albums of her precious grandchildren. Trina was coming. It would give them time to talk into the wee small hours of the morning, the best time to share, no matter what anyone said. She stared at Cristin Nicole and

Elizabeth Joy, now eight and six. She remembered her own girls at those ages and quietly prayed that God would keep Trina's children safe, that they would both grow up, unharmed. Being a grandmother was life's greatest joy, and Dori made sure she saw her little ones as often as she could. The drive wasn't that far ... only eight or nine hours. There was nothing as flat and uninteresting as the drive from Muscatine to Lincoln though. Flat, flat, flat. But she and Daniel shared the driving and read to each other to make the time pass more quickly. When she faced the fact that they might never make that trip together again, her eyes welled up, blurring the photos. She closed the album, reflecting on how many lasts and firsts lay ahead of her. Her father had told her as a child that behind every negative was a positive waiting to be discovered. A positive regarding her husband's cancer? She didn't think so. Her father had been wrong.

****

Daniel was sitting in the swing on the porch with an afghan over his legs when the cab carrying Trina from the airport arrived. She dropped her suitcase on the sidewalk, ran to him, and hugged him like she was making her peace with him in his last minutes on earth.

"Dad, you look good," she said, with her eyes expectant of an affirmative response, as she pulled up the wicker chair with the pillow she'd made in her eleventh-grade home economics class.

"Honey, I feel fine. I'm not in any pain. Just very tired. But I'm getting a blood transfusion tomorrow morning which should perk me up for a day or two."

"Can I donate blood?" she asked, as she rubbed his hands as if warming them.

"If our blood types match. I'd love to know I had my daughter's blood running through these old veins. You can come with us to the hospital tomorrow, if you want." He smiled lovingly. "Let's go in the house and let your mother know you're here. She's cooking up a storm in the kitchen, you know."

Trina helped her once-robust father from the swing, and felt how bony his elbow was. He'd lost weight and appeared fragile to her for the first time in her life.

She sniffed the autumn air, expanding her lungs to fill them with memories of childhood smells, and said, "Dad, I can't believe it's October already, my favorite month of the year."

"It's colorful, all right," he agreed. "It probably won't be real cold until the rains hit. Appreciate the beauty when you can, every time you get the chance, Trina."

She knew that he was implying that this was his last chance to see the fall colors but filed it in her denial file, not to be addressed at the moment.

Immediately after dinner, at her father's request, Trina played "Fur Elise" on the piano.

"Would you like me to play some others, Dad?" she asked.

"No, play that one, honey. That's my favorite. Who wrote it again?"

"Beethoven, Dad. Beethoven." So she played "Fur Elise" a few times, until Daniel closed his eyes and Dori helped him into bed.

After doing the dishes, Dori had her daughter to herself to discuss what lay ahead of them and to hear the news about Bryan and her granddaughters. After a comprehensive walk through the past few weeks of their lives, Trina needed to talk about her father.

"Mom, Dad seems so weak but in good spirits."

"He is a remarkable man, Trina. He appears to be handling his prognosis better than I am. He isn't afraid to talk about it. I'm the one who tries to avoid the topic. But I listen. That's about all I can do for him."

"Is he open to talking about treatment? Is there anything I can say to change his mind?" Trina asked with pleading eyes.

"No, dear. He told me he doesn't want to discuss his decision with you. So please honor his wishes. He said the best medicine he could ever have is having you here with us." Dori began to cry. Trina held her mother while they rocked back and forth together. After taking an enormous synchronous breath, Trina changed the subject.

"Mom, let's talk about something else, something happy, shall we?"

Dori nodded furiously.

"Ingrid's wedding is next month. Have you changed your mind about coming with me? I'd love for you to meet the Monsons."

"No dear. Not now with your father's illness."

"Of course, I'm sorry, Mom. I'm not used to thinking about it yet. I understand. That was insensitive of me. I just want them all to meet you, and it would be the perfect venue with so many of them gathering for the occasion. But another time. I haven't even met the bride myself. Oh, and before I forget, Tia has invited a man she met in Italy, a bonified Italian. His name is Dominic."

"Well, I'm sure you'll have a wonderful time. I'll meet them on another occasion. Have you heard anything about the other subject?" Dori asked.

"Actually, we did. We don't know where *she* is but our contact in Italy has come across some possibly incriminating evidence that supports our theory that she was up to no good once again."

"What, dear?"

"Well, this PI we hired, Vinnie, gained access to a greenhouse that had been mysteriously emptied on the night before she disappeared. All of the plants had been destroyed but there appears to have been some new growth in the dirt between the stones on the floor. He thought they were weeds, but had some samples analyzed and discovered they were poisonous plants. He believes that she was growing poisons in that greenhouse, Mom."

"And?"

"And we believe she poisoned her husband for his inheritance. Not all of it but half of it. The old man's oldest son inherited the other half. But there's more."

"More? What could be worse than that?"

"Tia, Tess, Katie, and I surmise that poison is how she's killed all of her other victims ... her ex-husband (and the pilot); Yvette Vandal, Tia's friend in France; our Cristin; and her parents."

"But our Cristin died in a fire."

"Yes, but they were all found together in the same room. They weren't trying to escape, were they?"

"Perhaps it was carbon monoxide poisoning before the explosion, like the policeman said."

"Maybe. But remember that book you used to read to me called *The Secret Garden*? Hunter Cross used to tell me she had a secret garden that she tended. I presumed it was a flower garden. And Tia remembers her talking about a garden as well. Then we found out that in Italy she had a greenhouse that no one was allowed to enter. It all adds up. She's been growing her own poisons and killing people."

"Trina, that's a lot of guesswork. What makes you girls so positive?"

"The kinds of poisons he found, Mom. They aren't local or indigenous to Italy ... one of them was an ugly plant from South Africa. Nobody grows poisons from other countries unless they plan to use them."

"I can't argue with that. Did this Vinnie send you a report? I'd be curious to read it. Gardening fascinates me."

"Sure thing, Mom. I'll email it to you as soon as I get home."

The following morning after it was determined that Trina's blood type matched her father's, she donated blood. When his transfusion was over, Daniel looked at her and said, "Why is it that I suddenly feel the urge to play Beethoven, honey? Where is that piano?"

Daniel's humor, injected into serious matters, had often saved the day, and this was no exception. The family laughed and relaxed.

The following days were underlined with sharing memories, mostly of the girls' childhoods: their annual trips to the north shore of Lake Superior, their visit to the lake cabin, their school plays, their boyfriends, and their 4-H trips to the State Fair. When Dori and Trina openly spoke of their Cristin, Trina noticed that Daniel was reticent to talk. He'd sweetly smile but quickly withdraw.

By the time Trina left Iowa, she'd booked her next trip back, knowing that her time with her father was limited. How much time was left was unknown but the doctors concurred that he would probably not see the following summer.

Dori missed her daughter more than she had thought possible. Her visit had been revitalizing at a time when she most needed the support, but her departure commensurately left behind an emptiness Dori couldn't fill. Daniel's comfort and state of mind became her constant concern. Their lulls in conversation became more frequent but she rationalized that the silences were necessary to focus on their thoughts.

One night in their kitchen where the clock ticked loudly and the refrigerator hummed, Daniel spoke in his gravelly voice.

"Dori, I only want to talk about Cristin once. It's still too difficult for me to discuss. You've always known that. But I can't ignore how much she meant to me so hear me out, please."

Daniel adjusted himself in his chair and looked down, avoiding eye contact, apparently to get through what he needed to say.

"Mortality has been hard to face. There's no other way to say it. You can't really deal with Mortality until It bangs on your door and you're forced to open it. I stare at Mortality every day now and It's not going away. So It has forced me to figure out who Daniel Shanihan really is and tell someone. And that someone is you. First, I want you to know how much I love you. So anything that I say doesn't diminish the love I feel for you."

He paused, blew his nose, and never once lifted his eyes.

"When we first lost our Cristin, the world became a different place. I was in it but as a stranger, in a world foreign to me, as if I'd awakened on a dirt heap on another planet with no home and no sense of identity or belonging. Why would I want to belong to a world so cruel? The world I lived in was devoid of color; everything and everyone looked like a photograph negative, a black and white transparency. The beauty I once appreciated, the kindness in voices which I once cherished, disappeared. I thought life was over and I was waiting to die. Life asked me, 'what are you doing here?' and I had no reply. It sometimes felt like I was on the ceiling looking down at myself, lost, without enough purpose to take the next step. It was frightening but in a strange sort of way, sometimes comforting, as I felt closer to Cristin and what she might be experiencing after death.

"I will not pretend by saying I ever found the zest for living I had before Cristin died, but gradually, time took the edge off my despair, so that I once again saw color, recognized kindnesses, and could talk again. You and Trina were directly responsible for my tenuous recovery. I guess that's what's implied by love healing all. Your love brought me back to you, Dori."

His wife squeezed his weathered hand, then retracted her hand into the skirt of her apron as he continued.

"There are things in my life that I'm proud of and there are things I'm not. I want you to know the truth so that when I leave, there is someone left who knew the real me. There was a time when our girls were young, that I thought I could never be happier." He paused and swallowed as if he were dislodging an object stuck in his throat. "And I was right. After we lost Cristin, I never recaptured that feeling. Even after ten years, Dori. It's been over ten years. Most mornings when I wake up, for a few seconds, I'm content. Then bam! It hits me that she's gone, and I don't feel that peaceful feeling again until the following morning, if I'm lucky to feel it at all. Sometimes it's days before I do. I'm fortunate to know what happiness is because I suppose there are people who don't. They think it's a fairy tale. Well, I knew what it was every moment of every day until we lost her. I ache to know that feeling again. I used to think that time would make me stronger, and I suppose it did. But now that I'm sick, I don't feel strong anymore. I remember Vince Lombardi saying 'Fatigue makes cowards of us all.' That applies to me. I feel like a coward because after losing our girl, I was never able to be the man I was. And I'm sorry."

He looked up to see his wife with downcast eyes, pursed mouth, attentively listening. He continued but now looked intently at her.

"I heard you and Trina talking the other night about Hunter Cross. I know you've wanted to spare me the details but I get the gist of it. She's alive somewhere, isn't she?"

Dori nodded.

"She may have killed our daughter, taken her name and identity. She used information about Trina's birth mother to make a new life. I may not live long enough to witness this monster brought to justice but I want you to know that anything we can do to help these girls find her, you have my blessing to do so, no matter what it takes. Do you understand? No matter what it takes."

With tears running down her cheeks, Dori nodded vigorously, unable to speak.

"I'm not proud of these feelings but they are real. Daniel Shanihan wants justice, so never wonder about that."

With that said, he stood on his own and walked to their bedroom. Dori followed him without exchanging words. As he lay down on the bed and closed his eyes to rest, she leaned over to kiss him on the forehead and covered up her prince, her courageous prince.

****

Unbeknownst to the world, that night under the stare of the moon and the light of the stars, saturated by sun and quenched with rain, deadly plants continued to grow on a remote section of the old Cross farmland.

CHAPTER TWENTY-SIX

Wen storm come
Yuh bawl
'get flat'
—Jean Binta Breeze

Every day Katie thanked God that her daughter had not chosen a destination wedding to some exotic land, as so many of her friends' daughters had recently done. There was no doubt that the destinations were beautiful but the expense, time, and planning involved were so exponentially disproportionate to the intimacy of the event that she quietly, gratefully, embraced the decision of a church wedding in Boston.

Many of the leaves had fallen, dropping blankets of color on Boston's autumnal floor. Any day the winds and rain would shake them all loose, exposing nothing but branch silhouettes and mistletoe. But November had been the best month for Ingrid and Adam's wedding because Heidi could be home from Dubai, and Adam's brother, who was a consultant in China, could also attend.

The Monson women gave their full attention to the wedding and its surrounding events, taking a vacation from their mutual mission which consumed emotional hours of each day, even if only subliminally. On the day before the wedding, the anticipation bloomed into a full lotus of joyful reality. People convened at Katie's home throughout the day to meet and greet. The caterers supplied trays of food, the bartender took his post, and the florist worked her magic, transforming the home into a nuptial wonderland. Katie greeted her family, inquired about their trips and accommodations, and tried to relax into the arms of the hours before the big day.

The doorbell rang and Ingrid answered it.

"Dad! You're here!" she cried, as she threw her arms around her father's neck.

Stefan had made the trip from Atlanta, and at his side was a girl Ingrid's age.

"Allow me to introduce Lynnie."

Ingrid nodded her head in deference to the young woman, and took her father's arm, ushering him into the room, and leaving Lynnie to follow. It was the first time Katie had seen him in years and he was met with reserved courtesy.

"Hello, Katie. This is Lynnie. Lynnie, Katie," he said as he pulled the young girl forward. Both women coolly acknowledged one another before Katie moved on, turning to her brother Troy.

Throughout the afternoon, the out-of-towners arrived. Tess and Ren, Sondra and Joe, and Troy settled in the living room. Ingrid and Adam entertained their friends in the basement. Heidi and Lindsey hung out in the backyard with Heidi's friends from college, and Katie worked the crowd.

Just before the evening buffet, Trina arrived. Katie answered the door and once again, feeling she was looking into a mirror almost thirty years ago, embraced her daughter. Meeting her in D.C. the year before had been a shock to both of them but the year had given them the gift of time to think and to bond with each other, on the phone, in their letters, and in their hearts.

Trina beamed at her birth mother and Katie asked, "Are you ready? Ready to meet the family?" Trina nodded energetically with the enthusiasm of a puppy, and they walked into the living room where Katie announced her daughter with pride, like a coming-out at a debutante ball.

"Everyone, this is my daughter Trina," she said with the emphasis on *this*.

Tess rose from her chair to assist with further introductions. Across the room, Stefan turned pale.

"I thought you had two daughters," said Lynnie, addressing Stefan.

"I do," he responded. "This is my ex-wife's love child."

"Wow! They look identical, don't they?" Lynnie naively continued.

"Yes, they do. Come with me," he instructed her. "Take my arm. Now."

"Hello, Trina. My name is Stefan. I'm your mother's ex-husband," he said impetuously.

"Stefan, stop it," Katie implored, nervously laughing as if to disparage his insinuation.

"How do you do, Stefan," Trina continued without missing a beat. Then turning to Lynnie, she asked with enthusiasm, "Are you one of my sisters?"

Katie snickered, instantly realizing that Trina knew better but had found it too irresistible to let it pass.

"No. She is not," Stefan replied defensively.

Obviously sensing her mother's amusement, Trina continued. "Oh, I'm sorry. A date?" she said with an air of incredulity

"No. My wife," Stefan responded angrily.

The room stood still.

"Your wife?" Katie interjected.

Trina addressed the girl. "I'm pleased to meet you. I'm Trina. I didn't catch your name."

"Lynnie Shepard," she said quietly.

"I'm pleased to meet you, Lynnie Shepard." Then turning her back on the rudely-met ex-husband and unfortunate bride, she addressed Katie. "Now I'd love meet my sisters."

Trina's entry and meeting of the rest of the family was stellar. Ingrid, Adam, Lindsey, Heidi, and their contemporaries embraced the shockingly similar countenance of Katie with open arms. Stefan and his new wife slipped out of the house unnoticed sometime during the early evening but when their disappearance was finally mentioned, the remaining family, including the bride-to-be, transparently relaxed.

By the time Tia and Dom arrived, the party was lively, loud, and exactly what Katie had hoped it would be. Everyone welcomed Dom and found it necessary to tell him about either their memories or dreams of visiting Italy. Everyone loved Italy. The food, the music, the shoes, the designers, the cars. What was not to love? And of course there were questions, such as, had he ever seen Diane Lane in *Under the Tuscan Sun* and what was his favorite part of *The Godfather* trilogy?

"Not all Italians are mobsters, you know," he responded while laughing.

Later in the evening when the bartender found out that Dom could tend bar, he invited him back to swap drink recipes and concoctions which led to raucous stories that everyone enjoyed. After all, who heard better stories than a bartender?

"My favorite stories are the animals walking into the bar," said Troy.

"I like the genie in the bottle stories, myself," Adam chimed in.

"How about the priest, the rabbi, and the minister stories," suggested Joe. "Or the Irishman, the Pole, and the Italian."

"Hey, hey ... watch it. You're getting a little personal there," Dom responded affably, waving him off and laughing at the same time.

After hours of jokes, stories, and toasts, Katie laid down the law. "May I have your attention, everyone?' she asked, after gently clapping her hands together twice with a flair-of-the-wrist chaser. "Okay, everyone, the bride needs her sleep. How 'bout we call it a night? Tomorrow is a big day, and tomorrow night we can stay up all night as far as I'm concerned."

Everyone agreed. By 1 a.m., Katie was in her home with her three girls, Ingrid, Heidi, and Trina, sleeping down the hall. For the first time in her life.

Twenty-five miles away, Maddie Thomas and Nico Gherardini made love in a Boston hotel. Twenty-five hours later, they would deliver a message that would stun the Monson women. And the game was on.

Weddings were not passive events. Through the years, Katie had noticed that there was something about a wedding that made happy couples happier, unhappy couples unhappier, single people wish they were married, glad they weren't, or wish they were anywhere but a wedding. There was nothing in-between or unemotional about the event. The most compromised attendees seemed to be those with a partner, unmarried and undecided. She didn't know who they were that day but after years of attending weddings, she knew they were out there. But Katie's only hope was that this would be, to date, the happiest day of Ingrid's life.

On wedding day, the sun was brightly shining through crystal blue sky and autumn cool air. Just as Katie had pictured it. By the time the organist began, indicating the seating of the guests, her nerves were frayed but her daughter's demeanor was bridal in every sense of the word. Just as Katie had pictured her. The floral color scheme was composed of orange gazanias, red asters, and gold and white chrysanthemums. Just as Katie had pictured it. The room was filled with well-wishers and high spirits and smelled like happiness. Just as Katie had pictured it. When Stefan walked his daughter down the aisle, the congregation was communally smiling; the wedding party, holding their breath; and the groom beaming. Just as Katie had pictured it.

The ceremony was brief and the vows were personal and touching. After the bride and groom had been pronounced husband and wife, the double doors to the narthex opened as the organ played the rousing Widor Toccata as the recessional music, the same piece played at Katie and Stefan's wedding years before. Katie turned her attention to the stunning wedding party and noticed Lindsey craning her head toward the back of the church as if searching for someone.

Within a half hour, the guests caravanned to the country club for an "island reception." The reception line was exhausting, but Katie didn't care. All was unfolding without a hitch. She overheard one of the bridesmaids say that the Reggae music was happy music and the Caribbean cuisine, divine, which made her beam with satisfaction. The guests danced to Bob Marley and Maxi Priest, and enjoyed jerk chicken, island rice and beans, conch fritters, stuffed red snapper, and pepper pot soup. Those guests with delicate stomachs had a less spicy version of the fare.

Five hours later, the bride and groom waved goodbye to their guests and were on their way to their bridal suite at the Hampton Hotel, then off to the Bahamas for their honeymoon the following morning. Once again, Katie was grateful that her daughter didn't need to fly to Tahiti or Bora Bora. The Bahamas off the eastern seacoast was perfect for Adam and Ingrid, as long as hurricanes didn't surprise them. It was hurricane season, after all.

The rest of the family changed into comfortable clothes and convened at Katie's to chat about the day's event and party on. At one point, during a pause in the fast-paced conversations, Tia asked Dom why the wedding coordinator had asked to speak to him.

"She gave me an envelope. But there was so much going on, I stuck it in my inside pocket. It was probably a request to be part of the clean-up committee. Frankly, I forgot about it." He smiled his irresistible smile.

Lindsey chimed in. "I saw the lady who handed it to her. I was still up front in the wedding party, just as the doors opened at the back of the church when the recessional started. I remember wondering who she was."

"She must have been a guest," Tess suggested.

"I don't think so," Lindsey continued. "She was wearing a navy Chanel-style suit and a hat with a dark netted veil. I didn't see her before the ceremony and I don't think she was in the sanctuary. I know she didn't stay for the reception … we would have noticed her. She didn't exactly blend, if you get my drift. She was right out of, like *Vogue.* But what really struck me was the man beside her. He looked so much like a man I saw in a casino when we were in Lucerne.

Remember, Aunt Tess? I think I told you about him. Maybe not. It was on the twenty-first of January. I remember because I thought how ironic it was that I wasn't twenty-one yet but I was legal in Europe."

She suddenly realized that her father was in the room. "Sorry Dad. I was only there for an hour." She shrugged her shoulders and smiled.

He smiled and nodded, deferring to her story.

"But he couldn't have been the same guy. What's weird though, and I hate to bring this up, but he had the same last name as the man who married *her*."

"You mean Gherardini?" asked Trina with apparent trepidation.

"Yes, but you said his name was Rudolpho. This man, this gorgeous man ... he like smiled at me and said '*Buonasera, Signorina*' ... his name was Nico, not Rudolpho."

With wide eyes and open mouths, the Monson women incredulously looked at Lindsey as if she had suddenly turned into a giant tarantula.

Tess nearly choked. "Why didn't you tell me?"

"Tell you what?" cried Lindsey indignantly.

"Dom, where's the envelope?" asked Tia.

"It's in my suit coat pocket, in the car. Do you want me to get it?"

"Yes!" the women yelled simultaneously, as if cued for their response.

"All right. I'll be right back." He stood and walked out the door to the car parked in the driveway.

"What's going on?" Lindsey asked in an unusually high-pitched voice.

"I guess we haven't kept you up to speed, little one. Let's hope that you did not see your Prince Charming this afternoon," said Tia, then continued to break the news to her. "Nico Gherardini is *her* lover. If he was here today, she may have been the one in the Chanel suit."

There. She had said it. The thought was incredibly outlandish and disturbing. She continued, "I'm hoping that the note for Dominic is from an admirer. I would trade the sinking feeling I have in my gut right now for sleepless nights battling the green-eyed monster."

Ren jumped in to calm the seas. "I think your imaginations have gotten the best of all of you. Hunter, or whatever her name is this month, wouldn't have risked being seen at this wedding, knowing that you're hunting for her."

Tess supported her husband. "Rennie's right. We're jumping to a ludicrous conclusion. She wouldn't have the nerve."

Tia disagreed. "She'd have the nerve but Ren's right. We're all hypersensitive. We'll know soon enough. I just heard the car door slam. Dom now has the answer in his hand."

The room's conversation halted, and the inhabitants of the proverbial tomb actively waited for the bartender from Italy. He walked in waving the unopened mystery envelope in his right hand, then ceremoniously handed it to Tia.

"It has your name on it, Dom. You open it," she responded.

"Well then, as you say at your awards programs, 'The envelope please.' "

She handed it back and without discussion, they watched him open it and silently read the contents. He looked up at them with a blank yet somewhat reserved expression and read it aloud.

Tell your brother to stop.

"Who's your brother?" asked Lindsey

"Vinnie," Dom answered. "He's the private investigator on this case."

"But how did she know you were here?" Lindsey continued.

Katie stood up and spoke. "That's the big question, isn't it? I hate this. It's like she's the storm and we're the trees. We bend in terror any time she blows," said Katie.

"It's a threat," said Trina. "*Tell your brother to stop* or what?"

"It's implied," Ren suggested. "Girls, I think you're over your heads on this one. From what we know, no one wants to be on her black list, and I think that in her mind, she's branded you as her enemies."

Joe unexpectedly jumped in.

"Excuse me. I've never met her, but from what Sondra has shared with me, this broad is dangerous. She knew that all of you would be in that sanctuary together today ... all of you. None of you would be roaming the hallways of the church during the actual ceremony. She also knew that if Dom happened to ask the wedding coordinator who delivered the envelope, she would describe the woman and the man with her, and Dom, you would share the information with the family. That didn't happen but thank goodness Lindsey was so vigilant. This horrible human being accomplished exactly what she intended ... let you all know that she knows you're on to her, that she's not afraid of you, and she's not going to put up with your continued search. She's an angry bitch. She's now labeled a missing person, and a missing person can't collect an inheritance. You've cost her an Italian mansion and estate, and probably her inheritance. If I were you, I'd drop it unless you're willing to live with the future consequences of her wrath, which there will be, if you pursue her."

"Joe's right. This could get ugly," Sondra said as she looked from side to side at the Monson girls.

"So you're suggesting that we halt the investigation? That it's all right if she's free to continue doing what she does?" asked Trina. "I'm the one who started this ball rolling. I admit it's unfortunate that she found out that we had tracked her to Italy, but we've all lost loved ones at her hand."

"You have to ask yourselves ... are you prepared to lose more?" asked Ren as he took Tess's hand in his.

The ambience turned cold.

"Of course not, but her actions need to be avenged! Don't they?" Trina yelled.

The room was ill with tension. Eventually, quietly, Trina sliced the abysmal silence.

"We're just going to have to be extremely careful. Look at how far we've come. We're holding the cards. She doesn't know that we've discovered what she was growing in the greenhouse. She doesn't know that we think she was having an affair with Nico, establishing a motive for killing her husband. She doesn't know that we think she's in Vancouver. If Vinnie lays low for a while, she'll believe we were intimidated by this note and we've given up our search. I think we need to wait her out, be patient. From where I sit, what we really need is to figure out her name and pinpoint where she is so we can have a Canadian investigator nail her."

"Well. I'm glad to finally be caught up to speed. Why didn't anyone think to tell me all of this? I'm part of this family too," added Lindsey, in a shaming voice.

"You're right, honey," said Tess. "With the wedding preparations and activities, we overlooked filling you in. We apologize."

Katie spoke. "Sorry, Linz. And just for the record, I agree with Trina. We should lay low."

Suddenly Tia stood up and addressed Dom. "When did you tell me your grandfather died?"

"In 1997."

"No, the date."

"January 21. We light a candle every year at Santa Angelo's. Why?"

"And that's the night Rudolpho Gherardini died, right?"

"Right."

"Linz, are you sure you saw Nico Gherardini at the Lucerne casino on the night of January 21?"

"I'm positive."

"Then there's his alibi. Where was she?"

Katie stood up and addressed the room. "All right everyone, it's late. We're all tired. We can continue to talk about this another time but please don't bring it up to Ingrid. It would cast a shadow on the memory of her wedding."

Everyone agreed. The blemish on the face of the beautiful day would need to be covered, but they all left Katie's living room that night knowing that it was festering and eventually needed to be treated, one way or the other.

CHAPTER TWENTY-SEVEN

There are very few monsters
who warrant the fear we have of them.
—André Gide

Immediately after the wedding, Tess and Ren returned home to Minnetonka, Minnesota, The audacious visit from the woman they had known as Cristin had punctuated the wedding events with a surprise ending which accentuated that they were dealing with a perfidious persona. Ren voiced that he was against pursuing her any further, believing that no good would come of it, or more poignantly, that there could be collateral damage to some of their loved ones, possibly themselves. Tess honored her husband's concerns and also understood her sisters' and nieces' desire to proceed with caution and patience.

Minnetonka was brilliant this time of year. They'd seen the last days of Indian summer. The trees were stripped of their colors, and everyone anticipated the first snowfall of the year as an event, like the opening day of the Minnesota Twins at the Metrodome or the first day of the hunting season. Sometimes the first snowfall came in October, and neighbor kids had to plow through unshoveled sidewalks in clumsy snow boots to trick-or-treat. But that was rare. It was the end of November already, and not a single snowflake had landed on the *Land of Sky Blue Waters*.

Since they'd just spent a week with family in Boston, the Monson women agreed to honor Thanksgiving separately with their immediate families and friends. To Tess, it was time to dress their home once again, and display what she playfully referred to as "The Changing of the Gourds."

Among Tess's greatest blessings was her appreciation of family. Prior to their marriage, Ren's daughter Lissa was his only family. But he had embraced her sisters, brother, and their families as his own, and Tess loved him more deeply because of it.

Lissa and her boyfriend joined them for Thanksgiving dinner. They spent the day together preparing the meal, which always, for some inexplicable reason, made it taste better. Ren had concocted Father Capone's gravy recipe which amply smothered the mashed potatoes, chestnut dressing, turkey, and vegetables. Lissa had taken baking classes at The Baker's Dream and baked flaky pastry crusts to showcase her contribution of pumpkin and mincemeat pies.

The crowning moment of the day for Tess was holding hands to share the prayer of thanks for their many blessings, and blessing the ravaged victims of Hurricane Katrina in New Orleans, and the military troops in the Middle East who could not be with their families that day. It made her feel connected to her world.

By the next day, just like clockwork, it was time to re-dress the house for Christmas. Down came the boxes from the attic. It would be a three- to four-day labor of love to bejewel the Parkers' Christmas home. Tess opened each box as a ritual, as if visiting old friends, who had gone away for eleven months, only to return, a year older and dearer. When she opened the angel collection, she found the letter that Cristin had written to her, on that magical Christmas in 1995 when her family had visited from Boston and California, and their beloved neighbor Serena was still alive. Fond memories. Bittersweet memories. If only they had known then what they knew now.

One morning the following week, the first snowfall threw a surprise party for early risers. From her bedroom window, the white quilt looked soft, like feathers, and sparkled in the morning sun like Mylar sprinkles. The breezy, leafless branches of the maple trees tickled the ground with shadows, creating moving patterns that looked like a Jackson Pollack/Ansel Adams collaboration in live theater.

Ren had traveled to Santa Fe on business the day before, so as usual, when he was gone, she hunkered down at home, with a fire in the fireplace, a crock pot of homemade soup simmering in the kitchen, and an island of finite time on which to write. For years, she'd wanted to write a psychological drama about a woman being stalked .This was as good a time as any to cross over the boundaries of her reality and explore her imagination.

But despite her intentions, her mind wandered. She was bothered by the boldness exhibited in delivering in person the note addressed to Dom at the wedding. She was disturbed by a phrase that Ren had used on that ominous night, so she examined it again. He had said that the Monsons had become enemies ... in her mind. *In her mind.* Perhaps they needed to try to think like she did. What would be her next move? This monster didn't want to be discovered but she wasn't afraid of surfacing to threaten them. How else could she threaten them? What would it take for her to retreat? The good news was that she didn't know that they suspected where she was. If that came out, they'd never find her. In the meantime, they would have to lurk under the radar. No mistakes.

The phone rang, jolting her out of her evocative reverie. The caller ID showed Trina calling from Nebraska. Tess answered the phone.

"Trina, what's up?"

"Hi, Aunt Tess. I just spoke to my dad in Iowa and he sounds so weak. I just need to talk to someone other than my mom about it. You don't mind, do you?"

"Of course not, it gives me a reason to take a break from my writing."

"I've always wanted to ask you something. How does that work? Do you know the ending at the beginning? Do you map it out? Work from an outline?"

"Well, every writer is different. I usually start with an idea and follow my instincts. It's more fun to be surprised. When it's no longer fun, I'll stop. As my father used to say, *Work isn't work unless you'd rather be doing something else*."

"I love that. Do you have to edit a lot when you're finished?"

"Oh yes. I'm not a Mozart, you know."

Trina laughed. "I needed that, something lighter to fill my mind. I'm so scared for my parents, Aunt Tess. Dad's prognosis is poor and my mom is so reliant on him. It really terrifies me. I don't know what she's going to do without him."

"She'll survive, Trina. Time will heal and she'll find her way. From what you've told me about her, she's a special woman," said Tess using her most reassuring voice.

"Yes, she is. Just not particularly self-sufficient, or perhaps I mean, worldly, street smart. She's never lived alone. She went from her parents' house to marrying my father."

"I bet she'll surprise you. She probably has a reservoir of untapped strength and courage. I wish you were here, Trina. I can smell my pot of potato-cheese soup with thick chucks of red potatoes and onions in a creamy broth."

"I'm coming right over." Trina laughed. "Go back to your writing. It's so good to hear your voice, Aunt Tess. I'm trying not to think about *her*, but just to let you know, I've asked a friend of mine to find us some help in the Vancouver area, in case Vinnie can stealthily come up with a lead for us. But I promised my husband that we'll have a Christmas season without talking about this. I hope you can do the same."

"Thanks, sweetie. I'll keep your parents in my prayers and no more discussions about *her*, until Christmas is over, I promise. Bye for now."

Tess went back to her computer. The snow had stopped falling, leaving a blanket of untainted white that sparkled under the street lights. *It must be 5:30 or 6 o'clock*, she thought to herself. Evenings came early this time of year, and she hadn't adjusted to the premature darkness that would continue through December before rounding the corner and starting the annual journey toward light-suffused summer skies.

She stood, stretched, and exercised her keyboard fingers to ward off the feared carpel tunnel syndrome that haunted so many writers. In the kitchen, she dished herself a bowl of her bragged-about potato soup, and walked into the dining room.

As she was taking her second bite of creamy, chivy potato, and staring out the window, she noticed fresh footprints on the sidewalk leading to her front door. She'd been home all day and hadn't heard the Federal Express man ring her doorbell, so rather than suffer from curiosity, she put her spoon down, walked to the front door, and opened it.

There was a box with her name on it, just "Tess," with no address, and no return address. Obviously, hand-delivered. The stiff fingers of cold air pricked her face as she leaned over to pick it up. She brought it in the house and tore off the brown wrapping. On the front of the box was a picture of an angel. Inside she discovered an angel statue, similar to the one "Cristin" had given her in 1995. Around her neck hung an inscribed medallion which read, "I am Sofia … I'm watching over you" … but the word 'over' was crossed out, as if a mistake, so it read, "I am Sofia … I'm watching you."

Tess felt a chill, similar to a daunting reaction she'd had to a *Twilight Zone* episode when she was a child. Her ears began ringing. The realization that "Cristin" had defiled her doorstep that day, while Tess was safe inside her own home, was terrorizing. An iron claw had reached from outside her front door inside her chest and threatened to rip out her heart. She was frightened to her core at the prospect of ever standing face-to-face with this stalker and instantaneously withdrew from the family coalition.

She walked to the phone to call her sisters and recognized what it took to break the promise she had moments before made to Trina.

****

Tia wasn't home to answer the call because she and Dom were finishing a two-week trip from Massachusetts to D.C. before he headed back to Italy. Long distance romances were tough. Tia was in love, but geography was a formidable adversary. So she didn't talk about it.

"What was your favorite place, so far?" Tia asked him one night while visiting his first sushi bar.

"That's not a fair question. I've had many favorites," he said as he rubbed his hands together as if to warm them.

"Humor me," she goaded him.

"Okay. I loved Cape Cod, eating lobster. New York City was unbelievable. I've seen pictures but could never have imagined standing on the sidewalk and looking up to nothing but skyscrapers. The hotdogs from the street vendors were excellent but my pizza is better than New York pizza. And seeing the Statue of Liberty, then the Liberty Bell in Philadelphia, and having a Philly cheese steak sandwich. So American."

"Do you rate cities by food?" Tia chuckled.

"No, of course not. Well, maybe." He smiled his adorable smile. "But when am I going to taste American apple pie?" he asked, squinting his eyes as to throw out a challenge.

"Tomorrow. We'll be back in D.C. I know the perfect place near my home."

"You know I have imagined what your home looks like … a little picket fence with flowers in the window boxes and big area rugs over wood floors."

"You've got the wood floors right but it's not at all like homes in Italy. It's on the fifth floor of a condominium development."

"Who owns the other rooms?" he inquired.

She took a sip of her miso soup, then looked up and admitted, "I don't know."

"You don't know the other people in your building? How is that possible?" he persisted.

"We're busy. We don't pay attention to each other. We come and go as we please."

"So you don't know your neighbors?"

"Not one."

"America is a very strange place," he said as he leaned back in the booth and crossed his arms.

"Yes, it is," Tia acquiesced. "But you'll love D.C. There's so much to do. I'll take you to a place across the street tomorrow night where you can try some Virginia wine, have a slice of apple pie, and paint a picture."

"I'm not a painter, Tia. I appreciate, but paint, I don't do. Did I say that right?"

Tia smiled, moved closer to him in the booth and kissed him. She thought to herself, *what am I going to do without this man?* But she'd think about that later.

The next evening after Dom had seen and been amazed by her home inside someone else's building, they walked to Arte e Vino. Sarah was there to greet them, offer them wine, and get them started with their paintings.

"This is going to be bad," Dom said as he grimaced while pulling his fingers through his thick mane of dark Italian hair.

"No one's judging. No one's watching for that matter. Just have fun with it," Sarah responded. She demonstrated by mixing paints on her palette and suggested brushing lines of colors on a practice paper before tackling the canvas. Her encouraging approach to the new experience seemed to ease his reticence, and Tia rather enjoyed seeing her boyfriend who was always so self-assured, unsure of himself.

"So did you two meet in Italy when you were there last spring, Tia?" Sarah asked.

"We sure did. And his brother has helped us with the investigation I told you about."

"How's it going?" Sarah inquired while cleaning some brushes with a foul-smelling astringent.

"Slowly, but we're determined to resolve it, as long as the money holds out." Tia took a sip of her pinot grigio and looked at Dom for support. He smiled.

"Well, I probably shouldn't bring this up but my husband did hear back from that banker your sister talked to in Lucerne. Apparently the banker put her in touch with a Swiss patroness who knew the woman you're investigating, and the patroness wants nothing to do with it. She was spooked by the fact that your target, so to speak, disappeared after she found out that you were looking for her. The patroness will not be your ally. She refuses to cooperate any further."

"Well, that answers one of our unanswered questions. We wondered how Sofia knew we were on her trail. She must have spoken to the patroness."

"I hope I haven't spoken out of line," Sarah said.

"No. It only confirms what we believed to be true. Thank you."

After their paintings were finished, they decided to leave them there overnight and Tia would pick them up the following day. She drove Dom to Dulles the next afternoon, promising him as a romantic notion, that she'd hang their paintings side by side in her home until he returned.

That evening she listened to her voice mail and discovered Tess's distressed message, but was so miserable about having said goodbye to Dom, she postponed a return call. She knew she'd miss him but hadn't felt as romantically heartbroken since Jimmy Bethesda dumped her for Rosie Mantua in the eleventh grade. Paralyzed from sadness, she just wanted to be alone, with no family drama.

The next day, she figured that hanging the paintings might be a partial antidote for her aching heart so she walked to Arte e Vino to retrieve them.

Sarah was tutoring a girls-day-out group when Tia caught her eye. Sarah excused herself, gave Tia the high sign, and disappeared into the back room. She returned with two brown-wrapped, canvas-sized packages and handed them to Tia.

"There are actually three, not two, but I wrapped yours and your boyfriend's masterpieces in one package. The other is a gift."

"Sarah, that's so sweet. You shouldn't have." Tia momentarily felt touched by a random act of kindness.

"Sorry, it's not from me. There was another lady who came in last night. She sat back in the corner, over there." She pointed to a station hidden behind a column. "She thought the two of you were such a cute couple, she sketched you and asked that I give it to you when you returned to collect yours. Unusual but generous. She had one condition however. She insisted on wrapping it herself so I didn't see it. She was a beautiful woman. Striking, actually."

"Describe her to me, please," Tia requested, not only with words, but with intense, pleading eyes.

"Sure. She had long, thick dark hair and beautiful eyes, although I couldn't tell you what color. Her face was perfectly proportioned like a Grace Kelly or a Jaclyn Smith. I know that sounds weird but what can I say, I'm an artist. I notice those things. Anyway she was about 5 ft. 9, slender, late twenties … she was gorgeous."

"Did she tell you her name? How did she pay?"

"No, she wanted to remain anonymous and she paid cash. Why?"

"I don't even want to tell you what I'm thinking. I need to go, Sarah. Thanks for everything."

"Aren't you curious to open it?" Sarah asked, peering over her blue-rimmed glasses.

"In private, Sarah. I need to open it in private." She waved her hand to say goodbye and brusquely walked across the street to find sanctuary behind the closed doors of her private space as quickly as she could.

She could tell by the weight of the packages which one was "the gift." Her heart hammered against the walls of her chest, and her hands trembled as she ripped the brown paper away from the canvas. Just as she'd suspected, there were two Munchian-type horror figures, elongated faces with open mouths embracing one another but looking directly at the viewer.

Tia let out a yell that filled her home, while the floor beneath seemed to swallow her as if she were falling into a deep, hollow well.

The woman they'd known as Cristin had followed her and Dom into Arte e Vino and watched them from twenty feet away that evening. And then had the daring to let Tia know that she'd been there.

The message was loud and clear. In a month's time, the predator had violated their private lives in Boston, in Minnesota, and now, had metastasized in D.C. The last thought that entered Tia's mind that night, like a benediction, was *thank God the bitch didn't know about Trina.*

CHAPTER TWENTY-EIGHT

How doth the little crocodile
Improve [her] shining tail
And pour the waters of the Nile
On every golden scale.
How cheerfully (she) seems to grin
How neatly spreads (her) claws,
And welcomes little fishes in,
With gently smiling jaws"
—Lewis Carroll

For two months following her visits to the lower forty-eight, Maddie Thomas heard nothing inflammatory or startling. Her hostile appearance in the cities of the American sisters seemed to have worked. Nico had given strict orders to Lucia and Jonas that no one was to be admitted to the estate without his permission. There were no rumors that Vinnie Vingiano was chasing his instincts and no reason to believe that anyone but Nico knew she was in Vancouver. So she relaxed, satisfied that she was safe for the time being, and ready to put into motion the last pieces of her plan.

February in Vancouver was colder than any month she'd thus far experienced in Canada but she'd been told that it was temperate for a Canadian winter. Winnipeg, Manitoba, was the icebox of civilization, so she didn't complain about her west coast existence. She established habits that gave her comfort but were not unusual, like visiting her corner coffee shop every morning to start her day. Living so close to Seattle where coffee in North America had been put on the map, she was exposed to varieties and combinations she'd never dreamed of, and it became one of her daily pleasures. A vanilla latté with a shake of nutmeg and a cinnamon stick was her favorite despite the objection of Delores behind the counter, claiming that the sweetness covered up the true flavor of the coffee bean. But what did Delores know?

Every morning at the coffee shop, Maddie read the paper while inconspicuously feeding her disdain for the mediocrity of humanity, reinforcing both her self-reliance and isolation. The news articles were generally uninteresting except for the stories of missing people, FBI searches, or unsolved murders. The Canadians were preoccupied with hockey which she'd learned from the stranger in Nova Scotia, so that was no surprise. He'd said that Vancouverites were friendly and he was not mistaken. But their natures were neither her concern nor her interest. She wasn't looking for her new best friend.

She opened an envelope she'd picked up at a local travel agency and spread the pamphlets on the table. She would move to a tropical climate, perhaps an island, before the end of the year. Somewhere warm where it never snowed, somewhere breezy without insects, somewhere remote.

Delores came by with a refill. "Because you're such a valued customer," she said with lilted voice.

Maddie nodded with a faint smile, feeling entitled to the service, but not calling attention to her privilege. The employees of the shop were officious considering the relative unimportance of their jobs and looked plebeian in their Birkenstocks and aprons. Maddie took a sip of her sweet coffee and thought about the California senator she'd met at the art gallery opening the night before, and about what she would pack for her trip to meet Nico in Toronto. Thank God her trysts with the Italian were coming to a close.

A week late, Maddie checked into the Four Seasons Hotel in the Yorkville business district of Toronto an hour before Nico was expected. Her view of the CN Tower dominated the skyline, and the ground below was covered with snow and bustling with activity like a

Christmas movie set. She unpacked, then paged through some city literature while waiting for Nico to bring her good news.

The hotspot in frigid Ontario that month was Ottawa's Winterlude, a tribute to outdoor activities in the dead of winter ... a snow playground, a snow maze, snow sculptures, ice carvings, and a triathlon of running, skiing, and skating. The showpiece of the event was the five-mile-long Rideau Canal, groomed for skating. She remembered the story her mother had read to her as a child about Hans Brinker and his silver skates. She remembered the almost frozen pond on their farm where a few years earlier, she'd stood by and watched the neighbor's dog drown.

In every magazine, there were photos of the famed Niagara Falls, the century-old honeymoon destination that she saw as a prank on the public, like Hallmark greeting cards or cholesterol medication.

She was bored. He was late. She swept her hair into a French roll, anchored it with a gold clip, and dressed in a black pencil skirt, a transparent white blouse with a lacy bra, and four-inch Jimmy Choo's. She sashayed into the hotel's Avenue Bar and Lounge, and sat at the bar for a drink. She crossed her long, lean legs, aware of the slit on the side of her skirt, and asked the bartender to surprise her. The men at the bar ogled as they always did, but no one dared approach her. She had mastered the art of narcissistic aloofness, but relished the attention. She checked her watch and during the following hour, her temper heated up like the Amazonian jungle.

By the time Nico arrived, her mood was foul but her acting ability, matchless. As he approached, she slipped from her stool and kissed him, long and deeply, with an eye on the men at the bar gawking with envy. She then slipped her arm through his and exited her stage.

Their first night was always romantic, passionate, and devoid of talk about business or future plans. This night was different. Nico had news. He had purchased a home on Stromboli, one of the Lipari Islands, north of Sicily. It was a gorgeous estate, but more importantly, remote. According to Nico, they could live their lives in a paradise without interruptions or concern of discovery.

"It sounds perfect, Nico. I don't know what to say," Maddie responded with her most ebullient voice, knowing full well that she would never be there, at least with him.

She started unbuckling his belt.

"It will be ready in two months, darling. Then you can leave the land of snow and ice and be where you belong … with me."

While she removed his shirt, she said, "It's wonderful, Nico. You are so good to me."

As he backed onto the bed, she undid the tiny buttons of her blouse, one by one, slipped off her bra, and unzipped her skirt, watching him watch it drop to the floor, never taking her eyes off of him.

"By the way, before I forget to ask you, Flaviano didn't know where you were going this time, did he?" she asked as she mounted him.

"No, I won't be mentioning my destinations to anyone. Relax."

"You're wonderful. Baby, we do need to figure out how we'll get our hands on my inheritance, a minor detail. I have an idea."

Nico stroked her legs as they faced each other.

"I thought we discussed this," he said without taking his eyes off of her breasts.

"Be patient. We're not going anywhere. How well do you know our family attorney, Nico?"

"Why?" he looked up at her.

"Do you trust him?" she asked.

"With my life. He and Rudolpho went back to boyhood days. He knows everything about our business. He's unimpeachably loyal. He's been the family consigliere for forty years."

"Does he know about us?" she questioned.

"No. No one knows about us."

"Just checking. If we told him, would he keep it a secret? Not the part about us being lovers, of course. But what if he, and only he, knew that your father's wife had been in danger and you have been protecting her whereabouts as a loyal son should. Would he tell the police or would he safeguard your secret under the auspices of allegiance?"

Nico urged her on. "Keep going."

"Well if you trust him, I could fly to Italy under my current passport. No one is watching it. Then he could secretly meet with us, to obtain my signature as Sofia Gherardini, rightful heir to half of your father's estate, and we'd have it all. Let's face it, darling ... it will be years before you can have me proclaimed dead and all that lovely money is just sitting there for us to enjoy."

"I like it. I'm scheduled to sign the settlement papers as soon as I return. We're keeping the mansion in Castiglione, Sofia ... Maddie. I couldn't part with it."

"No problem, Nico. I completely understand. Can we call him tomorrow?"

She leaned over him, holding his arms back and feeling him flex as her large nipples grazed his chest.

"I guess so. First thing in the morning so we catch him before he leaves work. Now come here and give Nico what Nico wants." He pulled her down to him.

"Oh Nicolai, I missed you, baby," she cooed.

The following morning the call was placed to Santino Scardina. He was shocked to hear that Sofia Gherardini was not missing, but rather, hidden. More importantly, he was willing to meet them at his Firenze office and to keep the inheritance proceedings among the three of them. Nico booked Maddie on the flight subsequent to his so they would not be seen traveling together. Just as a precaution, she bought a blonde wig which she would wear in Italy to circumvent detection. The plan was that she would be in and out of Italy in one day.

Two days before they departed, Nico informed Maddie of Luca's change of circumstance.

"I suppose I should have asked. How is he doing?"

"As you know, he's turned four. Mia and Marco are quite relieved that he is gone as he's a handful. But boys will be boys. Anyway, I enrolled him in that academy in Switzerland. They're the only place that would take a child that young. Of course, I made it worth their while."

"Good."

"And speaking of Luca, he is the beneficiary of both of our settlements and stands to inherit it all someday. Is that what we want to do, truly?"

"Do you have someone else in mind? I don't have anyone but you and Luca," she said.

"Well, I have a couple of cousins who could use the money if something happened to me. I know Luca's my brother but he's a kid."

"I think we should keep it as we initially planned with Rudolpho We keep each other the primary beneficiaries of each other's trusts, then Luca the secondary beneficiary? Let's leave it as is. I'm getting dizzy from this senseless money talk." She deferred to Nico.

"I'm just saying that Luca is your child. I don't even really know him. I think I'd rather give my cousin Mia a shot. This is morbid. We're talking decades from now. You and I will probably have spent the lot by then and there won't be anything left. Now there's a dream worth dreaming. Do you mind if I fuck you instead?"

She walked over to him. She smiled and dropped her lose fitting dress to her ankles. As she bent over, she whispered in his ear, "Lie down. I've been saving a surprise for you and this is the perfect time."

An hour later, Nico sat on the edge of the bed, hiked up his pants, and pulled his thin black shirt over his head. He searched for one of his hand-rolled cigarettes and headed for the balcony. "I'm going to crack the door open but I'm not going out. It's freezing."

Maddie nodded, put on one of his shirts, and rubbed lotion on her legs until he finished his smoke. When he closed the door, she said, "Will you teach me how to roll one of those things?"

"You really want to know? I thought you were kidding when you mentioned it last time," he said as he rolled his sleeves up.

"No, show me. You're the only man I know who rolls his own. I had a neighbor who flew a plane in WWII who rolled his own, but I've never met anyone else who did."

The lesson was quick but thorough.

"I see now why you roll them," she said with a giggle. "It takes so long; you smoke a lot less."

"That's true. You're on to me." He broadly smiled, revealing his adorable dimples.

Maddie thought to herself, *I'm on to you, all right*, and continued her charade.

"Are you ready for your surprise?"

"I thought I just enjoyed it," he said with a grin.

"Nope. It's a big one. Come sit next to me."

He obliged. She took his hands and began.

"Nico, before your father died, I took Luca to the hospital to have a test."

"What? Why? What kind of test?"

"A paternity test."

Nico looked at her quizzically. "I'm sorry. I'm lost. What are you getting at?"

"Nico, your father was not Luca's daddy. You are."

He stared at her.

"Do you hear me? You are Luca's father, Nico. He's our child."

"I don't understand. You said you took precautions. I believed you. Why didn't you tell me before now?"

"I had to make sure you loved me because even though I'm not a good mother, I'm still his mother, and he's all I have in the world. But you do love me, don't you, Nico? You do love me." Maddie's voice quivered as her eyes teared.

Nico held her and kissed her hair, her eyes, her cheeks, her lips.

"You have made me the happiest man in the world, my darling. I love you, I love you, I love you. And Luca is ours? I have a son? I can't believe it." He paused, then said, "But I don't understand, why didn't you tell me before now?"

"I told you. I had to make sure you really loved me."

"How do I know that you really love me?" he asked.

Maddie paused. "You don't."

It was his turn to pause. Then suddenly, he started to laugh and picked her off her feet and twirled her around.

"That's one of the things I love most about you. You make me laugh," he said. That night, Maddie let him hold her for hours, as she cradled his trust, his simplicity, and his credulity, qualities she needed in him for her to succeed. What was another untruth in a web of lies? She did what it took to assure Luca's position in the line of inheritance, so that she would always have access to it. Nico was putty in her hands. His gullibility was a concomitant partner to his neediness for her. And once again, she had won.

Days later, she deplaned in Firenze, detoured to the restroom to put on her blonde wig and dark glasses, and took a taxi to Scardina's office. She loved the Florentine streets and hadn't realized how much she'd missed Italy, its smells, its sounds, and its fashion. It was a Saturday so there was no secretary in the waiting room. Scardina heard the door and walked out to meet her.

"Well, aren't you a sight for sore eyes," he said, as he hugged her. "Please come in. Nico is waiting for you."

The office was dark with navy blue walls and cherrywood furniture, very fitting an attorney. Nico embraced her, kissing her politely on each cheek, as was the custom. He then offered her the seat next to his.

"So as I understand it, we are keeping all of the money in the family. Nico and I are each other's beneficiaries and my son Luca is the beneficiary to both trusts until we change it, which we can do at any time, correct?"

"That is correct. You realize that we have created these trusts so that according to your separate wills, funds can be transferred in and out of your trust accounts with ease, bypassing the court supervision or intervention."

"We're so grateful to you, Santino. And if either Nico or I die prematurely, the survivor would be the guardian over Luca's estate, indefinitely, and may disburse funds as deemed appropriate by the guardian, is that correct?"

"That's correct. Do you have any other questions?" Santino asked in a paternal tone.

"Yes, one more, Santino," she said. "If God forbid, something would happen to both of us, and Luca was a minor, who would be the executor? You?"

"If that's what you wish, of course."

"I do. You are family, Santino. Right, Nico?"

Nico nodded.

"I have taken the liberty of drawing up the documents, to save you time. We can make any adjustments if necessary. Please take time to read them," Santino said as he handed them both respective copies.

After thoroughly reading the documents, both parties signed where directed.

"Then it's settled," she continued. "When will the transfer take place?"

"In about a month, my dear. There are some loose ends that must be put in order. Your sudden reappearance caught me somewhat off guard, as you can imagine. Dare I say that I'm so happy that you are well, Sofia, and I do hope that whatever difficult predicament you find yourself in will pass. I'm sure your friends and the staff at Bellaterra would be thrilled to have you back once again but until that day comes, your secret is safe with me."

"Thank you, Santino. Here is my wiring information. And my cell phone number. You and Nico are the only people who have it and we want to keep it that way. Thank you, Santino. Our family is blessed to have you in our corner."

"Yes, we can't thank you enough," Nico said as he shook Santino's hand.

They left the office separately, but met briefly at the end of the corridor to say goodbye.

"I love you as a blonde. Can we have some fun with your new look when I see you in Montreal next month?" Nico squeezed her hand.

"How about if I'm a redhead for a night?" she whispered.

"I'll take you any way I can," he said.

"I love you, Nico. I have a plane to crash. I mean, catch." She laughed.

"Why did you say that?" Nico asked with obvious alarm.

"It was a slip. I've never felt comfortable flying. Must be nerves," she lied. "Love you, Nico." She kissed him, then disappeared behind the elevator door.

The Florentine interlude had been performed with impeccable technique, without a mistake. She would have her money in weeks; she would have his in months. Then no one would ever hear of her again.

CHAPTER TWENTY-NINE

Oh what a tangled web we weave
when first we practice to deceive.
—Sir Walter Scott

Maddie liked it when a plan materialized, when a puzzle fit together. She always held in her closed hand the missing pieces that no one else could yet see. Timing was everything. In a matter of a few weeks, she would evaporate, as a crassly wealthy woman, without a trace. The Monson women, the trio from hell—Tess, Katie, and Tia— had been an unexpected deterrent from her original plan; but Maddie, being a master of improvisation, had escaped their detection, and proved once again that she was smarter than they, even as a combined force. A true victory. But brewing beneath her sense of satisfaction was a seething anger. They had prematurely uprooted her from Italy. Despite her evading them, they'd chased her from her home. When she allowed herself to think about it, she felt unbridled fury. Now she was a fugitive, who if discovered, would lose her freedom, her fortune, and her future,

Her mind switched gears. The next step was to meet Nico in Montreal to celebrate the successful disbursement of the "missing person fund." Meanwhile, she would virtually decorate their Stromboli estate so when the time came for them to be together, it would be designed, at least in mind. Her enthusiasm, albeit false, fed his security and assured his trust.

Until that time, the only constants in her life were visiting her coffee shop which had become a ritual for starting the day; and tending her indoor garden to dry her plants. The one social enjoyment she allowed herself was visiting art openings, showings, galleries, or museums. She'd met an American politician who took her to exclusive private parties and didn't want an entanglement or publicity any more than she did. He was married and she didn't want to be married. He might come in handy someday. She was willing to meet him privately in small, controlled settings, so she surmised that she held a mystique unlike any woman he'd ever met. She chalked his attention up to his having an infatuation with someone he could never have which made her grippingly appealing. Nico didn't know, of course, but he was on the other side of the world. No harm done.

When she met Nico in Montreal, he whisked her away through charming townships to Quebec City where they stayed at the Fairmont Le Château Frontenac. He booked an odd-numbered room for a view of the St. Lawrence River. She felt like she was back in France; in a flash of a moment, she even missed her former husband, Shep. But only for an instant. After they settled in their room, Nico poured the Taittinger 1998 and handed her a Baccarat glass from a set of two he'd purchased in France, transported in a velvet box, and stored deep in his suitcase.

He first toasted their happiness, then continued. "As you know by now, the funds have been released from my father's estate to mine, and your funds have been wired into your account in the Caymans."

"I didn't know. Santino was supposed to call me on my cell," she said with intentional irritation.

"I decided it would be more celebratory to hear it directly from me, darling."

"It is. It is," she concurred, relieved to hear that it was handled.

"At what number did we settle?" she asked.

"In the neighborhood of 600 million euros to your account."

"That's a very respectable neighborhood." She smiled, acknowledging that it was even more than she had expected. "Whatever will we do with over a billion euros?"

"We'll bathe in champagne and dress you in diamonds, I suppose. Keep in mind, these are just the liquid assets. There is more to come."

"Nico, I apologize for the mess we've had to go through in order to be together. I know it's not what we wanted but we did what was necessary. Thank you for not pressuring me to talk about my past life. It's in the past, it's over. And although we've taken some detours, we're together."

He put down his glass and asked, "Do you mind if I smoke?" while he took out a cigarette he'd rolled earlier. "I only roll one at a time, you know, so they are fresh; but I try to roll a spare in advance for times like this."

She smiled and permissively nodded.

"Sofia ... Maddie, come here."

He opened the window overlooking the river and wrapped his arm around her shoulder while he took his first satisfying drag.

"I want you to remember this moment, because the next time we look out at water together, it will be at our home on Stromboli, overlooking the azure blue Tyrrhenian Sea."

She kissed his neck as he smoked, then he extinguished it prematurely, lifted her off her feet, as she kicked off her shoes, and took her to bed for a sexual *pas de deux*.

On the last day of their rendezvous, Maddie showed him her one-way ticket to Sicily, dated two weeks from that weekend. He was thrilled.

"There is something I need to share with you," he stated with a sense of unease.

"That sounds ominous. What?"

"Well, it probably doesn't mean anything but because it happened and it involved you, I do need to tell you. Remember that man who was poking around Bellaterra a few months back? Vingiano? Well, he's been snooping around again."

"And you waited five days to tell me this?" Maddie was outraged.

"I knew you'd be angry and I didn't want it to spoil our time together. Besides, it doesn't matter anymore. It's all over."

She postured, placing her hands on her hips. "What's all over?"

"We've got all the money, you're coming home to Italy, and no one knows where you are. Let's not be melodramatic."

"Tell me what happened."

"Well, you heard from that publisher who printed one of your paintings a couple of years ago. He sent a letter addressed to you at Bellaterra. Lucia gave it to me and I opened it."

"Never mind the fact that it was addressed to me and you shouldn't have opened my private mail. How did that art thief find me?"

"Art thief?" Nico asked, looking puzzled.

"Never mind. What did he say?" She shook her hands, waving off the irrelevant question.

"Apparently, after those American women came looking for you, someone told them about your marriage to my father and the town where he lived, so they wrote back to the publisher, asking that if he ever heard from you again, perhaps using the name Gherardini, to please inform them. Well, Vinnie Vingiano showed up a couple of weeks ago, asking if the publisher had heard from you recently, possibly using either Gherardini or another name."

"What? You've got to be kidding me!" she shrieked.

"And ... he hadn't. So Vingiano didn't get any new information, and you're fine. In the clear."

"Why did he write to me? He didn't even like me. The last time I talked to him, I was furious that he'd printed the painting. It ended badly."

"It must be some kind of artist courtesy. I don't know. Maybe he doesn't like Americans. But he thought that it was odd that on two occasions, people had contacted him asking about your whereabouts. He addressed it to Bellaterra and I intercepted it. He thought you should know that someone else was looking for you."

"He was right about that." She turned her face toward the window so Nico couldn't read how scared she was.

"And there was one more thing. He mentioned in the letter that when those Americans came to see him, the older woman referred to her niece from Nebraska, someone called Trina, who was the one who discovered the reproduction of your painting in the magazine. Does that mean anything to you?"

"Trina? Are you sure he said Trina?" Maddie felt like a supernatural force had grabbed her insides and started shaking her. She heard sloshing in her temples and the sound of Nico's voice became distant and muffled as she watched his lips move but heard no words.

She watched him walk to his briefcase and retrieve a letter.

"You have it with you? Give it to me!" she yelled as she ripped it out of his hand. She quickly read the contents.

She shook her head, grabbed Nico's arm and shouted, "What else do you know?"

"That's it. Maddie, they don't know where you are. They don't know your name."

"I don't believe it any more. I never thought they'd figure out as much as they have. I'm going to Nebraska to put an end to this." She started to pace, knocking over her wine glass on the table, without acknowledging the accident.

"Isn't Nebraska a big state?" he asked ingenuously.

"I'll handle it, Nico."

"Don't blow it now. There's too much at stake," he warned her.

"Shut up, Nico. I said I'll handle it."

Turning his back, he walked toward the bedroom.

"You know, sometimes you can really be a bitch, Sofia," Nico retorted with the emphasis on Sofia. "I'm going to bed. It is our last night for a couple weeks. Are you going to join me?"

"I need to think. I'll be there in a bit."

"Someday I'd love for someone to define what 'a bit' is."

He walked away and slammed the door.

Trina? Cristin Shanihan's sister? Could it be that her distant past had come to haunt her after all? Had Trina contacted her birth mother and discovered the family that Maddie had infiltrated? There were not three but FOUR Monson women?

Trying to keep her wits about her, she suddenly switched gears. She'd been waiting for an opening all day to accomplish what she needed to do. She'd never thought that news of this magnitude would provide her with her opportunity, but it did. She waited until she could hear him snoring, put on surgical gloves, and opened his tobacco pouch. She took a wrapping paper as he had shown her and mixed the correct amount of tobacco with bee pollen and grains of dried plants from her garden for insurance, rolled the mixture, and licked the paper to seal it. She then closed up the pouch and put it back in his briefcase where she'd found it. She placed the deadly cigarette in an envelope, sealed it, and wrote on the front, *Baby, This may be the first and last time I ever roll for you. Thinking of you, my love. S & M.* She then placed it in the side pocket of his briefcase next to his small framed picture of the two of them, so she knew he'd find it, but only after he'd returned to Italy.

Then back to the problem at hand. She'd had no problem tracking Katie and Tess in their respective cities. Tia had been tougher to find, but when Maddie signed the guest book at the church under a former, assumed name, she made note of the address Tia had written, and discovered she was in D.C. But never dreaming that Trina Shanihan was involved, she hadn't looked for her name in the register.

Now she'd formulated what needed to be done. Nico was taking his final trip to Italy, and Maddie was going to Nebraska.

CHAPTER THIRTY

Along came a spider
And sat down beside her,
And frightened Miss Muffet away.
—Anonymous

On the first of April, Trina received a message from Katie. Tess had been hospitalized after a car accident only a mile from her home. She'd been driving down a hill when her brakes failed. No other cars were involved but in trying to avoid oncoming traffic, she slammed into a tree, resulting in a broken right leg and fractured pelvis. Apparently, she'd done the right thing by swerving away from oncoming traffic; she instinctively pulled to the right, missed a cement barrier, but hit the tree. Questions regarding the failing brakes had surfaced.

"What are you implying, Katie?" Trina asked.

"You know what I'm saying. Tess and Ren are responsible car owners. Why in the world would they have breaks fail on their Mercedes? It's too bizarre to believe it was their negligence."

"So you're saying someone may have tampered with the brakes?"

"It isn't outside the realm of possibility, is it?"

"You're saying that *she* tried to kill Tess?" Trina's voice had grown louder in only a few words.

"I can't prove it, Trina. But this is so random and improbable, once again. We need to let go of our investigation."

"Katie, why would she try to hurt Tess at this point? We've virtually come to standstill. Vinnie can't do anything until she surfaces there. She doesn't know that we suspect she may be in Vancouver. Christ, we don't even know her name! I don't understand why something terrible has to happen for the police to be involved." Trina sounded on the verge of hysteria.

"Trina, take a deep breath, sweetheart. This is a horrible situation to be in. None of us wants to let go, but now if we don't, someone may be hurt, or worse."

"This is what Bryan has been saying for months." Trina cracked her knuckles, a nervous habit from her teenage years, hard to break.

"I think he's right, honey."

"Katie, there is one loophole in her information about us. She doesn't know I'm involved. I could continue somehow, but frankly, I don't know what to do next."

"Well, we can talk about that later. First, I think your Aunt Tess would appreciate a call from you. I don't have the number handy but she's at Abbott-Northwestern Hospital. And it's fair to say that Tia, Tess, and I are pulling out of this investigation. We're scared."

"I understand, Katie. I can't blame you. Thank you for the call. Talk to you soon. Bye."

After she hung up, she placed a call to Tess Monson Parker at Abbot–Northwestern Hospital in Minneapolis. Ren picked up the phone.

"Hello, I'm calling for Tess Parker. This is Trina McClaren."

"Hi, Trina. This is Ren. I met you at the wedding." He sounded reticent.

"Oh yes, Ren. I just received a call from Katie. I'm shocked to hear about the accident. How is she doing?"

"She's resting now, Trina. I'll tell her you called. And Trina, she doesn't want to hear anything about this witch-hunt. She's out of the club, understand?"

"Yes, I do, Ren. I'm so sorry. Goodbye."

Trina hung up the phone and her mind wandered into wonder. She wondered if Hunter Cross had actually tampered with the brakes. She wondered if the accident was unrelated and they had all become sickly paranoid about their lives. She wondered if they left the monster alone, if she would disappear, and their lives could return to normal. She wondered if she would lose her newfound family if someone else's life was compromised. She wondered where the justice was. But most of all, she wondered if she could let it go.

As the self-appointed liaison from the family, she emailed Vinnie to get his read on the accident. That evening he called her.

"Hi, Trina. I've been in touch with your mother and aunts. They are clearly intimidated by their close encounters with this vicious woman so I guess at this point, I'll be talking to you."

"Yep, they're really scared, Vinnie. I am too but the difference is, she doesn't know about me."

"Trina, as I understand it, she's gone out of her way by visiting each of their cities and coming within feet of each one of them without their knowing it. She had the audacity to sign your cousin's wedding guestbook as Cristin Shanihan. Her message is clear. She doesn't want to be found and threatens your safety if she feels you're still hunting her. The problem is that she knows where they all live and has been watching them, giving her the upper hand. And after all of our digging, to say nothing of the expense, we can't watch her because she's managed to remain invisible, undetectable. She's a piece of work."

"Did you hear the latest about Tess's accident?" Tia asked.

"I did. Actually through my brother Dominic. You met him in Boston at the wedding. How is she doing?"

"She'll hopefully recover but she faces extensive physical therapy. Katie and my aunts think that *she* may have fixed the brakes on Tess's car. What do you think?"

"I doubt it. Tia said that Tess always keeps her car in the garage, and tampering with brakes in a public place would draw attention. I seriously doubt it. People tend to become paranoid when they think someone may be out to get them. It was probably a simple malfunction."

"That might have killed her. Vinnie, have you learned anything I don't know?"

"I visited the banker who was Tess's first contact in Lucerne, and he was tight-lipped about the patroness who knew her … Klara Zutter?

Then I took a trip to meet the publisher in Lausanne in hopes that he'd heard from her, perhaps using another alias. Regarding Nico, his chauffeur who is my contact, isn't privy to his destinations anymore, and the few times I've been able to track him, he's gone to several different cities in Canada. I don't have Canadian provincial contacts who could physically track him, and I don't have the funds to follow him myself."

"Good point. Listen, Vinnie, if you ever have to reach me immediately, try my new cell phone number. I'll keep it on me all the time, okay?"

She shared her number, talked for a few more minutes, then said goodbye. After the phone call, she was left with the feeling that their target had successfully eluded them, and perhaps had won. Vinnie had parenthetically suggested that he be released from their employment because they had no further leads and he had other business he'd neglected. They had all become obsessed with a phantom, an idea, which left clues, but no body.

Later that night, Bryan showed her the features of her new cell phone. She would never have believed once upon a time that her first entry into her cell phone address book would be a private investigator from Italy. Bryan bought her the phone because of one breakthrough, stellar feature. You could take photos with your phone. He was certain she'd be thrilled by the new technology that would allow her to take photos and send them to other cell phone owners. Perhaps she'd buy one for her mother so she could shoot pictures of Cristin and Elizabeth at ballet class and instantly share them with Dori. There was no one on the planet whom Dori loved more than her two granddaughters.

The following day, Trina contacted a private investigator, a Scott Holgate in Vancouver. He returned her call to inform her that because they had nothing to go on, he refused the job. His most compelling reason to decline it, as he had so indelicately put it, was the fact that in examining their evidence, though persuasive, the only crime he could have proven and arrest he could have legally facilitated, if he did find her, would be on the grounds of identity theft. But the statute of limitations had run out on that charge. No news there. They were facing a dead end.

****

Daniel died on a Friday. Trina received the call at 4 a.m. and was in the car an hour later. She suggested to her mother that she pull the girls out of school, or that Bryan and the girls drive to the funeral once the arrangements had been finalized. But Dori was insistent that the service be simple, and she'd visit the family in Nebraska when she felt stronger. Trina was all she'd need. Trina acquiesced to her mother's wishes. This time, Dori was the boss.

The plan at home was simple as well. Bryan would postpone some of his appointments, and Trina's friend Annette Evans from across the street would pick up and deliver the children to and from school. It would work because there wasn't an option for it not to work.

It was practically a straight line from Lincoln to Muscatine if she took Interstate 80. It would take her eight hours so she could be there by 1 p.m. It was cheaper than flying at the last minute, and she probably wouldn't arrive any earlier. Besides which, she needed time by herself to think about what she'd say in her eulogy. As she looked at Iowa on the map, she saw a hundred little boxes, counties to be exact, most of them the same size and stacked uniformly like wooden alphabet blocks.

The snow had melted across the state. The air was cold but the ground was warming, preparing itself for the planting that was soon to come. Trina had been so emotionally consumed with her family and the saga of Hunter Cross, she hadn't called her dad as often as she had wished, and guilt hung over her spirit like the sword of Damocles. By the time she arrived in Muscatine, she was ready to walk into her childhood home and concentrate only on her mother's well-being and her father's memory.

Dori looked like she'd aged ten years since Trina had last seen her. Her hair was grayer, her wrinkles more pronounced, and even her voice was weaker. She'd lost the love of her life, and when Trina walked in, she broke down and sobbed. Over the next few days, Trina notified everyone who needed to be informed, including her Aunt Kathryn from Australia whom she'd met only once when she was eight. Their family was small but Dori's church community was sure to show up in force for the funeral service.

Since Daniel's daughter's death, he hadn't attended church regularly, and when he had, it was in loving deference to his wife, nothing more. So knowing that her father wasn't openly religious, Trina chose two scriptures that she knew he would approve: Philippians 4:8 and Psalms 51:10. Everyone who knew him would also approve. He had once shared with her that it bothered him when ministers made religious references that the deceased didn't believe. At his funeral, there was to be no preaching or proselytizing.

By the time the day came, they were both ready for it to pass. The flowers were assortments of spring lilies, and the church, as expected, was packed. Trina made it through the deliverance of the eulogy without crying, her voice cracking only twice. But she broke down, as did nearly everyone, when the church tenor sang "Danny Boy." The day was long, but as every day comes to an end, so did this one. Trina and her mother had stood through the interment, had greeted the mourners at the church reception, and had fallen asleep an hour after returning home.

They slept late the following morning, but Trina awakened first to make breakfast for her mother, as Dori had so often done for her. The tables were now turned. She would need to care for her mother as if she were the mother. She would insist that Dori come home to Nebraska for a while so she could watch over her and feel comfortable that she was not too depressed to be on her own.

When Dori rose, they reviewed the events of the previous day, how beautifully it had gone, the kindness of specific people, and they both expressed gratitude that the day was over. They agreed that there was nothing worse than waiting for something inevitable to happen.

"You know, I asked your father how he felt about knowing that his death was around the bend, looming. He said he would have much preferred not knowing. I mean, we all know we have a finite amount of time, and we should live like we'll die tomorrow. Who said that?" asked Dori, her swollen eyes almost pleading with Trina to come up with the answer to the big question.

"Gandhi, Mom. How many times did we hear Dad repeat that quote? 'Live like you'll die tomorrow. Learn like you'll live forever.' "

"Well, his prognosis hung over him like a storm cloud. He knew that the storm wouldn't pass, and he would die in it. But I know he was at peace about making sure his affairs were in order. We did have time to talk and say our goodbyes. All I can say is that I suppose it's better for us that we knew what lay ahead because we could say goodbye and tell him how much we loved him. But it wasn't easier for him. I guess you can make a case for knowing or not knowing ahead of time. I just want to slip off in my sleep but that probably wouldn't be better for you, Trina."

"Oh, Mama, I can't talk about that now. I'm so sorry I wasn't here more often to help you," Trina said, reaching across the table to grasp her mother's hand.

"No dear, we both know that you must be with your young family. I just wish you weren't so far away."

"It's only eight hours by car, Mom. That's not too far. What if I lived in Maine or Arizona or Canada?

"I'm not complaining, dear. I just miss you." She suddenly raised her right index finger, and paused thoughtfully, looking up, as if trying to recollect a dream from the night before. "That reminds me. The day before your father died, a young lady called here looking for you. She said she was on the high school reunion committee and needed your address in Nebraska to send you an invitation. If I'd known that Daniel would die the next day, I would have asked her to send it here."

"Did she say her name?"

"No, I don't think she introduced herself. If she did, I didn't recognize it. You had a large class, dear."

Suddenly with her elbows on the table, Trina's face fell into her hands as she thought.

"Did you give her my address, Mom?" she said in a muffled voice.

"Well of course, dear. I wouldn't want you to miss your high school reunion."

"Mom, my high school reunion was last year. I didn't go."

"Well, why then did she want your address?"

Trina looked up as her hands slid down her face, still covering her mouth, and stared at Dori.

"What if it was *her*, Mom? She'd know where I live."

Dori burst into tears. Trina held her mother, rocking her back and forth, just like Dori had held her as a child.

Trina whispered, "Mom, it's going be all right. I promise." A few moments later, she added, "I think I'm a little paranoid these days. It was probably a legitimate call about a reunion photo book they wanted to send me or something like that. It was probably an innocent phone call. I'm sorry I upset you."

Trina looked at her mother's bloodshot eyes and felt ashamed that she'd jumped to a conclusion. Dori was the dearest, kindest, most loving person she'd ever known. She vowed never to hurt her again. Then she prayed that her gut reaction was misguided.

That night after Dori was asleep. Trina checked her new cell phone. There was a message from Bryan and one text message. Almost too weary to address them, she called her husband just to hear his voice.

"Hi there," she said. "I love my cell phone, baby. Thank you so much. My days here are so exhausting, I just want to listen to you talk about the girls and you. Ready, begin." She muffled her laugh to not waken her mother.

"I'm glad you called. All is well. The girls are fine. Annette is a good neighbor, a good friend. The girls adore her, so really, it couldn't be going better. She even brought over a hamburger casserole for our dinner tonight. We miss you though."

"I miss you too. All of you."

"How is your mom?"

"Struggling, but relieved. Like me." Trina removed her watch and set it on the bed stand.

"Now that the funeral's behind you, when are you coming home?" he asked, sounding eager, but appropriately compassionate.

"Oh, in a few days. I just need to be with Mom a little longer, Bryan. That's okay with you?"

"Of course. Oh, by the way, you received a mysterious note this afternoon."

"No doubt from an admirer," she joked.

"To the contrary ... it's from a woman. When Annette picked up the girls from school, the school secretary handed her a letter with your name on it. She said it was delivered personally by a stunning woman with dark hair and who 'wore' a Prada purse, whatever that means. Anyway, the reason she bothered to describe the woman is that she could tell she wasn't from around here. She said she looked like she stepped out of a Gucci ad. She wore expensive Dolce & Gabbana sunglasses and it was a typical cloudy April morning, no need for sunglasses ... and once again, I had to write this down, as I don't know what this means, but she was wearing Ferragamo heels. Now either this was suspicious or our secretary has an over-stimulated fetish for fashion."

"Bryan, what does the letter say?"

"It was addressed to you so I didn't open it."

"Open it!" Trina screamed.

She could hear her husband rip the envelope open.

"It says, 'Your girls are beautiful. H.' "

Trina's wail woke up her mother. Dori appeared at the bedroom door in time to hear Trina say, "Bryan, Hunter Cross was at our children's school today. Oh, my God. I'm driving home tonight. This search is over. We're done. She has won and I never want to hear her name again!"

She hung up after promising to leave early in the morning. She knew she wouldn't sleep but asked that her mother stay with her that night, in her room, just like when she was a little girl. Dori's role changed dramatically in a matter of minutes. Instead of the weak, older woman Trina had put to bed minutes before, Dori now acted strong, protective, and resolute. They talked for a while, then rolled over to try to sleep.

Just before they turned out the light, Trina checked her text message. It was from Vinnie and it read, "Nico's dead."

CHAPTER THIRTY-ONE

The way to find a needle in the haystack is to sit down.
—Beryl Markham

Sondra Rampling Mahr had been in the pipeline of Monson women for years and was informed like a sister, through Katie, when there was a development regarding the person they had known as Cristin. She supported her best friend Katie and her family in any way she could but their circumstances didn't consume her emotionally like it did the others. She'd weighed the value versus potential damage of involving herself in others' lives. If she assimilated their lust for revenge, if she allowed their problem to devour her hours with empathetic attention, she could harm herself, or perhaps even her marriage. She couldn't afford that. But she needed to listen and be there for her friend because *she* was inevitably a topic of conversation whenever they spoke.

Sondra walked a tightrope of sanity, learning to be present when speaking to Katie, keeping her eye on her footing, but purging herself of the ordeal when she hung up the phone, having landed at the platform. She felt a bit guilty that she chose not to make it her problem. She loved Katie, but Katie sometimes wore her wrath like a suit of armor. Then again, Katie had lost a son at the hands of *Cristin*. Sondra had not. And therein lay the difference. When stripped to the bone, people were islands, and ultimately had to battle their demons, alone.

Sondra justified her disconnection by believing that no one would choose to take on her problems either, and neither would she want them to. That morning she'd heard that not only had Katie, Tia, and Tess all received phantom visits from the alleged murderer, but now, so had

Trina. They were justifiably spooked enough to bury their investigation. Sondra was relieved. It was horrifying knowing that someone so threatening was still out there, but then again, there were a lot of sickos out there ... just because they weren't obvious, didn't mean they weren't there. Nevertheless, it didn't warrant being paranoid about living one's life.

Joe would be home for dinner at five that night, and she was in the mood to prepare a special dinner for him. He loved meatloaf, twice-baked potatoes, and grilled asparagus with oregano, olive oil, and garlic. That was easy enough so she went to the market to pick up two large baking potatoes and a mixture of ground beef, pork, and veal that her local butcher had prepared specially for her.

It was raining and her new lime green rain boots felt like slippers, soft inside and impervious to water, so she stepped in every puddle she could find, enjoying the sound and sight of each splash while admiring her boots. In the market's produce section, she ran into her friend Krystal Archer, smelling cantaloupes to check their ripeness.

"Krystal, hi!"

"Hi, Sondra. Ray and I were just talking about you guys last night. Joe has to be pretty excited about the Canucks making the playoffs."

"Well, it's the first round, but yes, he's pumped. How are you?"

"I'm fine. Busy. We're going to a party tonight at the Pan Pacific. It's black tie, and apparently, there will be American royalty in attendance."

Sondra prodded. "Sounds intriguing. Who do you think it will be?"

"I don't know but I wish it were British royalty. They're a lot more interesting ... and royal." She laughed as she put the chosen cantaloupe in her shopping cart.

"Call me tomorrow and let me know."

"I'll do better than that. I'll be in your neighborhood tomorrow so I'll stop by in the afternoon and tell you all about it. I want to take a few sneak shots with my new phone but Ray says no."

"You can take pictures with your phone?"

"Just came out, had to have it. You know me. I'm a techie girl." She tossed her head and smiled at her audience of one.

"And a poser," Sondra said as she laughed. "See you tomorrow."

Joe arrived home an hour late. The house smelled of meatloaf, cheese, and garlic.

"You made my favorite," he said, as he shook off his raincoat in the entryway. He grabbed his wife for a hug and kiss, then like a puppy dog, followed his nose to the kitchen where he opened the oven for the full olfactory effect.

"Hmmm. What makes me such a lucky man tonight?"

"I'm just feeling grateful, Joe. I talked to Katie today. Her family's life is so complicated. We don't have the problems other people have. We're truly blessed."

"I agree." He picked up the Vancouver Sun and took off his shoes before sitting in the family room adjacent to the kitchen. "What did Katie have to say?"

"Well, remember after the wedding, I mentioned the other incidents of receiving communication from that *Cristin*? They were terrified. It must be awful to wonder if you're safe or not." She pulled the meatloaf from the oven, placing it on the granite counter to set. "Evidently, somehow, and God only knows how, this stalker bitch found Trina, Katie's other daughter. You met her at the wedding. She visited Trina's daughters' school in person and left a message addressed to Trina. That was too close for comfort. The nerve!"

Joe put down his paper and gave his full attention to his wife.

"What if they've pushed her too far, Joe? What if she hurts one of them ... or those little girls?" She wasn't hiding the fact that she felt frightened.

Joe thought for a moment, then spoke.

"If she were going to harm them, she probably would have by now, Sonni. It sounds as if she's warning them to stop tracking her. Hasn't her past *modus operandi* been to establish new identities for money? These women don't have substantial assets, do they?"

"Not that I know of but they do know she's alive, and they believe she's a murderer," Sondra replied.

"But from what I understand, there's no definitive proof. She may be a psychopath, but do you think she'll make it her life's mission to destroy their lives if their means didn't better serve her end. I don't think so. The bottom line is she doesn't want to be found. She's intimidating them, until they relent. If they leave her alone, she will leave them alone. I think that they need to drop it, forget it, bury it, and get on with their lives."

"For the first time in over a year, I think we're all in agreement. But there is one more interesting piece of news. Are you ready for this one?"

"Born ready," he replied.

"Do you recall that the person we knew as Cristin changed her name to Yvette and then to Sofia? She married a rich guy in Italy? A year after they were married, the husband mysteriously died. You knew that but I don't know if you knew that the private eye over there had reason to believe this Sofia was having an affair with the husband's son, Nico. She and Nico were the two heirs to the fortune. Guess what happened."

"Nico mysteriously died," he said in a cavalier tone.

"Bingo! He died. Suddenly. How did you know?" she asked as she anxiously twisted the silver bracelets on her wrist.

"It's predictable. Young beauty marries older rich guy, knocks him off and inherits half of his fortune. Realizes she wants more. Seduces the other inheritor, handsome dude, right? Knocks him off. So she inherits the whole burrito, right?"

"But she's missing. That's where the theory falls apart. A missing person can't collect. The girls think she killed the son, too. But how could she? She hasn't been seen in Italy for over a year."

"We'll never know. Let's eat." Joe put down his paper and walked to the kitchen table, leaving his wife's unanswerable questions unanswered.

The next afternoon, Krystal popped in on Sondra while she was planting annuals in her front yard. The ground in May was hungry for new friends, after waking up from a long Canadian hibernation.

"Come in. Planting always puts me in a summery mood. I made a pitcher of lime margaritas and fresh guacamole," said Sondra. "How was the party last night?"

"Outstanding. I wish you could have been there."

"Well, tell, tell. Who was the royalty? The Clintons? Caroline Kennedy?"

"No, nothing like that. Just a few congressmen and a senator from California. It was a lot of fanfare and hullabaloo but I didn't care. The party was fabulous ... the best tiger prawns and caviar I've ever eaten."

"Let's sit in the porch. I think it's warm enough," said Sondra, reaching for the pitcher of margaritas and motioning for Krystal to grab the guacamole and chips. "So what else?"

"Well, the dresses were right off the red carpet at the Oscars. The women were beautiful ... I felt very out of place but Ray looked smashing in his tuxedo. But what man doesn't! It's unfair."

"What did you wear?" asked Sondra.

"The only label dress I own ... my Vera Wang ... you know the flowered one?"

"I bet you looked fabulous. Describe the other dresses."

"Okay. Where do I begin? You know, the best part was that it actually was an intimate party so I could see all of them close up." Krystal sipped her margarita, then continued. "There was one woman who really stood out in the crowd. She was dressed in a red, floor length gown. I didn't have the nerve to ask her who made it but it was gorgeous. Ray couldn't keep his eyes off her. I hit him on the arm so often for staring at her, he's probably bruised." She laughed. "Anyway, she was the escort of the senator. I've never seen her before. Probably professional. I know I shouldn't say that, but it happens. Anyway, her name was Maddie, obviously not his wife. Apparently, the senator is married so Ray said to be hush-hush. But who am I going to tell, right? Whatever."

"Who catered? Or was it just a cocktail party?" Sondra asked.

"No, it was a full-scale, sit-down, intimate dinner for forty ... I should have asked for the caterer's card, not that we could afford them." Krystal sighed lightheartedly.

"I didn't know the Pan Pacific had private rooms that large...was it a cordoned-off ballroom or an actual suite?"

"A suite! It was ultra-private, Sondra, first class, thrown by the owner of Metrovan. Nice man, by the way."

"Sounds beautiful. In my dreams," said Sondra.

"Oh, come on, you go to plenty of nice functions."

"Yes, surrounded by jocks, agents, and scouts." She smiled. "Not exactly royalty. Did you take any pictures or was it too intrusive?"

"Well, there was a sign at the entrance that stated: *NO CAMERAS, NO SMOKING*, etc. You know the drill."

"So what did you do?" asked Sondra, hoping that her friend had defied the system.

"You know me. I took pictures. I didn't have a camera but I had my new cell phone. Remember? It has a camera application. They aren't very good. I couldn't very well ask them to say 'cheese,' if you know what I mean. I had to be careful, so I literally shot from my hip."

"Show me."

Sondra moved to the cushion next to Krystal who took her camera from her purse and touched the photo icon.

"Here. Here is the room. Isn't it gorgeous?"

"Wow, all the flowers are red. All of them. It must have cost a fortune."

"You've got that right. Here is a selfie of Ray and me that I took in the hallway because he didn't want me to make a fuss. Here's Mr. Metrovan. Weird angle so you can't see him very well. He's actually quite good looking but I had to be discreet, so none of these are head-on. Here's a picture of my plate piled with food ... that was a tough one to get when Ray's head was turned and everyone else was engaged in conversation. Timing is everything. Oh, and here's one of that woman, Maddie ... even with a bad camera angle, isn't she dazzling?"

Sondra stared at the tiny photo in disbelief. There on Krystal's camera was a woman who looked like "Cristin." It couldn't be...but it was.

"Oh my lord in heaven." Sondra inhaled and held her breath. She stared at the photo without blinking, hearing Krystal talking in the background, but not hearing a word she said. Finally Sondra spoke, interrupting whatever her friend was saying. "Krystal, I need a copy of this picture. Right now. And don't show this to anyone else. Promise?"

Krystal laughed out loud. "I know she's stunning but I wouldn't leave Joe for her," she teased.

"You have no idea how long my friends have been looking for this woman. Her name is Mandy?"

"No, I think it was Maddie, or Mattie. But, Sonni, hush-hush, remember? This senator dude is married. Ray would kill me if he knew I took a picture at that party. It was verboten. It was a very private party."

"I don't care about the senator. I care about the woman. I need to find out her full name and where she lives."

Alarmed, Krystal turned her phone off.

"Listen, Krystal. My best friend and her family have been tracking her for over a year now. They believe she's killed people."

"No shit!" Krystal's mouth dropped open, her lower jaw jutting forward.

"I need that picture. And somehow we need to find out her last name. Could Ray do that for me?" asked Sondra, panicky.

"What am I going to say? I want the name of the woman you were infatuated with at the hotel last night? He'll either think I'm uncharacteristically jealous or I'm gay."

"Okay. First things first. How can I get a copy of the picture? I promise I'll crop out the man. I don't care about the man. Please, Krystal," Sondra begged.

"All right, if you promise to crop everyone but her so you can't even tell where she is, I'll transfer it to your computer. On second thought, I'll crop it to make sure it's permanent, okay? You don't know how to crop photos anyway, right?"

"Please," Sondra said sarcastically.

"I thought so. The box for the phone is in my trunk. I think there's a cord I can use. Just a minute."

Sondra ran to the phone to call Katie who wasn't home. This was not the kind of news she could leave as a message, so she said, "Call me. It's urgent! Urgent!!"

Krystal returned with the magic cord and plugged it into Sondra's computer.

"Aren't you glad I'm a techie girl?" Krystal smiled.

"You have no idea." Sondra hugged her from behind.

She tapped some keys and voilà, there was Maddie's gorgeous face on Sondra's screen, bigger than life.

"Thank you. Thank you. Thank you. How can I ever thank you, my darling friend?"

"Just don't tell Ray I took it, okay?"

"Promise. My friend Katie will want to hug you to death when she meets you. But now, I need to know her last name. Somebody at that party knows her name. Please think of a way to get it. You are a lifesaver, Krystal. You don't even know how big this is."

"Glad I could help. Listen, this has been fun but I do have to go. I'll talk to you later."

The phone rang, Sondra lunged for the receiver, and waved goodbye to her friend, blowing her a kiss of gratitude.

"Don't worry about me. I'll let myself out," Krystal said as she shrugged her shoulders and shook her head.

"Katie, I'm so glad you called. You are never going to guess what just happened."

"Are you all right? It sounded like an emergency."

"I'm more than all right. Go to your computer. I'm sending you an email."

Katie whined, "Why?"

"Just do it! I'm not saying another word until you're in front of your computer."

She could hear Katie walking to her office on the lower floor and turning on her new Mac.

"Okay, I'm sending it now. It will come as an attachment so click on the photo icon on the top line and tell me what you see."

A few seconds passed. Sondra said nothing.

Then from twenty-five hundred miles away in Boston, Massachusetts, Sondra heard the scream.

"Oh my God, it's her!!! You found her? Oh my God."

Sondra could feel Katie's alarm in her rapid breathing. "Where is she? How did you get this? What name is she using?"

"Her name is Maddie, or Mattie. That's really all I know. She showed up at a party my friend attended. Katie, she's in Vancouver."

"She *is* in Vancouver ... just like Vinnie thought," said Katie.

"I know you were all washing your hands of this ordeal but now that there's been a sighting, so to speak, what will you do?"

"I need to talk to my family. I really don't know what they'll say. Just when we'd let go of it all, this happens. I'm in shock."

"All right, you speak to them and call me later. We'd need a last name to track her at this point but at least we know she's here. At least she was last night. But whatever you decide to do, be careful."

"Oh, my stomach. Sondra, I feel like someone just punched me in the gut, like I've just been dropped ten stories on an amusement park ride. I can't catch my breath. I don't know if this is good news or not. I ... I need to make some calls. I'll talk to you later, okay?"

Sondra hung up the phone and stared at the photo. God, she was pretty, even more beautiful than when Sondra had met her ten years ago in Tess's home in Minnesota. How could beauty be so deceiving?

She poured herself a Scotch and waited for Joe to come home. It wasn't often that she would stop and not do anything, no reading, no working, no making dinner, no television. She felt paralyzed to do anything but wait for Joe. It was her sole objective for the remainder of the afternoon. She couldn't concentrate on anything else, anyway. By the time he walked in the door, the sun had set, and she hadn't moved a muscle.

No lights were on in the house and she heard him say, "Honey, I'm home. Sonni, are you here?"

"I'm in here, in the living room."

"What in the world? Why are you sitting in the dark?" he asked, as he turned on a light illuminating his wife wrapped in an afghan in the recliner. "What's going on?"

"Come with me. I need to show you something," she said.

"What's with the cloak and dagger, honey?"

"Just come here and look at this picture, Joe."

He stared at the photo and looked puzzled, as she had expected.

"This is the woman, the monster that Katie has been trying to find for over a year. This is the monster!"

"What is she doing on your computer?" he asked innocently.

"One of my friends took it … she wants to remain unnamed, but that part doesn't matter. This is the right person. She's here in Vancouver, Joe. In our backyard!"

Joe leaned over her shoulder to take a better look.

"Joe, her name is Maddie, or Mattie."

He leaned close to study it with uncharacteristic interest. "Yes, it is."

"What do you mean, yes it is?" she asked in a curious but interrogating tone.

"I've met this person, Sondra. I met her in Halifax, Nova Scotia, having a beer at a café on the boardwalk. I met this woman. She told me she was headed for Vancouver."

Sondra looked at him incredulously. "What was her name?"

"She introduced herself as Madison, Maddie, somebody … it was in passing."

"Did she say her last name, Joe?"

"Yes, I'd probably recognize it. Maybe. It was a man's first name."

"Think, Joe, think. Andrews, Johnson, Charles? Think."

"Okay. Okay. Give me a minute."

"Let's go through the alphabet." Sondra urged him on. "Murray, Roberts, Russell. Stuart, Thomas, Vincent, Wallace …"

Joe suddenly yelled, "Thomas! Maddie Thomas. That was her name!"

CHAPTER THIRTY-TWO

Every year without knowing it I have passed the day
When the last fires will wave to me
And the silence will set out.
—W.S. Merwin

Spring in Vancouver was beautiful because it was so lush and verdant, the greenest city she'd ever seen. And although it had recently rained almost every day, there was nothing as lovely as a clear day in British Columbia. The purity of a deep breath was like wearing an oxygen mask, without the mask. The cherry blossoms had bloomed and the boulevards were dressed in their finest, fullest blossoms.

Maddie hadn't heard from Nico in two weeks which was dramatically atypical, so she figured the plan had worked ... he was dead. She pinned her hopes on it. Her phone rarely rang because only three people had her number. Nico, her attorney Scardina, and the senator. She was reasonably certain that the next time it did ring, it would be Santino Scardina, delivering the news. She'd told the senator she didn't want to see him anymore. Although he'd balked at her new game rules, she'd made it clear that if he persisted, she would go to his wife. That had stopped the pathetic, irritating, late-night calls.

She ritualistically stopped at her coffee shop, where Delores served her regular vanilla latté with nutmeg and a stick of cinnamon. Maddie rarely acknowledged Delores with so much as a glance, but always recognized her man-hands, gnarly with blue veins, which served the coffee. Once upon a time, Delores had tried to engage her in conversation but had learned not to expect a response. While making some notes regarding the logistics of her upcoming move, Maddie's cell phone rang. It was Scardina. She braced herself for a performance worthy of an academy award.

"*Ciao,* Santino."

"*Ciao*, Sofia." Scardina had never been privy to her Canadian name, knowing her only as Sofia.

"Are you calling to confirm the transfer of funds? No, I remember, it happened a couple of weeks ago. Thank you for facilitating the transfer. Nico and I so appreciate your discretion."

"When did you last hear from Nico, Sofia?"

"I don't remember. We don't have reason to talk often. I'm so looking forward to coming back to Italy ... but I'm still not in a position to return to Bellaterra, as you well know."

"When was the last time you spoke to him, Sofia?"

"Well, I think it was a couple weeks ago."

"So you have not heard?"

"From him? No. Why?"

He repeated, "So you have not heard."

"Heard what, Santino? What are driving at?"

"Sofia, Nico Gherardini died ten days ago. The funeral was yesterday."

She paused dramatically, then started to cry with no attempt to stifle her performance.

"No, no, this can't be true. You're lying! Why are you saying this terrible thing? I saw him at your office a month ago. He was fine!"

"I know, I agree."

"What happened, Santino?"

"He apparently had a severe allergic reaction. Since you left the estate, he has cut the servants to a minimum. No servants stay overnight anymore. So he was alone. He must have realized he was in trouble and dialed for an ambulance, but you know how far out of town Bellaterra is. It took them a half hour to get there and by the time they arrived, he was dead."

"Oh my God, Santino. Did they determine what killed him? Was it something he ate?"

"I presume so. All I know is that his windpipe had swollen shut. He suffocated."

"How dreadful for him. And no one was with him? He was alone? Did they do an autopsy?"

"No, they didn't. There was no inquiry. He only had two cousins from the south, no immediate family, and no one requested an autopsy. The cause of death was asphyxiation by allergic reaction. What more is there to discover, you know?"

"I guess so. Santino, I'm in shock. I don't know what to say. Nico was so young, so alive. This is tragic."

"Sofia, I probably should have called earlier. My apologies. I knew you couldn't return but you should have known before this. What prompts this call is we need to chat about Nico's trust. Your son Luca is the primary beneficiary of Signor Gherardini's assets, but you are Luca's guardian, so we need to transfer his inheritance into an account which you will oversee. We need to discuss this, perhaps at a later time. This is what Nico wanted so I must respect his wishes."

"Of course. But not now, Santino. I need time to think, to mourn my late husband's son's death. I can't believe this has happened. What could possibly happen next?" She began to sob.

"Call me when you can, Sofia. Again, my condolences. Goodbye."

She hung up to celebrate. Delores appeared to offer her a refill and comfort.

"I'm so sorry you received bad news. Is there anything I can do for you?" Delores said in her most compassionate voice.

Maddie brushed her away with her left hand, then put both hands on her face to hide her true feelings from the world.

Within a half hour she was home where she could close the doors and celebrate her victory privately. The Gherardini fortune was hers. And she had orchestrated every movement of the opus. However, there was a cadenza to score before the finale.

She could hear the clock ticking in the hallway. She listened and wondered at what second Nico's heart had stopped beating. *Had he realized that it was the cigarette that had killed him? Had he thought of her? Had he realized that the cigarette was the one she'd packed?* She wondered when her heart would stop ticking. Every day, the clock ticked at that time. She just didn't know which second it was, and she didn't want to know in advance. *What a strange feeling it must be to know the second you're dying, especially if you know that it is at the hand of another.*

The clock continued to tick, and she thought not about time, but about timing. She needed to keep a clear head. When would it be appropriate to call Scardina to discuss the trust? When would it be appropriate to bring up the sale of Bellaterra and the home on Stromboli? And how long would it take? Another six months, a year? She remembered her father saying, *Pigs get fat; hogs get slaughtered.* But she didn't care. She wanted it all. Santino had set up the inheritances in separate trusts so money could flow in and out of them with ease and with no court surveillance. Her Cayman Island account was the golden pot to hold her funds, and she'd pour Nico's inheritance from Luca's golden pot into her own, for safekeeping. It was a magnificent visual. Any proceeds from future liquidations would have a home in the Caymans. No one knew about the Cook Island account.

What to do about Luca? Maddie certainly couldn't care for him. But Nico had set up a fund to take care of him until he was out of school, and she'd ask Santino to oversee his financial needs. And if, God forbid, something ever happened to her? Santino had agreed to be the executor of their estates if either she or Nico died prematurely. Well, Nico was dead. She had no intention of leaving the planet before her time. Santino was the only one who knew she was alive, except for the Americans, but they had no idea where she was and what name she had assumed. Santino alone knew how to reach her so it would have to be Santino as her executor and trustee with Luca as the sole beneficiary. She'd probably never know her son but it made no sense to die intestate or will the Gherardini fortune to the government. She'd most likely live for another sixty years anyway so it was most likely a moot point but it was her nature to plan for all conceivable scenarios.

Another issue loomed. Should she leave Vancouver or stay until all of Nico's inheritance was transferred, then make her move to the South Pacific? She'd already settled on the French Polynesian islands, possibly Moorea, or Raiatea, where it was warm and remote, the planet's answer to paradise. She could deal with that another day; it was the least pressing issue. She needed to settle her mind which felt like a hamster wheel, spinning at full speed.

She took out five sheets of paper. She had replayed these directives in her mind a hundred times, and the time had come to write and send them. Four would not be added to Santino's office file, but kept by him somewhere safe other than his office. The fifth letter would be slipped into his office file for legal reasons.

On the first, she authorized Santino Scardina to be the executor and trustee of her estate; and in the meantime, gave him the power of attorney to sell the homes, and asked him to transfer all of Nico's funds into an account for Luca which she would oversee and administer, as previously set forth. Any future liquidated assets would be funneled into her island account. Santino Scardina, Rudolpho's lifelong friend, was her lifeline to the future, her only lifeline. She sealed the instructions in an envelope marked, 'PRIVATE, NON-OFFICE FILE, OPEN UPON RECEIVING.'

In the second letter, she wrote that if she were to die, Luca would have access to her Cayman Island account and any assets that were not already in his name, but in hers. Santino was to direct Luca to a safe deposit box which only Luca would be allowed to open, after he turned eighteen, and only if she had not contacted him herself, and she was confirmed dead. She sealed the instructions and marked them, 'PRIVATE, NON-OFFICE FILE, OPEN UPON RECEIVING.'

On the third page, she made a copy of the inside pages of her passports as Sofia Gherardini and Madison Thomas, proving that they were one and the same, so a death certificate could be issued, opening up the access to her accounts. The only eyes that would ever see these photos would be Santino's. In the event of her death, he would have to prove that the island account under her Italian name in the islands was the property of the deceased Madison Thomas. Once again, marked, 'PRIVATE, NON-OFFICE FILE, OPEN UPON MY DEATH ONLY.'

The fourth directive was to Luca, with the location of the safe deposit box in Vancouver, along with a letter telling him that if he was reading it, she was dead. And although he would never have known his mother, from the grave she would, in great detail, give him a mission in her memory, to be found in a safe deposit box in Vancouver. This letter was left unsealed until the following morning when she would deposit a key in it before sealing the envelope, marked, 'TO LUCA ONLY UPON MY DEATH.'

Lastly, she wrote a letter for the office file, confirming that Santino was the executor of her estate, and an abbreviated message to Luca. She put this in an envelope marked 'OPEN IMMEDATELY-FOR OFFICE FILE.'

At this point, she believed her affairs to be in order. The following morning, Maddie Thomas walked into a bank to have her authorization letter notarized. She then rented a safe deposit box with two keys, dropped one of the keys in the letter for Luca and sealed it, deposited all five directives in a large envelope marked CONFIDENTIAL, and mailed it to Santino Scardina in Firenze, Italy.

****

Meanwhile, the sisters and Trina talked about Sondra's discovery. They had halted their investigation but now that they knew where she was, they needed to think it through again. Trina rehired her private investigator, Scott Holgate, in Vancouver to find out where Maddie Thomas lived. When he did, Trina wanted her followed for a while, until their funds ran out, in hopes that they could tie her to a felony or misdemeanor.

But it didn't take Scott long to find her. He had connections with the ICBC and found her at 1703 Oak Street. So every morning he sat in his car, a block from her home, and followed her to the coffee shop, and sometimes to her hair stylist, a manicurist, and/or her bank. She didn't appear to meet anyone, and her only outing of any consequence was to local galleries where she perused the art by herself. After being paid for reenacting *Groundhog Day* for a couple weeks, he asked to be relieved of his duty.

On a call to Trina, he admitted he was bored. "Either this Maddie Thomas is the dullest person on the planet, or she's waiting for something to happen. I will say one thing for sure … she's a real looker. If I weren't married, I'd go undercover and ask her out. Not that she'd say yes but …"

"You'd be a fool, Mr. Holgate. Stay away from her."

"Please call me Scott."

"All right, Scott," said Trina. "I know I'm ranting but it's just a crying shame that we've come so close and there's nothing we can do. Can we track her passport so we know if she leaves the country? We're all on alert because she's threatened our families."

"Well, have her arrested then."

"She lives in another country, Scott, and we never know when she's here until after the fact. Besides, any of the threats to us wouldn't appear threatening out of context. She delivered two messages, a painting and a Christmas gift … nothing punishable by law. I'm beginning to think there is no justice."

"Now, lassie, you know better than that. This isn't the Middle Ages."

"I know. We're just frustrated. What do you think we should do?"

"To tell you the truth, I'd drop it. You found her. She's no immediate threat to you. She's hasn't been stalking you lately. If I were you, I'd take your own advice, and leave this whole business alone. You're probably right about her past, but the past is the past. She's on to greener pastures."

"She killed my sister and her own parents. She killed my cousin, my aunt's best friend, and probably those two Italian men, Scott, and those are the ones we know about. She's dangerous."

"Then stay out of her way."

"I have half a mind to show up at her front door, and tell her off, just to show her that we did find her, and although we don't have iron-clad proof, we know what she's done."

"Bad idea, Mrs. McClaren. If what you say is true, there could be repercussions. She'll eventually make a mistake. You may not be around to see it, but she'll eventually make a mistake. Karma, you know."

Trina could hear Scott Holgate yawn on the other end of the phone. She bit her lip, hung her head in defeat, then added, "You're right. Thank you, Scott. If you read anything, hear anything, or decide to moonlight on your own, and find out anything about Maddie Thomas, you know who to call."

"You betcha, Mrs. McLaren. It's been a pleasure. I'll email you a written report—her address, her haunts, her habits, etc. It's part of the friendly service. Good luck. Bye."

Hours later, Trina received the file from Scott Holgate, along with the final bill. She sent the report on to her moms, Katie and Dori, and asked Katie to forward it to Tess and Tia. It felt like the end of a long, long road. It wasn't a satisfying destination. Justice had been the dream and sometimes dreams didn't come true.

CHAPTER THIRTY-THREE

If you don't break your ropes when you're alive,
Do you think ghosts will do it after?
—Kabir

Dori reread the latest letter she'd written to Trina, none of which she'd posted. But this time she read it aloud, to hear the words, and anticipate how Trina would receive them.

Dearest Trina,

The death of your father is unlike any loss I've ever endured. I don't know what to say to you, except I never want you to know this feeling. I hope we all live long lives but as much as I want to live to see my darling granddaughters marry and have children, I can't live forever and don't want to outlive you. I never thought I'd outlive your father, Trina. He was the stronger of the two of us. He would have fared better than I. One doesn't think of dying when one is busy living, Trina. It's a harsh and cruel business, dying. I wish I could promise you that you'll not feel this lonely but I can't. Be safe, my darling daughter. I love you.

Mom

Sensing she'd never send this letter either, Dori put it in the drawer on top of the others and sat down in Daniel's wicker chair on the veranda, to think.

During the first days after Daniel's death, waves of grief pounded over her, threatening to drown her; and at other times, lifted her to the surface for a gasp of air. But day after day, she was pulled farther from the shore of her former life, until she could barely see the memory of it. Then someone would hug her, and she'd climb upon the raft of a kind gesture. Another wave would pull her down into the riptide of grief, and she would lose her bearings and will to struggle any longer, until an act of kindness buoyed her up for another breath. This undulation of dying and living went on for weeks.

Life without Daniel was initially so empty that Dori felt un-human. At times she robotically moved from one place to another as if at the mercy of someone else's remote control. Her stilted movements were aimless and random, with no compass to guide her. Her only feelings were relatives of heartbroken sadness—loss, grief, anxiety, depression, anger, futility, and all of their nasty cousins. She knew she'd never feel joy again and the concept of happiness felt long-lost and irretrievable. If she heard one more person say that Daniel was in a better place, or time would heal her heartache, she knew she'd scream.

Daniel was gone, not for the weekend, not on a business trip, but gone for good, forever. She'd never see his face again; his kind, loving face with each wrinkle, earned though years of laughter and pain; his clear, blue, Irish eyes that smiled on her every day of their lives together. She'd never again hear his voice that humored her when she was cranky, that grumbled when his eggs were cold, that lilted when he told her that he loved her. She'd never hear the voice that went away when their daughter died, but returned when time opened a merciful window one morning and lessened the pain of his muteness. She'd never again feel him search for her hand when they walked together, or roll him on his side in bed because he was snoring ... what she wouldn't give to hear him snore once more, and to roll him over, just one more time. If only she had known when these experiences and myriad more had been the last times. There was never a second last.

Now all she had was a litany of firsts to face, the first Thanksgiving without him, the first Christmas without him, his birthday, his death day, the first drive to Lincoln without him, paying the bills, shoveling the sidewalk in the winter, planting the garden in summer … all without him. She was trapped in a vortex of endless firsts to face.

Firsts were not what they were cracked up to be toward the end of one's life, bordering on unbearable at times, like staring at a yellow police tape that warned, "Stay out. You have never been here before and you're not going to like it." But there was no avoiding stepping past the yellow tape into the zone of the unknown. Thank God there were never second firsts in this zone. The paradox was unnerving. At one time she would have died for a chance to relive certain firsts in her life … their wedding, her girls' birthdays as children, the night in the canoe in the middle of McConnell Lake. But not now. She wanted to just make it past the firsts without Danny in hope that the seconds and thirds would be less painful.

The only aspect of her loss that didn't scream of loneliness was the fact that she had joined the billions of souls who had already experienced the loss of a beloved partner. Eventually, day by day, she worked herself out of the hole where there had been no light, no joy, no hope. Eventually, the ladder she discovered and began to climb, one rung at a time, brought her closer to a light she called grandchildren. Eventually she could see the faces of little Cristin and Elizabeth, smiling at her at the opening of the hole, extending their pudgy little hands for her to grasp. And mysteriously, they had the strength to pull her out. "The child is father to the man." The child is mother to the woman. The hope, love, and protection of the children would be her salvation. Day by day, Dori realized that Daniel would not want her to suffer. She felt his presence, urging her to live, to give her heart to their daughter's family.

Two and a half months had passed since Dori had lost her husband. She had not gone to Lincoln as she'd initially planned. After gradually working her way back to the world, she preoccupied herself with her garden during the day, and at night she studied on the Internet. She thought about what Trina had reminded her ... the Gandhi quote that people should live like they'll die tomorrow and learn like they'll live forever. She learned that the technology her computer offered exponentially expanded her knowledge in selected fields of interest. Staying busy was a key. Staying focused was a key. Believing in her fate was a key. A complex key that opened her survival door and gave her life meaning.

She'd received the news of locating the woman she'd known as Hunter Cross, and was relieved that despite the news of the siting, her daughter had the good sense to discontinue her compulsion to bring the woman down. Trina's children's safety would always come first. Trina's job was to care for them and protect them, at the expense of not avenging her sister's death when she'd come so close to doing just that. Dori's job, the reason she'd been left behind, was also to protect her grandchildren so she could guide their innocent hearts and minds. They were the future, the dreamers, the hope of the world. They were the barometer of her aging and the recipients of her guardianship. That weekend, when she made her call to Trina, Dori had made a big decision.

"Hi, Mom. How are you feeling?" Trina asked upon picking up her phone.

"Stronger, honey, much stronger than I thought I could ever feel again. Your father would be proud of me. I have my moments, don't get me wrong. I miss him terribly."

"Of course, you do. And he was always proud of you, Mom. What did you plant in your garden this week?"

"The usual suspects; some exotics; and new plants. I do love growing plants, always have. By the way, I have some news. I've decided to take a road trip."

"What? Bryan, Mom wants to take a road trip!" she yelled to her husband in the family room. "From Muscatine to Davenport?"

"Very cute, dear. No. I have friends who have moved away and I want to see them. I never would have asked your father to make a trip like this, and I'm really looking forward to it. I'll be coming through Lincoln to see all of you ... I miss the girls so much. I'll be traveling through South Dakota, Wyoming, and as far as Montana. Tell Bryan that all those stories he's told about the beauty of that Gallatin River area got to me. And I have a friend who lives outside Bozeman."

"Who?" asked Trina, obviously surprised.

"Oh, Sheila Evans. I don't think you ever met her, dear. We served on the communion committee at church for years after you left. But it's all set. I'm leaving in less than a week."

This was a woman who had traveled only to Lincoln, Omaha, and Des Moines in her lifetime. "Mom, I can't believe my ears. Why now?"

"Like I said, dear, your father was a homebody. He didn't like to leave the area. Just to see you, of course. But I have pent-up wanderlust. I'm excited."

"I think it's wonderful, Mom. When can we expect you?"

"On Friday. I'll call you from my cell phone when I'm an hour out, okay?"

"Okay, Mom. I love you."

"I love you, Trina. Bye," Doris said cheerfully. She hung up and sipped her tea, aware that her throat had gone dry.

Five days later, Dori Shanihan arrived in Lincoln to spend two days with the family she loved more than her own life. She could tell that Trina and Bryan were shocked to see her feeling as strong as she was. Was there something inappropriate about holding it together after the death of her husband? She didn't quite understand where her strength had come from. Perhaps it was her body's way of coping with her loss and her days ahead. But she didn't argue with it. She was thankful.

Leaving Lincoln, she drove long hours, so many hours, that when she laid her head down at night and closed her eyes, all she could see was the centerline on the highway in front of her. She skipped South

Dakota and drove straight through to Cheyenne, Wyoming; Ogden, Utah; Boise, Idaho; stopping only to eat and sleep. But during her journey, she called Trina every night to tell her tales of the wonderful visits she was having with her friends, using her cell phone with her Iowa area code. She never saw a phantom friend named Sheila and she never saw the Gallatin River Valley, although she described it perfectly to Bryan when Trina put him on the phone. Instead, on one glorious late June afternoon, Dori Shanihan crossed from Bellingham, Washington, into British Columbia, Canada, at the Peace Arch border crossing, with her shiny new passport that had never been stamped.

She'd mapped out her route to Oak Street where the cherry blossoms were mashed on the pavement and innocent children played on the sidewalk outside a house of evil. For the next few days, she followed the glamorous woman using the name of Maddie Thomas as she walked for four blocks to a coffee shop, just as Holgate's report had indicated. Every day, Dori cried as she watched through the window of her car as Hunter Cross sipped her coffee and worked on her laptop. Every day, Dori reigned in her rage that eleven years ago Hunter Cross had murdered her daughter and taken her name. Every day, Dori mustered her courage to do what needed to done.

On the fourth day, Dori drove to The Coffee Grind where on the door was a sign that read, *PART-TIME SUMMER HELP WANTED*. She parked her car, walked in the door, and asked the hostess for an application.

When all of the customers were served, a frumpy waitress wearing a cardigan sweater, comfortable-looking shoes, shapeless pants, and a gray ponytail sprouting from the side of her head, sat down next to her.

"Hi. I'm Delores. It sure is nice seeing a mature woman apply for work. This time of year we get kids out of school and as soon as September comes around, poof, they evaporate. What's your name?"

"My family and friends call me Sissy."

"So what should I call you?" asked Delores.

"I prefer Sissy."

"Where are you from?"

"From the states. But my son lives in White Rock so I decided to move up here to be close to my grandchildren. Where are you from?" Dori asked, trying to divert the focus from herself and feeling uncomfortable about her newly acquired skill, lying.

"Me? I'm from North Van but I live around the corner from here. I walk to work. Been here for over fifteen years now. Now listen, Sissy, the man who owns the shop is a good guy. He'll be back in a half hour. You should stick around to meet him. It would probably help you get the job. I'll put in a good word for you. It would be nice having a contemporary around here instead of a giggly, teenybopper who looks down on me as a lifer, even if it's true."

She laughed a smoker's laugh, followed by a bout of coughing. "Would you like a coffee?"

"Sure. Just black. Regular."

"Come on, honey, there are dozens of choices in a place like this. Why would you order something you could get anywhere else?" asked Delores.

"You're right. I guess I'm not very adventurous. Let me try what you like for starters. I'll have to learn the menu, right?"

"That's the spirit. Coming right up."

Just as Delores stood up, the owner walked in. Before getting back to her customers, Delores made a beeline for him to direct him to his new applicant.

"Hello, Sissy," he said. "I'm Said Assizi, the owner."

Dori stood to hand him her application. "It's nice to meet you, Mr. Assizi. I saw your sign out front and would be interested in working here. I could start right away and would prefer mornings, if it were possible."

Having overheard her, Delores materialized, and said over Said's shoulder, "That would work for me, boss. These weary bones could use a couple of mornings a week to sleep in. These 5:30 a.m. calls are killing me."

"Go back to work, Delores," he said with a chuckle in his voice as he waved her away.

Delores winked at Dori, turned her back, and skipped a few steps.

"Did you write down a number where you can be reached?" he asked. "I'm looking for a part-time employee who isn't going to leave as soon as she's trained."

"I need the work, sir. I have no intention of leaving. Because I was a full-time mother, I don't have any references. My apologies. My children are grown and my husband recently died so my hours are my own."

"I'm sorry to hear of your loss. Just a minute, Sissy. Give me a few minutes to look at this now. If it looks good, I'll have Delores start training you and check the schedule for the rest of the week."

Dori's heart jumped. This was easier than she had imagined. She sat down and texted Trina about her virtual visit to Yellowstone the day before. She described the paint pots, the elk meadow, and Old Faithful, as if she were gazing at them as she wrote.

After a half hour, Said approached her table. "Can I have a copy of your driver's license for the records, Sissy?'

Her adrenalin punched in as she felt herself about to deliver answers from a world of untapped untruths.

"I've misplaced my U.S. license but have an appointment to replace it next week, so I'll bring that in as soon as I have it in hand. Or I can show you my passport but it's at home. Would that work?"

"That's okay. Your new driver's license will suffice. Bring it in when it arrives. Welcome to The Coffee Grind, Sissy. Delores will train you this afternoon and you can start work in the morning."

Delores acted as if she'd found her new best friend, and Dori was stunned and overwhelmed.

"You'll start by taking orders and learning the cash register. Making the specialty drinks will come later. Welcome to the wonderful world of coffee." Delores beamed as if she'd just landed a professorial post at a major university.

That night, Dori studied the menu, the names, the combinations, and the sandwiches. She would be the quickest study they'd ever had. It was her first job and an unexpected satisfaction of competence awakened her from decades of relative passivity.

The following morning, as she took her first orders and watched Delores make the coffees, Maddie Thomas walked into The Coffee Grind. She took her seat and opened up her laptop computer. Dori felt paralyzed, panic-stricken to be standing feet from her daughter's alleged killer and granddaughters' proven threat. She focused her attention on the next person in line, while taking quick glimpses at the woman she'd known to be Hunter Cross. She watched Delores bring Maddie her coffee, and Maddie, not even glancing up, handed her a card to punch.

After an hour, Maddie left as inconspicuously as she had arrived, right on schedule. When Dori found a moment, she asked about the beautiful woman who hadn't stood in line like the rest of the customers.

"Oh, her? Her name is Maddie. I don't know her last name. She's a bitch but the boss has a crush on her so he asked that we serve her. She gets the same drink every morning, so she's not demanding, just aloof. But she doesn't bother me. I just punch her card and get back to my customers. Come to think of it, if I'm not here some morning, Sissy, she gets a vanilla latté with nutmeg and a cinnamon stick; sickeningly sweet, but to each her own."

Another week went by before Dori worked the morning shift alone. She was there by 5:30 and asked Miguel to show her how to make a vanilla latte with nutmeg, which he did. By 8:30, Maddie walked into The Coffee Grind, sat down at her usual seat, and opened her laptop. With the steady hands of a surgeon and a will of steel, Dori Shanihan walked to the coffee machine to make a vanilla latté. She sprinkled it with nutmeg but before adding the cinnamon stick, she opened up a tiny bag of finely-crushed plants from her garden in Muscatine, Iowa, and pinched the appropriate amount, stirring the granules until they were blended into a sea of floating nutmeg. All of the hours of studying poisonous plants on the Internet, having used Vinnie's lab analysis as a guide, was about to pay off. It would be a couple of hours before the full effect took hold, and Maddie Thomas would be back in her home, as she always was after her morning walk and coffee. The only people who would wonder where *she* was for a few days would be Delores and Said.

With a dizziness of intoxicating lunacy, Dori Shanihan served the cup of coffee. Maddie looked up, possibly sensing it was not Delores. They locked eyes, and for a split second, Maddie looked as if she recognized her server. But even if she thought Dori's face was vaguely familiar, she would never have placed her. As a child, Hunter Cross had never met Dori. Dori chalked her unease to paranoia. After all, it was the first and only time she would serve a human being a lethal drink.

She returned to the serving counter and took two orders, while watching her target out of the corner of her eye. Maddie hadn't yet taken a sip, intently working on her laptop. After Daniel died and the woman they had referred to as Hunter Cross had paid a visit to her granddaughters' school, Dori had come to the conclusion that what the system wouldn't take care of, she would, and she had Daniel's blessing. As she swiped a credit card for her next customer, she looked up to watch Maddie sigh, sit back, and pick up the drink of death. Then came the moment of watching her crime actualized.

Maddie Thomas took a long swallow of her last coffee. Her facial expression didn't change. She set it down without taking her fingers from the cup handle. She brought it back to her lips and took another drink from the cup that she now held in both hands. She looked intent in thought, not once looking around the coffee shop at her surroundings, then finished her latté, stood up with her laptop, and walked out the door and down the street to her home.

Dori thought how ironic it was that a woman who was obviously laying low until she made her next move, thought that a consistent, unsuspicious behavior like a daily visit to a random coffee shop in a foreign city, was safe. When in fact, the very under-the-radar routine, as unsuspicious as it was, would set the stage for her downfall.

The longest day of Dori Shanihan's life was underway. She worked through her shift and held her breath until the following morning when Maddie Thomas would either enter The Coffee Grind, or not. That night, Dori called Trina and shared her day at Glacier National Park. She recounted the stirring drive on the Going-to-the-Sun-Road, describing the alpine meadows and sharp-toothed glacial crags. She talked about her fictitious friend Sheila who was entertaining company and helping her with the driving.

She suggested that someday Bryan and Trina take the girls to Glacier, and she'd like to join them, to see Glacier's grandeur once again. Then she said goodbye, and put down her Montana guide book from which she'd described her counterfeit day.

The following morning, after barely sleeping, Dori walked into the coffee shop. By 9 a.m., a half hour after Maddie's customary visit, there was no sign of her. Delores said nothing so neither did Dori. The next morning, Dori wasn't scheduled to work so she drove her car and parked across from The Coffee Grind and waited. Maddie didn't show up. Then it occurred to her, *what if she'd left town? What if she wasn't dead?* Dori resigned herself to the possibility that she'd have to try again, if given the chance. She read the papers and watched for an obituary. *And if she was dead, who would find her? Who would have reason to check on her?* Dori turned on the ignition and drove past the home on Oak Street. There were two newspapers and a book of yellow pages in a plastic bag on the sidewalk. The exasperating hours of the waiting game ensued.

Maddie didn't show up for coffee for four days but on the fifth day, Delores, with wide, rheumy eyes and puckered mouth, met Dori at the front door. Before Dori even stepped foot inside the coffee shop, Delores displayed the newspaper article.

"Look, Sissy, it's *her*! The bitch!"

Dori took the paper and began reading the article entitled *Local Woman Found Dead.* Her heart pounded as she tried to disguise her relief, hearing Delores babble in the background about how she'd known her for years and would miss her, blah, blah, blah.

"Who found her?" asked Dori.

"The article says that her landlady who lived next door saw mail and newspapers piling up. Apparently, Maddie always informed her when she was going out of town, and she hadn't received a call from her. So she knocked on the door for a couple of days, and finally used her key. She discovered her on the living room floor. Read it. They think she had a heart attack, because there wasn't any evidence of forced entry or anyone being there."

"That's so sad. She was so young," Dori heard herself saying.

"And beautiful. Read further down. Look at the end, at the end." Delores's age-spotted fingers tapped at the article's closing. "They ask for anyone who knew her to come forward because they don't know who to call to make her final arrangements, if you know what I mean."

"That's so sad, Delores. What a shock. We should get to work. Staying busy will make the day pass faster."

Delores nodded and walked into the kitchen.

After Dori finished her work day, she called Trina and told her she'd be coming home soon. The next morning she informed Said and Delores that her other son had been in a car accident, and she would have to care for him for a few months so she'd have to quit her job at The Coffee Grind. They appeared disappointed, but sympathetic, and she vowed to never lie again. Her charade had been a means to an end of which she hadn't thought herself capable.

Her drive home gave her days by herself to think. She came to terms with two personal truths. The first being that there is a love so strong, so protective that even speaking about it diminished its power. Had a polar bear mother the brains to understand that her cubs bore her grandchildren, imagine the power of that grandmother polar bear. Wasn't the visceral, violent animal defense of cubs the root of maternal protection?

Daniel was gone but she remembered his words—"No matter what it takes." She had translated those words and applied them to her most courageous defensive instinct. Her granddaughters were the reason she'd come back into the world, and she had exerted personal authority to protect them from someone taking them out of the world before their natural time. Hunter Cross's big mistake: She should never have come to Nebraska. She should never have set eyes on Dori's grandchildren, endangering their well-being. Dori would not lose another one of her cubs to the beast.

The second, but tougher, realization to face was the nature of her act of violence. She rationalized that in war, one killed. You were not a murderer in war. In America, you defended a higher ground ... liberty, freedom from tyranny, and freedom to be.

So how had this been different? She had defended the innocence and safety of her grandchildren against the evil force of Hunter Cross who threatened them. The perpetrator had to be destroyed.

Who else was going to do it? The legal system? Who else was going to die before justice was served? Who was going to put a stop to the uncertainty and violence? And who would suspect or trace a sudden death with no evidence of entry or violence to a grandmother who lived in Muscatine, Iowa, a lonely widow who lived a passive existence and was the proud owner of an unblemished civic and personal history? No one ... was the answer.

She also knew in the recesses of her mind that a human being could justify anything, and that didn't make it right. She knew that she'd compromised her code of ethics as a citizen of the world and assumed the role of vigilante this one time in her law-abiding life. She'd killed a woman and she could never look back. Any great general validated and defended his actions in the eyes of God and humanity for a higher good. She, Dori Shanihan, had completed her march to the sea.

Dori arrived home in Iowa four days later, bypassing Lincoln, in need of time to recuperate from her mission accomplished. She'd forgotten to hire the boy down the street to cut her grass, so her home looked ignored and unoccupied. The interior, although stuffy, was untouched, and Dori was safe at home. She called the neighbor boy, restarted her newspaper and mail deliveries, and called her daughter in Nebraska.

"Hi, Trina. I'm home!"

"Mom, why didn't you stop for a visit on your way? We were expecting you." Trina's voice sounded annoyed.

"I'm sorry, dear. I was so tired. I wouldn't have been good company. I planned poorly because I was driving through Lincoln at two in the morning; I was wide awake and I couldn't very well wake you up in the middle of the night. I was ready to sleep in my own bed. I'll come to see you at the end of the month. I promise."

"All right. Now that you're a world traveler, I guess I'm not concerned about you making the trip on your own. And by the way, from your phone calls, I feel like I've been on vacation." Trina laughed. "But tell me more."

"Honey, I just walked in the door. I'll call you on Sunday and by then I'll make a list of things I didn't share, okay? I love you, Trina."

"I love you, Mom."

Dori hung up. *Trina hadn't heard about the sudden death of Maddie Thomas.* Dori wondered if she ever would. But it didn't matter. Trina's children were safe and justice was served.

Before the sun went down, there were only two musts on Dori's list. The golden sunlight of late afternoon slanted on her garden as she walked up the aisles of plants. The wheels of the trash bin creaked as she pulled it behind her, leaving tread marks in the rich, black, fertile Iowa soil. She pulled the toxic evidence from the earth that hadn't been watered in a month. Ironically, the plants appeared dead but the dead must be buried, hidden from the eyes of the Universe.

When her first task was finished, she took a shower and prepared to a take a drive. Just as she closed the screen door behind her, the phone rang. She thought twice about answering it but out of dutiful habit, she walked back into the kitchen.

"Hello," she said.

"Mom, it's Trina, again. I just heard from Scott Holgate, that private investigator from Vancouver I hired? He said that a woman identified as Madison Thomas was found dead in her home last week! He's confirmed that it was her. Mom, she's dead! She can't hurt us ever again."

"Oh, Trina. I don't know what to say. I'm happy you're relieved, I guess. It was a dreadful business. I'm glad it's over."

"It just goes to show, Mom. The universe works in mysterious ways. She died alone, with no one in the world who cared about her. I know it's terrible for me to say, but I hope it was food poisoning. It would at least be poetic justice. I just thought you should know, Mom. Our Cristin's death has been avenged by the premature death of Hunter Cross. I need to call Katie and her sisters. I love you, Mom."

"I love you, Trina."

Dori hung up the phone and sighed. She felt as if she were having an out-of-body experience as she drove to the cemetery to Daniel's resting place. When she parked the car, she sat for a while, still, silent. Then came the time to have the talk with him. She exited the car; her legs, unsteady as she approached his grave. When she stood in front of his headstone, she felt her lower body buckle and give way as she fell onto her knees. Dori Shanihan cried until the salt from her eyes burned the lips she was biting. When finally she composed herself, she whispered, "Danny Boy, my mission is complete. God forgive me, I did what it took." She then knelt closer to his grave and touched his name. With a tremoring voice, she sang through a whisper,

You will feel me softly tread above you,
and your grave shall warmer, sweeter be,
and I will bend and tell you that I love you,
and you will sleep in peace until I come to thee.

EPILOGUE

Even the most rational approach to ethics is defenseless
if there isn't the will to do what is right.
—Alexander Solzhenitsyn

Five years later in Lucerne, Switzerland, Clement Germond was informed of his dear friend Santino Scardina's death. Because Clement had a license to practice law in Italy as well as Switzerland, Santino bequeathed Clement a number of his sensitive client files. One of the files most interesting to Clement concerned the Gherardini fortune, the heir apparent being Luca Gherardini.

Luca was a nine-year-old student at the Swiss Conservatory for Boys, SCB, a glorified boarding school, where he began attending shortly after he was abandoned by his mother. Her unsolved disappearance remained a missing person file for years, until she was declared dead.

Clement had served on the board of directors of Luca's school since 2003 and had heard on a number of occasions that Luca's behavioral problems caused the instructors concern. But that was their concern, not his.

One rainy evening, Fiona was knitting by the fire when Clement walked in from his study with a letter in his hand.

"Fiona, I need to talk to someone about a decision I must make in good conscience. Do you have a minute?"

Fiona put down her knitting. "Of course, dear. What is it?"

"As you know, I am charged with some of Santino's legal files, one of which is the Gherardini estate. There are three disturbing issues in this file. Of course this is confidential but I need your input. First, by virtue of my being on the board of directors, over the past couple years, I have been apprised of Luca Gherardini's aberrant behavior which has almost led to his expulsion. This is a very disturbed young boy, abandoned with virtually no family."

"Clement, surely you are not suggesting ... I mean, we can't. Gabriel is twelve. We're grandparents ..."

"God, no, Fiona. Hear me out. He is theoretically a very wealthy young boy. At this point, the trust money is paying for his health, education, support, and maintenance at SCB but there will come a time when funds will need to be disbursed. However, I am concerned with what the instructors have termed his "lack of conscience." Fortunately or unfortunately, I am in possession of this envelope that is supposed to be given to him on his eighteenth birthday. If there is something in this envelope that will set him off, as they say, is it not my moral duty to withhold it from him?"

"I don't know, Clement. We don't know what's in the envelope."

"That's the point. Unless I unlawfully open this confidential envelope, I may not be able to deter inappropriate behavior in the future. However, it may simply be a letter from his mother written before she disappeared which he is certainly entitled to. Secondly, there is also a reference to a key to a safe deposit box in Canada. But there's no key. It gets more complicated and mysterious. After Nico Gherardini died, all of his assets were to go to Luca, with Sofia named as Luca's sole guardian, having unlimited access to the trust funds.'

"What's mysterious about that?"

"Remember, Sofia disappeared after Rudolpho's death. She was declared missing."

"What are you saying?" Fiona asked.

"This brings me to my third point. Why would Santino have been transferring property liquidations into an account in the Cayman Islands under the name Sofia Gherardini if she were missing, and presumed dead? We're talking over a billion euros, Fiona. I checked it out. In

Santino's records, there is an offshore account in the Cayman Islands under the name of Sofia Gherardini into which he deposited those funds long after Sofia went missing. This is all according to hand-written instructions, dated weeks before Nico died and signed by Nico and Sofia Gherardini, witnessed by Santino. Santino could not make withdrawals, only deposits. Her signature suggests that Sofia Gherardini was not missing at all, and both Nico and Santino knew it."

"Are you saying she's alive, Clement?"

"I'm saying if she were alive, and she'd pulled off a ruse of this magnitude, who is she? And where? Isn't it bizarre that both my friend Rudolpho and his son Nico died within a year of each other? And if she is alive, she's treacherous, and should I not open this envelope to investigate the contents?"

"Clement. I think we ought to sleep on this. It would be against the law."

"I know, my dear, and I will not play God. That's why we're discussing it. Fortunately, the child is only nine. I don't have to make this decision now."

Clement waved the envelope over his head as he walked back to his study, and Fiona picked up her knitting.

Three months later, after Clement had been informed and gone to great effort to keep it out of the local newspaper, an article appeared in the Lucerne Gazette:

Student at the Swiss Conservatory for Boys Found Dead; Another Student Accused.

On Friday, a student was accused of murder by parents of a deceased seven-year-old student. The deceased was found hung in his closet, discovered by another student. The parents of the dead child were quick to accuse a nine-year-old boy, because of his history of bullying

*their boy. Names have been withheld due to the juvenile
element of the alleged crime. Investigation is underway.
Services will be private.*

When Clement arrived home, Fiona met him at the door.

"Tell me the accused boy is not Luca Gherardini," she said as she waved the paper.

"It is," Clement acquiesced. He walked directly into his study and brought out the envelope in question and sat down in front of his wife to open it.

Inside the envelope addressed to Luca, he found enigmatic instructions from Sofia Gherardini to her son to find four American women and avenge her exile. Their names and locations were listed in a safe deposit box, the whereabouts known only to Santino Scardina. There were references to bank accounts and passport photos, but no specifics … no other pieces of the obscure puzzle.

The final sentence was chillingly clear—

*Luca, if you are reading this letter and I have not
contacted you, these women are responsible for my
death. Find them.*

*Your beloved mother,
Sofia*

ACKNOWLEDGMENTS

A special thanks to Karen Feher and Lisa Hogue for their editing expertise; to Amber Jerome~Norrgard for formatting my manuscript; and to the artistic talent of JT Lindroos who designed my cover. I'm grateful for the professional advice of Barry Crowther, Bob Saadai, Lynn Goodlad Reiss, Frank Emma, Dede Soto, Karen Twichel, Shannon Ingram, Steve Concialdi, and John Haradon.

Thank you to those whose genuine encouragement has truly touched my heart ... Beverly Wallace, Heidi Wiessner, Liz Weatherhead, Sandy Hames, Donna Moore, Krystal Partridge, Kele Thompson, Suzanne Becker, Joan Halvajian, Terese Walton, Tracey Reimann, Ann Svensson, Barbara Pierre, Heather Haith, Carmen Heston, Pam Crowley, David Sheehan, Jasmin Parva, my husband Rich, and so many others to whom I apologize for not mentioning.

I sincerely hope you enjoyed reading *The Mind of a Spider*. Please tell your friends on Facebook and ask them to share it with their friends. I invite you to visit my website at trishastandrews.com to follow my blog and submit your comments. I am open to visiting book clubs in the Orange County, California area.

Most of all, thank you for your support. A writer's dream is that her readers truly look forward to her next book.

ABOUT THE AUTHOR

Born in Canada, raised in Minnesota, Trisha currently lives in southern California with her husband, near her three married sons and families. She graduated with honors from the University of Minnesota with a degree in the humanities and history.

Trisha has written this sequel to her first novel, *The Heart of a Lynx*, and intends to write a third book in the Heart/Mind/Soul trilogy to complete the story that spans over twenty years in the lives of her characters.

WHERE TO FIND TRISHA ST. ANDREWS:

www.trishastandrews.com

www.facebook.com/trishastandrews

www.twitter.com/trishastandrews

BOOKS BY TRISHA ST. ANDREWS

The Heart of a Lynx
The Mind of a Spider

Made in the USA
Middletown, DE
22 July 2018